In this study, Lynn Staley Johnson offers an illuminating critical reading of four major Middle English poems. Her close scrutiny of *Pearl*, *Purity, Patience,* and *Sir Gawain and the Green Knight* provides rich insights into the language and structure of the poems, and firmly grounds the works in their literary, social, and religious contexts. Emphasizing the parallel themes that link these poems, Johnson also advances critical evidence that the four pieces were, as many scholars now believe, the work of a single author. Scholars and students of medieval English literature, poetry, philosophy, and society will find this a compelling work of literary criticism, one that underscores both the individual complexities and artistic affinities of four medieval masterworks.

Lynn Staley Johnson

The Voice of the *Gawain*-Poet

The University of Wisconsin Press

Published 1984

The University of Wisconsin Press
114 North Murray Street
Madison, Wisconsin 53715

The University of Wisconsin Press, Ltd.
1 Gower Street
London WC1E 6HA, England

First printing

Printed in the United States of America

For LC CIP information see the colophon

ISBN 0-299-09540-1

Publication of this book was made possible in part
by grants from the National Endowment for the
Humanities and Colgate University.

For Linck

Contents

Introduction

The four poems of MS Cotton Nero A.x. Art. 3 are generally acclaimed to be some of the finest examples of Middle English literature, eclipsed only by contemporary works by Chaucer. Although there is no external evidence to link *Pearl, Purity, Patience,* and *Sir Gawain and the Green Knight,* the poems are commonly ascribed to one author. As the title of this study suggests, I share the general view that the poems are the work of a single writer, a poet of extraordinary talent whose works still interest and frequently puzzle a twentieth-century reader.[1] As my title also indicates, I believe that these four poems—though they stand on their own—deserve to be studied as a group. As Charles Moorman said in 1968, "Our greatest need . . . seems now to be for studies in which the works of the *Pearl*-poet are taken as a whole. . . . they should be devoted to establishing the central themes and techniques of the poet . . . [the poems'] organic unity, which is the poet's vision of life."[2] Although there are numerous studies of the individual poems, there are relatively few books dealing with all four.[3] But the poems need to be studied not only individually but as a group and in the context of medieval literary, social, and religious views.

In studying these poems within the context of the spiritual life of the Middle Ages, we need to recognize the degree to which medieval thought was influenced by medieval Christianity. Whereas the modern world is a secular one, in which a distinction is made between the concerns of religion and those of daily life, for the medieval world the two areas informed one another. For example, discussing the eleventh century's preoccupation with the doctrine of the Eucharist, Charles Williams helps us to understand the medieval interest in and awareness of religious matters: "It was not, I suppose, discussed as politics are to-day, but neither was its discussion confined to a particular class of the pious, as such things usually are to-day. A more general imagination, a more universal (almost—dare one say?—a more casual) intellect was aware of it; and even the people who did not argue had probably heard of the argument."[4] "Casual" is the key word here, and it is precisely that casual awareness of theological matters in the Middle Ages that can create difficulties for the modern reader of medieval literature.

Both implicitly and explicitly, the *Gawain*-poet demonstrates an awareness of traditional Christian views. First, and most obviously, *Patience, Purity,* and *Pearl* are, to greater or lesser degrees, based upon Biblical texts. In seeking to understand these poems, we must know how these texts were treated in order to understand the possible reasons the poet had for using them. In many cases, a survey of the commentaries on these texts illuminates the poet's handling of incidents in the poems and the reasons behind his emphasis upon certain themes. What may appear recondite to us was likely to be familiar to an audience whose members regularly attended church and, through sermons, were accustomed to hearing passages from the Bible interpreted figuratively.[5] This is not to say that the *Gawain*-poet wrote sermons or that he expected his audience to listen to a poem as though it were a sermon. It does, however, underline the necessity of understanding how a text, such as the Parable of the Wedding Feast in *Purity*, was commonly understood. Many of the same contextual methods that V. A. Kolve, Walter Myers, and Rosemary Woolf have applied to the English mystery cycles can be applied to the works of the *Gawain*-poet. In both the plays and the poems, we confront writers who used Biblical texts with an awareness of their figurative meanings, evoking or reflecting those meanings in their imagery, themes, and techniques.

It is equally important, however, to establish guidelines for a use of exegetical sources. It makes more sense to rely upon a series of common interpretations rather than upon those of one writer whose views, no matter how attractive they may be to a critic, have little in common with the consensus of medieval thought. Thus, when dealing with interpretations of Biblical passages, I have aimed for a broad range of authorities who echo one another and who can be said to constitute a single tradition. For example, as Yves-Marie Duval has recently shown, there were a wide variety of ways of seeing the Biblical figure of Jonah.[6] It would hardly illuminate the poem if we read it in relation to Byzantine or Jewish interpretations of the Book of Jonah, ignoring the work of Saint Jerome and others who followed him in establishing the ways in which the Christian West saw this puzzling figure. Furthermore, the *Gawain*-poet appears rarely to draw upon what we may call "university" authorities, but, instead, to reflect a tradition that begins most notably with Saint Augustine and is passed on by Saint Gregory, Bede, Rabanus Maurus, and others. When possible, I also refer to contemporary thinkers, writers, and preachers whose ideas shed light on the poet's more literary interpretations of traditional views.

The poems of this manuscript are also informed in more implicit ways by medieval religious life. *Sir Gawain*, clearly a secular romance, nonetheless is built around a calendar of liturgical time. The poet carefully alludes to the feast days on which each significant event of the poem occurs, and the whole poem describes a calendar rotation from January 1 to January 1, New Year's Day, the Feast of the Circumcision. Whereas these dates may appear simply ornamental to us, the poet's audience, which would have celebrated these feasts each year and thus participated in their significance, would probably have recognized that the poet evokes the lessons and themes of those feast days in his descriptions of Sir Gawain's experience. This in no way suggests that *Sir Gawain* is not a secular romance; it does, however, underline the necessity of looking at the poem in the context of the audience's common religious experiences and expectations.

But religion is not the sum of medieval thought. As many scholars have demonstrated, the late fourteenth century was a time of social unrest and reevaluation.[7] Chaucer, Langland, and Gower all voice a concern for the social world of their age. The *Gawain*-poet shares with these writers a recognition of the hierarchical nature of social bodies. In all the poet's pictures of societies—from the court of heaven to Arthur's court—degree and proportion are implicit. Like his contemporaries, the poet was also aware that, unless the hierarchy of social bodies was based on true values, it became the meaningless order we find in Balthazar's court in *Purity*. Thus, we find in these poems a scrutiny of human societies. Although Chaucer is the most well known critic of his age, the *Gawain*-poet may take his place beside Chaucer as a commentator upon the times. Particularly in *Sir Gawain*, we find a concern for the nature of chivalry, the ultimate strengths of human institutions, and a recognition of the sorts of weaknesses that can precipitate ruin. These were contemporary issues in the fourteenth century, an age that saw the young Edward III bring glory to England, watched his decline, and then found its hopes for a renascence dashed by the follies and weaknesses of Richard II. The social remedy the poet offers is one also advanced by his fellow Englishmen, whether they be playwrights, poets, or preachers; he prescribes individual penance for national ills. Looked at in his social or historical context, the *Gawain*-poet appears neither idealistic nor pessimistic about human societies. Rather, he offers a realistic appraisal of man's institutions, recognizing their inherent flaws and advancing individual reform for man's native imperfections.

As a writer, the poet shares with his age a comic view of man. As both D. W. Robertson and J. A. Burrow have suggested, fourteenth-century literature includes very little of the heroic since its picture of man is charged with irony and humor.[8] The poems of the *Pearl* manuscript are as rich in humor as they are in serious intent. The reader is, in various poems, faced with a wordy, querulous Jonah; a dreamer who stands sputtering and shaking, "as hende as hawk in halle";

and a perfect knight who resolutely braves the terrors of wild beasts only to pale when confronted by his importunate hostess. Again and again, the poet underscores the comic incapacities of man when faced with the unknown. While all of these characters fail in serious ways, their failures are comic, not tragic. The subject is man, but man undone and insufficient to the task at hand, not man heroic and capable of triumph.

The oral presentation of medieval poetry, a subject of sporadic critical discussion, no doubt underscored the humor within the poems of the *Pearl* manuscript. *Patience* is much funnier when read aloud, and the drama and humor of *Sir Gawain* and *Pearl* assume their natural prominence in an oral reading. The two most famous literary references to oral delivery are Saint Augustine's allusion in *Confessions* VI 3, to Ambrose's "curious" habit of silent reading, and Chaucer's account of the reading of *The Siege of Thebes* in *Troilus and Criseyde*. Larry Benson has noted the large number of formulaic phrases in *Sir Gawain*, an incidence that sheds light on the developing alliterative style. Benson speculates that what we call the alliterative revival was really a continuing, organic tradition within Middle English literature.[9] Recently, Rosemary Woolf has made a telling point by noting that medieval poems were not only read aloud, but probably read with vocal impersonation. She supports this remark by suggesting that the medieval conception of drama was not limited to the stage but included sermons, poems, and the liturgy as well.[10] To "do the police in different voices" was a natural method of delivery for generations without film or television.[11] In his *Richardian Poetry* Burrow emphasizes the interest of medieval poets in storytelling, observing that they were more willing to force a rhyme or to settle for a simple one than to sacrifice a story.[12] The medieval interest in narrative helps to account for the drama of medieval poems and suggests a certain amount of interaction between the audience and the poet, or his poem. The fact that medieval narrative poetry can sometimes appear ambiguous or mysterious may arise from its intrinsic dramatic appeal. In an age when books were rare and expensive, and literary entertainment was a social experience, we can assume that the listeners discussed what they heard, just as we discuss a play or a movie.

The works of the *Gawain*-poet reveal the poet's efforts to realize the dramatic potential of narrative poetry. He shares with such writers as the Wakefield-master a recognition of the drama of human situations. When dealing with Biblical episodes, the poet heightens the drama implicit in these scenes by inventing speeches, by adding descriptive passages, and by providing additional motives for some of the characters, motives that are revealed as all too often grounded in self-interest. His portrait of Jonah in *Patience* is a case in point. Whereas the Biblical Jonah has only an implied personality, the Jonah of *Patience* is verbose, self-absorbed, cowardly, and scornful of his fellow man. The poet emphasizes the humor of Jonah's incapacities by contrasting Jonah's wordiness and lack of dignity to God's verbal economy and forbearance. The same strategy is apparent in his handling of the *Pearl*-dreamer and of Sir Gawain, characters whose limitations are obvious in their misapprehension of the world around them.

The dramatic appeal of these poems, however, is not limited to comedy. In the *Pearl*-dreamer's grief and amazement and in Sir Gawain's agonized cry of failure, the poet demonstrates an awareness of a more serious human drama. He uses such scenes to draw his audience into the poems and to involve it in the problems the protagonists face. Despite the exotic situations the poet describes, we are drawn into the *Pearl*-dreamer's encounter with the supernatural, Jonah's problems with God, and Sir Gawain's dangerous mission and experience in Bercilak's court. The poet, however, only baits his hook with drama. Once caught, we are faced with intellectual puzzles and choices and are forced to consider the best responses to situations that highlight the frequently ambiguous problems of human life.

The blend of wisdom and folly in various characters points up the ambiguities of human nature in general. The poet's tendency to link the heroic or the serious with the bathetic reflects the medieval assumption that man will ultimately fall short of his goals and that the events and choices of human life can turn out to be important milestones along the road to self-knowledge.[13] Thus, the *Pearl*-dreamer, Jonah, and Sir Gawain are, at times, embarrassingly human, for each is inadequate to the task at hand, falling far short of those ideals that form the backdrops to their stories. The poet's picture of man is a familiar and an unsettling one; it is Adam or everyman.[14]

To some extent, recognition of the hero's failure has characterized critical appraisal of the poems. In his study of *Sir Gawain*, Benson reveals the types of changes the poet has made in his sources, changes that underline certain emerging themes in the poem. For example, *Caradoc* records the exchange-of-blows incident that reappears in the Green Knight's challenge to the court through Gawain. Among the *Gawain*-poet's changes are the rather unflattering picture of Arthur and the link the poet suggests between Arthur and the challenge itself; moreover, the changes "reinforce Gawain's position as a fit representative of Camelot." Noting that "the *Gawain*-poet seems to change the source so that it concerns the ideals of knighthood itself," Benson emphasizes the real test of virtue that informs *Sir Gawain* and the theme of self-discovery.[15] But, while they have recognized the failures of characters like Sir Gawain, critics have tended to underestimate the significance of such failures. As I seek to demonstrate, the poet treats a character's failure as a crucial moment, a point from which a character may either slide to destruction or take his first step in a momentous process of renewal. For example, only when we understand the significance of alternative responses to failure do we begin to understand the unifying theme among the disparate stories recounted in *Purity*.

Whereas the poet's view of human nature is implicit in *Patience*, *Sir Gawain*, and *Pearl*, in *Purity* his message is explicit. *Purity* is, in many ways, the least successful of the four poems. Because it contains very little humor and almost no sense of dramatic ambiguity, we are less engaged by its situations. The poet too often intrudes, telling us how we should respond to these situations and thus glossing the poem for his audience. But *Purity* illuminates the other three poems, for in it the poet focuses upon the willfulness of human nature, man's wish to have his own way despite the bounty God has prepared for his creatures. To this end, the poet paints a dark picture of man, who prefers his own imperfections to the perfection he might find in loving service. The light the poet offers is the light that shines in each of his poems—the possibility of renewal through penance. Only by recognizing his inadequacies can man avail himself of new life in grace. The emphasis in *Purity*, as in the other three poems, is upon personal recognition and choice, for through knowledge man may be released from his incomprehension and folly into the true freedom that is a gift of grace.

Although these poems cannot be understood without regard to their historical and literary context, an approach that skirts formal and poetic matters is equally inadequate. The four poems are neither tracts nor sermons; they are the work of a poet who organized his material carefully and who, for the most part, allowed his themes to remain unstated, implicit in his organization. Thus, though this study has its foundations in a contextual approach to the four poems, it is finally a critical reading of them, an effort to illuminate the poet's strategy, organization, and themes. My primary emphasis is upon the text of each poem and the ways in which the poet through language and imagery draws and expands upon traditional medieval views.

As the Contents indicates, I have changed the order of the poems as they appear in the only surviving manuscript. Charles Moorman has warned me that taking such a liberty amounts to heresy; so I should immediately note that the rearrangement is solely for the sake of clarity and convenience. It is fitting that the manuscript begins with the mysterious line, "Perle, plesaunte to prynces paye," but I felt that a critical study should begin with *Patience*, the most accessible of the poems, before confronting the mysteries and complexities of the others. Therefore, whereas in the manuscript *Pearl* is followed by *Purity, Patience,* and *Sir Gawain,* my chapter on *Patience* is followed by readings of *Sir Gawain, Purity,* and *Pearl.* That order is, I believe, very much in keeping with the thematic concerns of the manuscript. The first two poems in the manuscript appear to complement one another by focusing on purity, the subject of the sixth Beatitude, quoted in both poems. *Purity* is primarily concerned with outward purity, or right action, whereas *Pearl* describes the process of inward refinement, a process that should culminate in the spiritual marriage the maiden describes to the dreamer.[16] Both *Patience* and *Sir Gawain* explore human nature and human failure as they are revealed in characters who function as both ideals and figures for everyman. I have sought to retain or to highlight the links between the poems by keeping each pair together.

Perhaps the ultimate test of a poem, or of a study of a poem, is the reward involved. The poems of the *Pearl* manuscript certainly deserve scrutiny. They reveal a degree of subtlety and sophistication that underscores the remarks by both Derek Pearsall and Larry Benson that, in general, the poetry of the alliterative revival suggests aristocratic and literate patronage.[17] These four poems certainly suggest an audience capable of appreciating them and a poet willing to offer poems that demand attention and thought. Furthermore, the poems are not exhausted by scrutiny, for at each successive reading they reveal stylistic touches and thematic nuances not noticed the first or the second time. This study, the product of my own successive confrontations with the poems, places them in a new light. I have sought to highlight the richness of each poem as well as to illuminate the fine interconnecting tissues among all four. Through such detailed study I have also endeavored to offer a glimpse of the author and the audience, whose shared social and religious concerns found their most enduring expression in narrative poetry of the fourteenth century, in *The Canterbury Tales* and in the poems of the *Gawain*-poet.

While writing this book, I have been continuously and

generously supported by others. First, I am grateful for the faithful support of the Colgate University Research Council, which has supported much of the research and defrayed all the expenses of preparing the manuscript. I would like to thank Patricia Ryan for the care with which she has typed its various drafts. The manuscript was read by Kathryn Hume, of the Pennsylvania State University, and by Charles Moorman, of the University of Southern Mississippi: I would like to thank both for their help. Professor Moorman may not agree with everything in this book, but his clarity, humor, and shrewdness, together with his knowledge of and sensitivity to the *Gawain*-poet, led me to make a number of changes in the final version of the manuscript. I owe Professor Hume a special debt for the interest she has taken in this project, for the care and intelligence with which she has made suggestions, for her informed and logical approach to the issues of literary criticism, and for the extraordinary amount of time she has expended on the work of another scholar. I am enormously grateful to her and can only say that I feel honored by my debt to her and pleased to be able to thank her publicly for an association that has been one of the unexpected benefits of writing a book. John V. Fleming of Princeton University read and commented upon the manuscript in an earlier draft; I am grateful to him for the help and enthusiasm with which he has supported my work. I also owe a major debt to D. W. Robertson, Jr. Over the years, Professor Robertson has cheerfully and conscientiously read and reread versions of this book, following it through various transmutations, and offering suggestions from his vast store of knowledge of the Middle Ages. As both a teacher and a friend, he has given what cannot be measured or repaid. Wishing neither to measure nor to cancel a debt so happily incurred, I can thank him for over ten years of a friendship that grows fuller as it grows longer. Finally, I thank Linck C. Johnson, who, as husband, friend, and colleague, has read this book almost as many times as I. What he has given is truly rare—genuine and knowledgeable support, honest appraisals, humor, and conversation as rich as any could wish.

Audited, I must count myself a bankrupt, but I feel blessed in my debts to friends and colleagues; it is with pleasure that I ascribe the good things in this study to their encouragement and care.

The Voice of the
Gawain-Poet

One

Patience

Patience is, on the simplest level, a poetic retelling of the Book of Jonah. Rather than merely paraphrasing the Biblical story, however, the poet sets the career of Jonah within a narrative frame by providing a first-person narrator who tells the story of Jonah as an exemplary tale. Though the account takes up the bulk of the poem, the narrator uses the figure of Jonah to illustrate the necessity of aspiring to the virtue of patience. To this end, the narrator begins by providing us with a preliminary definition of patience; moves to a consideration of the Beatitudes, focusing upon the first and the last (poverty of spirit and patience); and, finally, proceeds to an account of Jonah and his efforts to evade the will of God. At the close of the account, the narrator returns to a brief consideration of the virtues of patience and poverty.

Structurally, the poet's use of a first-person narrator unifies the poem; thematically, the presence of a narrator links the concerns of the poem to those of a contemporary audience, since the narrator intrudes upon the action of the poem, providing us with a contemporary point of view. The means by which the narrator shapes and expands upon the story of Jonah suggest a particular way of using the account of this prophet—as an illustration of the Christlike virtues of humility and patience. The narrator's account of Jonah is at once comic and serious, for in the comic portrait of this querulous prophet we may find a portrait of the old Adam whose life typologically foreshadows the life of Christ. The narrator thus uses the figure of Jonah as a means of exploring human incapacity and of stressing a Christlike perfection that can be achieved only through penance.

Although the Biblical account of Jonah describes a man who is both disobedient and uncharitable, Jonah, for the Middle Ages, was a type of Christ.[1] The incidents of Jonah's flight to Tharsis—the storm at sea, his willingness to be cast overboard, three days and nights in the whale, "resurrection"—and his successful mission to Nineveh were seen as foreshadowing events that would be fulfilled in the life of Christ.[2] Jonah's flight to Tharsis was thought to foreshadow Christ's prayer in the Garden of Gethsemane that the "cup be passed from him"; the storm at sea was linked to the turbulent nature of the world; Jonah's voluntary sacrifice, which quelled the storm and saved the sailors, was likened to the Passion; the days in the whale were viewed as foreshadowing the events of Holy Saturday and Christ's descent into Hell; Jonah's release from the whale was seen as a type of the Resurrection; and Jonah's success in Nineveh was thought to look forward to the salvation of the Gentiles through the New Law sacrament of penance. These events of Jonah's life were conceived of as "historical manifestations of principles set forth in the New Law," whose meaning and reality were fulfilled through Christ.[3] In fact, Christ himself was thought to have distinguished Jonah as a type (see Matt. 12:40).

The story of Jonah was not only considered typologically; it was also scrutinized for its tropological lessons. Thus, Jonah was used as an example of human disobedience. Frequently both typological and tropological discussions of Jonah occur within the same commentary as a means of exploring human nature in relation to the divine nature. For example, Rupert of Deutz discusses Jonah's flight to Tharsis, which was linked to Christ's anguished prayer in the Garden of Gethsemane. Saint Augustine had discussed this prayer as a manifestation of the tension Christ experienced between his two natures, divine and human. Rupert applies this interpretation to Jonah, saying that Jonah's flight is intended to remind us of the conflict between Christ's human and divine wills and the very real weaknesses of the human will.[4] Saint Gregory in his *Moralia*, Petrus Berchorius in his *Super Jonam*, and Thomas à Kempis in a sermon to the novices regular also scrutinize the moral implications of Jonah's flight to Tharsis.[5] Saint Gregory discusses the futility of attempting to disobey God. Berchorius discusses Jonah's flight and the resulting storm at sea in terms of spiritual discord, a theme that also appears in the poet's treatment of Jonah's noisy and jangling character. Thomas à Kempis, writing fifty years after the probable date of *Patience,* combines the story of Jonah with the moral of patience in a sermon entitled "Of Having Patience amid the Slothful and Perverse." Like the poet, Thomas à Kempis links the virtues of humility (poverty of spirit) and patience, exhorting the novices, unlike Jonah, to bear adversity humbly and patiently in exchange for the kingdom of heaven.

Patience indicates that the poet was aware of these various and often paradoxical approaches to Jonah. The poet takes full advantage of the tradition that was available to him, creating a figure who displays the characteristics of both Christ and everyman. In general, the poet is faithful to the Biblical account of Jonah, but the occasional liberties he takes with his source, the use he makes of the narrative voice, his organization of the story of Jonah, and, finally, his invention of a comic personality for Jonah suggest a treatment of the prophet that is intended to be understood both typologically and tropologically. The figure who emerges from that combination underlines what is the poem's central theme, the need for penance. Taken tropologically, Jonah remains a bad example, inadequate to the demands God makes of him. Taken typologically, Jonah is an ideological construct and both less relevant to the difficulties of the human condition and less engaging than the "human" Jonah. However, as both a figure for humanity and a type of Christ, Jonah speaks to the realities of human failure, while pointing toward an ideal of Christlike perfection. The poet thus uses Jonah to stress the need for penance if man is to become more than merely comic, employing Jonah as one element of a poem that proclaims the idea of change inherent in the sacrament of penance, the catalytic process by which base metal may be turned to gold.

The Story of Jonah

The story of Jonah in *Patience* is divided into four sections.[6] The first section describes God's calling of Jonah, Jonah's flight by ship to Tharsis, the storm at sea, and the sailors' decision to throw him overboard. Section 2 contains an account of Jonah's descent into the ocean and his three days and nights in the whale. Section 3 records Jonah's repentance for his disobedience to God's command that he preach penance to Nineveh, and Nineveh's repentance for her sins. In section 4, the poet recounts Jonah's wrath over Nineveh's salvation, and the episode of the woodbine, which God causes to grow over Jonah and then destroys as a lesson in patience. Although *Patience* is faithful to the details of the Book of Jonah, the poet exploits the dramatic potential of the story by elaborating upon the figure of Jonah, by interpolating speeches, by emphasizing certain themes, and by organizing his material so that only one section describes a truly typological Jonah. The result is a tightly organized story, focused by the poet's interest in vivifying the New Law lessons inherent in Old Law history.

The first section of *Patience* corresponds to the "Passion sequence" of the Book of Jonah, events which at once foreshadow Christ's passion and suggest Jonah's weaknesses. From his first appearance, Jonah is distinguished by his unwillingness to hear the voice of God. God's voice, calling him to Nineveh, sounds discordant to this discordant prophet: "Goddes glam to hym glod þat hym vnglad made, / With a roghlych rurd rowned in his ere" (63–64). After the voice has ceased and Jonah is left with an unpleasant memory of its command, he becomes angry because he does not wish to suffer. The Biblical account states simply that Jonah rose to flee to Tharsis from the face of the Lord, omitting any motive for his flight. However, the poet devotes lines 75–84 to the possible dangers of warning Nineveh. Jonah's fears are entirely physical, encompassing the terrors of prison, the stocks, foot shackles, blindness, and possible death:

"If I bowe to his bode and bryng him þis tale,
And I be nummen in Nuniue, my nyes begynes.
He telles me þose traytoures arn typped schrewes;
I com wyth þose typþynges, þay ta me bylyue,
Pyneӡ me in a prysoun, put me in stokkes,
Wryþe me in a warlok, wrast out myn yӡen.
Þis is a meruayl message a man for-to preche
Amonge enmyes so mony and mansed fendes,
Bot if my gaynlych God such gref to me wolde,
For desert of sum sake, þat I slayn were."

Jonah's language here bears witness to his excitable and hyperbolic nature. The first word he utters is "if," a word that suggests his effort to calculate the advantages and dis- advantages of this mission for him, and a word that easily leads into a series of imagined fears. He also assumes that God's command is a punishment for some offense Jonah has unknowingly committed (83–84). Jonah's frame of mind is childlike, for he sees God as a judge, a strict principle of justice whose ways are mysterious and arbitrary. His fears center on physical harm. The humor of Jonah's instant hy- perbole, his childish reaction to God, and his fear of physical suffering are underlined by his decision to run away: "'And lyӡtly when I am lest he letes me alone'" (88).

Jonah's human inadequacies remind us of Christ's perfec- tion. Those things that Jonah fears—shackles, pain, the power of malicious men, death—recall similar terrors foreseen and feared by Christ in the Garden of Gethsemane. Christ con- quered those fears and accepted the cup of the Passion; Jonah decides to run away from the cup. The comedy of the scene— God's stern voice, Jonah's fantasies, his intent to steal away— prevents us from sympathizing with Jonah. The poet's use of hyperbole enlarges the realities of human fear and anger to the point where they appear absurd, thus shifting our allegiance from the very human figure of Jonah to the figure of Christ.

Until Jonah voluntarily agrees to the judgment of the sailors, he is characterized by his human shortsightedness and by his cowardice. His ability to delude himself is most evident during the storm at sea. The Book of Jonah states simply that as soon as Jonah took ship, God sent a great wind that raised a storm. The poet embellishes the Biblical narrative by conveying Jonah's delusive feelings of safety and relief and by describing the power of the storm, thereby emphasizing those aspects of the sea that are associated with chance or risk. The connection between weather, especially weather on the sea, and chance is, of course, a common one, and Jonah's security is manifestly false from the beginning of the voyage. The poet further undercuts the figure of Jonah by commenting upon his shortsightedness: "Lo þe wytles wrechche, for he wolde noȝt suffer, / Now hatȝ he put hym in plyt of peril wel more" (113–114). The narrative intrusion underlines the irony of Jonah's situation: the man who ran away from suffering is, in fact, running toward it. Jonah's childish desire to run away from God elicits the punishment he feared in Nineveh, for he finds himself in acute physical peril. The prophet who first heard God's voice as a harsh clamor now hears real clamor in the howl of the winds, the noise of the waves, and the sounds of a ship in distress (137–140).

Whereas Jonah does not recognize the providential source of the storm, the sailors do, casting lots to determine the man responsible for the ship's distress. The outcomes of the sailors' game of chance and of Jonah's flight are, within the sphere of the poem, determined by Providence, for both "games" focus upon Jonah himself.[7] The poet hints at the thematic relationship between the two events by linking them with the word *lotes*. The sailors lay "lotes" (173), and Jonah flees to the bottom of the boat because he is afraid of the "flode lotes" (183). The two words have different roots, but in the plural they appear the same. "Lotes" in line 173 comes from Old English *hlot* and had as one of its meanings the lot that is cast in a game of chance. "Lotes" in line 183 comes from Old Norse *læte, lot,* and means noise.[8] For Jonah, both the game and the sea are risky ventures, and he finds himself caught by lot and caught by his own fear.

Jonah is not only caught; he is relieved of a good deal of his dignity. To this end, the poet begins the storm section with the magnificent power of the storm, goes on to describe the sailors' terror and their vain efforts to right the ship, and finally focuses upon the ignominious figure of Jonah who lies in the bottom of the ship, "Slypped vpon a sloumbe-selepe, and sloberande he routes" (186). The Book of Jonah says merely that Jonah fell into a deep sleep. The poet, by noting that he snores and slobbers, provides us with a picture of man at his most bathetic.[9]

The comic bathos of the scene is heightened by the sailors' reaction to Jonah. One of them kicks him and then calls out a rather rude awakening, " 'What þe deuel hatȝ þou don, doted wrech?'" (196), a summons similar in purpose, though not in tone, to "Why are thou fast asleep?" (Jon. 1:6; quotations from the Bible are from the Douay-Rheims Version). The comedy highlights the more serious implications of Jonah's condition. He has fallen into a deep sleep, sluggishly ignoring the storm and the sailors' realization that the storm is the result of spiritual disobedience. Rude as they are, the sailors identify Jonah's problem, asking him, " 'Hatȝ þou, gome, no gouernour ne god on to calle, / Þat þou þus slydes on slepe when þou slayn worþes?'" (199–200). In the Biblical account, the sailors do not ask this question because they know the reason for Jonah's flight; there, they ask him why he did such a foolish thing. Their question in *Patience* provides Jonah with an opportunity for confession after he has revealed his identity, a confession noteworthy for its brevity and simplicity: " 'For I haf greued my God and gulty am founden'" (210). All of Jonah's efforts to have his own way end in a statement that, like Adam's words in the mystery plays, realistically describes everyman's shortcomings in relation to God.[10]

Once Jonah expresses his willingness to endure punishment for his misdeeds, he ceases, for a time, to be a comic figure. He becomes the suffering servant, through whose sacrifice the ship is saved. That the poet was aware of the scene's typological associations is apparent from the sailors' anxiety that they be absolved from Jonah's death:

> Fyrst þay prayen to þe prynce þat prophetes seruen,
> Þat he gef hem þe grace to greuen hym neuer
> Þat þay in baleleȝ blod þer blenden her handeȝ,
> Þaȝ þat haþel wer his þat þay here quelled.
>
> (225–228)

Jonah, like Christ, takes on himself the consequences of heavenly wrath, or justice, so that the sailors may reach harbor in safety and, eventually, Nineveh may repent its own wickedness. By his sacrifice, he thus opens up an avenue of mercy for others.[11]

The poet's description of the sailors' relief and Jonah's dread intimates the new life Jonah embodies for others:

> Þaȝ þay be jolef for joye, Jonas ȝet dredes;
> Þaȝ he nolde suffer no sore, his seele is on anter;
> For what-so worþed of þat wyȝe fro he in water dipped,
> Hit were a wonder to wene, ȝif holy wryt nere.
>
> (241–244)

Jonah, of course, will receive new life by being dipped in water, just as the sailors will receive life in exchange for his immersion. But line 243 also reminds us that, for the poet, everyman may receive new life if he imitates the death and resurrection of Christ by dipping himself in baptismal water.

Section 1 presents us with a picture of Jonah's spiritual progression from anger and fear to submission, but section 2, which records his descent into the depths through the belly of the whale, makes it clear that Jonah is not yet truly humble and obedient. Jonah's three days and nights in the whale were thought to foreshadow Christ's death and descent into hell on Holy Saturday, a convention recalled by the poet's allusions to the hellish aspects of the whale's belly:

> And þer he festnes þe fete and fathmeȝ aboute,
> And stod vp in his stomak þat stank as þe deuel;
> Þer in saym and in sorȝe þat sauoured as helle,
> Þer watȝ bylded his bour þat wyl no bale suffer.
>
> (273–276)

LIke Christ, Jonah descends into the depths. He goes down into the water and, once in the whale, moves downward through its body—from the throat, to the gills, to the stomach (267–272). Although the poet's description of the whale's stomach suggests the smells and darkness of hell, and though Jonah is as unhappy as if he were in Hell, the similarities between Jonah's descent and Christ's descent are physical rather than spiritual.

The poet underlines Jonah's lack of spiritual renewal by providing him with a prayer that does not appear in the Biblical account:

> "Now, prynce, of þy prophete pite þou haue.
> Þaȝ I be fol and fykel and falce of my hert,
> De-woyde now þy vengaunce, þurȝ vertu of rauthe.
> Thaȝ I be gulty of gyle, as gaule of prophetes,
> Þou art God, and alle gowdeȝ ar grayþely þyn owen;
> Haf now mercy of þy man and his mys-dedes,
> And preue þe lyȝtly a lorde in londe and in water."
>
> (282–288)

This is not a prayer of repentance but a bargain. Jonah admits his duplicity, acknowledges God's omnipotence (because he is now trapped in the whale), asks for mercy, and finally suggests that God prove his power by releasing him from the depths. This prayer does not win Jonah his freedom but, instead, three days and nights in the whale. Section 2 concludes with the narrator's telling us that, in the next section, he will recount another prayer, a prayer that follows Jonah's three days in "hell."

Whereas Jonah's prayer in section 2 does not appear in the Book of Jonah, his prayer in section 3 is a translation of the successful prayer of Jonah 2:3–10 (see 305–336). This prayer is the cry of a man in despair, and the poet captures both its power and its tone of spiritual anguish. We have a sense, not that Jonah is bargaining with God or angry with him, but that he cries from "hellen wombe," from a spiritual hell he chose for himself. In the first lines of the prayer, he acknowledges the folly of his own willfulness, the omnipotence of God, and the providential nature of his experience in the whale:

"Þou dipteȝ me of þe depe se in-to þe dymme hert,
Þe grete flem of þy flod folded me vmbe;
Alle þe goteȝ of þy guferes and groundeleȝ powleȝ,
And þy stryuande stremeȝ of stryndeȝ so mony,
In on daschande dam dryueȝ me ouer."

(308–312)

Rather than accuse God of petty vengeance, Jonah now appears to recognize that the sea and the whale and the storm are God's. He begins to move toward an understanding that he, too, is a servant in a providential universe. He goes on to state his despair at being cast away from God, trapped beneath the waves in the prison of the whale.

Jonah calls on God because only God can save him, but he does more than sue for mercy. He offers God a new will, or a humble and contrite heart:

"Bot I dewoutly awowe, þat verray betȝ halden,
Soberly to do þe sacrafyse when I schal saue worþe,
And offer þe for my hele a ful hol gyfte,
And halde goud þat þou me hetes, haf here my trauthe."

(333–336)

That the poet intends us to mark the spiritual change in Jonah is clear from the first word of the following line,

"*Thenne* oure fader to þe fysch ferslych biddeȝ / Þat he hym sput spakly vpon spare drye" (337–338, emphasis added). Jonah has moved beyond a simple recognition of God's strength and now offers God his own will, his true obedience as a sign of his penance.

Jonah's second prayer, a model for penitential humility, illustrates the poet's familiarity with both the Book of Jonah and the traditional glosses on these verses. Jonah's prayer in the Book of Jonah contains an insertion from the psalm that was linked with the sacrament of penance. Both Psalms 68 and 129 were associated with this stage of Jonah's career, and both bore the rubric "De profundis." While fourteenth-century English illuminators included a picture of the whale devouring Jonah next to Psalm 68, the commentators usually connected Jonah to Psalm 129.[12] Jonah's prayer in *Patience*, which follows that in the Book of Jonah, strongly suggests these traditional associations of penance. Jonah's grief here suggests the grief of man, for he laments the fact that he has removed himself from the presence of God. In the end, he can offer God only what any man can offer— what God made for service.

The remainder of section 3 describes a new Jonah. The poet points to Jonah's new condition first by referring to his clothes, the outward sign of his inward state: "Þenne he swepe to þe sonde in sluchched cloþes; / Hit may wel be þat mester were his mantyle to wasche" (341–342).[13] After the reference to cleansing, we again hear the voice of God, commanding Jonah to Nineveh. Jonah's reply, after his former hyperbole, is remarkable: "'Ȝisse, lorde,' quoþ þe lede, 'lene me þy grace / For-to go at þi gre; me gayneȝ non oþer'" (347–348). The Book of Jonah does not contain Jonah's reply to God's second command; these lines of *Patience*, which are brief, obedient, and humble, emphasize Jonah's spiritual renewal.

Jonah then begins to use his "new speech" for purposes other than excusing himself. Like John the Baptist, whose speech and mission directly anticipate Christ, Jonah preaches penance to a corrupt and doomed city. He preaches, or, as the poet says, "he cryed so cler" (357) that the message of penance reaches the hearts of the Ninevites. Jonah's change of heart is especially manifest in his ability to speak clearly; he is succinct and purposeful. Moreover, his voice is now at the service of God, for he preaches the message of his spiritual lord. Rather than noise and self-absorbed jangling, we hear the voice of a man who appears to have moved outside himself.

Lines 353–408, which describe Jonah's mission to Nineveh, his preaching, and the penitential sorrow of the city, are a faithful paraphrase of chapter 3 of the Book of Jonah. Jonah's speech is simple and direct, and there is nothing in the poetic account to suggest an unfavorable approach to Jonah. In this section of the poem, as in his voluntary sacrifice and his second prayer of penance, Jonah perfectly fulfills his function as a type of Christ. Nineveh's salvation follows Jonah's figurative death and rebirth and subsequent preaching, just as the salvation of the Church depends upon the Passion and Resurrection. The poet emphasizes the relationship between Jonah's newly found voice and the penance of the city in line 365, "Þis speche sprang in þat space and spradde alle aboute," a line that does not occur in the Biblical account. The speech exites fear, "Such a hidor hem hent and a hatel drede, / Þat al chaunged her chere and chylled at þe hert" (367–368), a dread that produces penance:

Heter hayreȝ þay hent þat asperly bited,
And þose þay bounden to her bak and to her bare sydeȝ,
Dropped dust on her hede and dymly bisoȝten
Þat þat penaunce plesed him þat playneȝ on her wronge.
                                                    (373–376)

By changing their garments for hair shirts, by throwing dust upon their heads, and by crying to God, the Ninevites act out the ritual of penance. Finally, the king hears Jonah's message and orders the entire town, including newly born children and beasts, into mourning and penitential fasting.

From Jonah's truly penitential prayer, which begins the

section, to the Ninevites' penitential acts, section 3 focuses on the sacrament of penance. The emphasis here is important for a number of reasons. First, this is the only section in which we see a truly Christlike Jonah, who functions as a model for humility and obedience and as a means of Nineveh's salvation. Jonah's descent, obedience, resurrection, and good stewardship during this interval of his career have an added power because, for the poet and his audience, they foreshadowed the central events of Christianity. The fact that Jonah appears to have lost his distinctive "personality" underlines his mythic or typological function. He is both a type and a model for everyman, for his figure bridges the distance between man and Christ. If a noisy, disobedient man can become, through penance and grace, the voice of God and a precursor of Christ, everyman can move beyond his own preoccupations, fears, and angers, through Christ, toward Christ. Jonah here presents us, not only with an ideal, but with the means of moving toward that ideal.

Second, not only do we have in Jonah a model for the Christlike life, but in the salvation of the Ninevites we have a model for the relationship between God and man possible through penance. Nineveh's salvation is the result of her penance, but her penance is the result of Jonah's "speche." Jonah's voice, originally used for justifying his own selfish acts or for complaining, awakens dread and fear in the city. That dread inspires contrition, a progression more explicitly outlined by Chaucer's Parson, who states that fear of doom can be such a spiritual catalyst, setting in motion the sequence of contrition, confession, and satisfaction that is man's means of conversion. That Jonah's "speche," the agent of this process, is the product of his own typological passion and resurrection recalls the divine movement of salvation, a movement that receives its impetus in heaven, is worked out on earth, and returns to heaven as a noise of penance: "Þe rurd schal ryse to hym þat rawþe schal haue" (396). The original noise that God's voice made in Jonah's ears, "a roghlych rurd" (64), has become a "rurd" of mourning which deflects the consequences of justice, for God substitutes for

Nineveh, as he did for Jonah, mercy for justice. However, Jonah, like everyman, is not pleased with the mercy extended to Nineveh.

Section 4, the final section of the poem, reintroduces the old, querulous, angry Jonah, whose language is hyperbolic, whose anger is comic, and whose response to God is hasty and disobedient. First, he is angry because God spares Nineveh. His anger is no longer marked by fear—he is simply angry. Although he follows the Biblical version of Jonah's complaint over Nineveh's salvation, the poet infuses a vigor and a despair into Jonah's speech that, in its comic self-involvement, suggests that of everyman:

"I biseche þe, syre, now þou self iugge,
Watȝ not þis ilk my worde þat worþen is nouþe,
Þat I kest in my cuntre, when þou þy carp sendeȝ
Þat I schulde tee to þys toun þi talent to preche?
Wel knew I þi cortaysye, þy quoynt soffraunce,
Þy bounte of debonerte and þy bene grace,
Þy longe abydyng wyth lur, þy late vengaunce,
And ay þy mercy is mete, be mysse neuer so huge.
I wyst wel, when I hade worded quat-so-euer I cowþe
To manace alle þise mody men þat in þis mote dowelleȝ,
Wyth a prayer and a pyne þay myȝt her pese gete,
And þer-fore I wolde haf flowen fer in-to Tarce.
Now, lorde, lach out my lyf, hit lastes to longe;
Bed me bilyue my bale stour and bryng me on ende,
For me were swetter to swelt as swyþe, as me þynk,
Þen lede lenger þi lore þat þus me les makeȝ."
                                              (413–428)

This speech exemplifies Jonah's comic self-involvement in section 4. He uses the first person seventeen times, while the second person, referring to God, occurs twelve times. Moreover, Jonah uses second-person pronouns only in the first eight lines; most of these are possessives, referring disparagingly to God's mercy and compassion, qualities that gained Jonah his release from the whale. He begins his speech

with words that connote humility—"I beseech thee, sire"—
but these words are merely a preamble to a complaint char-
acterized by spiritual pride and anger. As in the Biblical ac-
count, Jonah insists that his knowledge of God's inevitable
mercy inspired his flight to Tharsis, a statement that is comic
in its self-delusion. In fact, the speech is funny because of
Jonah's inflated ego, manifested in his delusive pride. Al-
though he pays lip service to God's superior position in his
use of "syre" and his final request that God snuff out his
life, Jonah speaks as one colleague to another: not only is
Jonah's pride hurt by Nineveh's salvation, but God has wasted
his time in directing him to preach there. Jonah's absurd
gesture toward equality is especially apparent beginning in
line 417, "Wel knew I. . . ." He goes on to speak of God's
mercy as though he were discussing a lamentable weakness
in a well-known fellow. Finally, in lines 421–422, Jonah not
only takes full responsibility for their salvation but dispar-
agingly refers to the Ninevites as "þise mody men." The
statement is noteworthy for its triple insistence in the first
line on the first person and for its complacent pride: "I wyst
wel, when I hade worded quat-so-euer I cowþe / To manace
alle þise mody men þat in þis mote dowelleʒ." As a *typus
Christi*, Jonah is responsible for the salvation of Nineveh; as
everyman, his arrogance and self-sufficiency are ridiculous.

The following sequence of events illustrates the difference
between God's absolute power and man's absurd preten-
sions. God's reply in Jonah 4:4 is a stern question, "Dost
thou think thou hast reason to be angry?" In *Patience*, God's
mature and scornful reply contrasts sharply to Jonah's child-
ish egotism: "'Herk, renk, is þis ryʒt so ronkly to wrath / For
any dede þat I haf don oþer demed þe ʒet?'" (431–432). Twice
in six stanzas the poet applies a synonym for man to Jonah,
in line 409 ("Muche sorʒe þenne satteled vpon segge Jonas")
and again in line 431 ("renk"). The poet thereby alludes to
the lesson the audience should draw from this section of
Jonah's career. But Jonah is a man, so his response to God is
"joyles and janglande" (433). Moreover, he thereupon goes
off to the east of Nineveh where he builds himself a bower

in which he is oblivious to the fact that God is preparing another lesson for him. After a restless night, a sign of his spiritual condition, Jonah awakens to find a woodbine now shading his tent, a vine that God will use to teach his recalcitrant servant more about the duties of man to God.

The vine of the Book of Jonah deserves attention because it appears to have vexed medieval commentators as much as it can vex a modern reader of the Bible or student of the poem. Literally, Jonah is delighted by the vine, rejoices in its shade, is grieved when a worm destroys it, and finally turns on God and wishes to die. Medieval interpretations of these events appear to ignore the text. For example, Saint Jerome, Saint Augustine, and Rupert of Deutz link the woodbine with the people of Israel, and Jonah's sorrow over its death and anger over Nineveh's salvation with Christ's grief over the fate of Jerusalem (see Matt. 23:37; Luke 13:34).[14] These interpretations, however, seem to ignore the fact that Jonah is less sorrowful than he is angry and despairing. Taken morally, Jonah's reaction both to the appearance of the vine and to its death seems to indicate a lesson in fortune, a lesson the fourteenth-century English preacher and bishop Thomas Brinton drew in two sermons.[15] Brinton uses Jonah's delight in the vine as a means of warning England of the dangers of luxury; he suggests that the worm that destroys the vine is beneficent because, when the vine dies, Jonah must turn again to God. Brinton connects Nineveh's penance with the episode of the vine, for as Nineveh turned away from the pleasures of the world in penitential grief, so should we turn from transient luxuries to the stability of God.

The poet's treatment of this incident also emphasizes the spiritual effects of prosperity or luxury. The poet calls the booth (umbraculum) that Jonah builds to the east of Nineveh a "bour." This "bour" recalls the "bour" he attempts to find in the whale (276).[16] Both his shelter in the whale and his shelter on the hill overlooking Nineveh are temporary refuges from his spiritual restlessness, and neither alleviates his sadness. Furthermore, the poet intimates a relationship between the vine which grows up over the "bour" and the effects of luxury by calling the vine a woodbine. The nature of the vine had been the occasion for some controversy between Saint Augustine, who felt it was a gourd (*cucurbitas*) and Saint Jerome, who thought it an ivy (*hedera*).[17] According to the *OED*, medieval treatments of this episode usually refer to the vine as an ivy or as a wild vine although Wyclif called it an "eder," and the Geneva translators call it a gourd. The poet chooses "woodbine," a word denoting a clinging vine, such as honeysuckle, that can envelop and destroy its host plant. In literature, the word is usually used in settings that are associated with luxury and amatory pleasure.[18]

The description of this vine, or woodbine, in *Patience*, far more elaborate than in the Book of Jonah, also suggests its association with luxury:

> For hit watȝ brod at þe boþem, boȝted on lofte,
> Happed vpon ayþer half, a hous as hit were,
> A nos on þe norþ syde and nowhere non elleȝ,
> Bot al schet in a schaȝe þat schaded ful cole.
>
> (449–452)

Whereas the author of the Book of Jonah says merely that the vine provided Jonah with shade, "for he was fatigued," the poet describes a shelter, completely enclosed, save on the cooler north side, a shelter that not only provides Jonah with shade, but also pleases him:

> Þenne watȝ þe gome so glad of his gay logge,
> Lys loltrande þer-inne lokande to toune;
> So blyþe of his wod-bynde he balteres þer-vnder,
> Þat of no diete þat day—þe deuel haf!—he roȝt.
>
> (457–460)

Jonah's despair vanishes; he begins to laugh and to relax; he takes pleasure in his new dwelling place, using the word "won" (dwelling, 464) to describe the shelter the vine affords. He seems to forget that the vine was not there yesterday and might disappear tomorrow. What is manifestly transient, at best incomprehensible, he takes for a permanent token of stability. Not only has Jonah accepted a gift of Fortune, but he has forgotten that it is a gift. In his euphoria, he falls into a "sloumbe-slep" (466), only to discover his woodbine died in the night. Losing his good fortune, Jonah loses his good temper, and he lapses again into despair and anger.

It is clear from the poet's handling of the incident that the woodbine is less important than Jonah's reaction to it. By suggesting that Jonah's equilibrium depends upon the existence of a plant, the poet alludes to the dangers of good fortune or luxury. Jonah's good nature in prosperity is no more attractive than his bad temper in adversity. The death of the woodbine thus exposes the potential for illusion inherent in good fortune. In the shade of the vine, the realities of Nineveh's salvation, the sun's heat, and Jonah's problems with God are far less compelling. Only when the vine disappears does Jonah once more address himself to God. He turns to God, but he does so in anger, accusing God of depriving him of his last earthly comfort:

"I keuered me a cumfort þat now is caȝt fro me,
My wod-bynde so wlonk þat wered my heued;
Bot now I se þou are sette my solace to reue;
Why ne dyȝtteȝ þou me to diȝe? I dure to longe."
(485–488)

This complaint reveals a good deal about Jonah and about human nature. First, like his earlier complaint (413–428), Jonah's speech is dominated by his use of the first-person pronouns, *I*, *my*, and *me*. Second, he perceives worldly comfort as something he deserves. Third, he takes bad fortune as a personal insult, and, therefore, he prefers to die. That the poet intends the audience to see in Jonah's predicament the humam predicament is evident in God's reply to Jonah's address: "Why are þou so waymot, wyȝe, for so lyttel?" (492). God addresses Jonah as "wyȝe" (man) and describes Jonah's state of mind as "waymot" (bad-tempered), a word that nicely amplifies the sound of Jonah's wrath in God's ears, "ronk noyse" (490).

Jonah's self-absorption prevents him from absorbing the real lesson of the second half of his career. He is far less concerned with Nineveh than with his own pride and comfort. He anticipates the destruction of Nineveh, a destruction he might observe from his comfortable shelter on the hill. Ignoring Nineveh's true penance, he awaits justice, not mercy. His real lesson lies in Nineveh, whose penance, like his own in the whale, is marked by contrition, confession, and satisfaction. In longing for justice for others, Jonah brings justice upon himself. Jonah exemplifies the plight of man in general, who wishes justice for others and mercy for himself, but who ignores the fact that mercy is the result of penance. God, unlike Jonah, waits for the opportunity to substitute charity for malice, mercy for justice, and patience for wrath.

As a sequence, the story of Jonah in *Patience* bears ample witness to the poet's talents, not the least of which is his ability to focus his material. As vivid and as rich in detail as the story is, only when we stand back from it do we realize that each detail serves a purpose, that the sequence is a triumph of economy. For example, in section 2, the poet goes to a good deal of trouble to describe the inside of a whale, a subject not treated by the author of the Book of Jonah; however, the description emphasizes the resemblance between the whale's belly and Hell, a resemblance that has nothing to do with literal whales but everything to do with the tradition that linked this stage of Jonah's career to Christ's descent into Hell. Similarly, the poet's account of the woodbine is far more lavish than that in the Book of Jonah; once more, his attention to detail alerts us to the relationship between Jonah's attitude toward his woodbine and the dangers of luxury or good fortune. Though the details themselves help to create a world that appears "real," ultimately these details, like the equally multitudinous details of late Gothic art, are at the service of a good beyond verisimilitude.

Similarly, in Jonah, the poet creates a character as real, with a voice as urgent, as any in medieval literature. Some of Jonah's speeches are as lively as any Chaucer gave to his pilgrims; and Jonah is more fleshed out than any of the Biblical characters who appear in medieval drama. With the Wakefield-master and Chaucer, the *Gawain*-poet shares an ear for the inflections of speech, an awareness of the dramatic potential of monologue. Like them, he is able to create characters who reveal themselves by patterns of speech, turns of phrase, and logical inconsistencies. Just as it is possible to "hear" the Reeve shape and comment upon his tale or the Wife of Bath shrug off the significance of the marriage of Cana and welcome her sixth husband, so we can "hear" Jonah calculate, bargain, and complain in his never-ceasing effort to outwit a God who has prepared one lesson after another for him. If Jonah's voice sometimes sounds too familiar for comfort, we are "hearing" clearly. For Jonah speaks with a human voice, the voice of a person whose speech is dominated by first person pronouns, whose first concern is always himself, whose allegiance is naturally to his own comfort and stability.

The fact that, individual and real as Jonah sounds, he speaks with the voice of everyman, of the unredeemed Adam, underscores the degree to which the poet has his comedy under control. The comedy of Jonah is, like the rich detail of *Patience*, at the service of the poet's broader thematic concerns. First, as I have suggested, the comic portrait of Jonah is intended to comment upon the human tendency to place self at the center of the universe. The comedy at once distances us from Jonah and awakens a nagging sense of kinship with him. The lesson Jonah should teach us is implicit in his character. Second, frequently the poet uses comedy to underline the distance between Jonah and Christ. For example, the events of sections 1 and 2 were thought to foreshadow events surrounding the Passion, but Jonah's behavior during this part of his career is un-Christlike in ways that can only distantly remind us of Christ's perfect response to fear, suffering, and pain. Within the poem, Jonah acts as a bridge between man and Christ because he is quintessentially the one while foreshadowing the other.

That the poet is aware of the medieval tradition behind the figure of Jonah and is consciously using the prophet to point up both typological and tropological lessons is borne out by section 3, where Jonah is obviously Christlike. Here, as a type of Christ, Jonah is a model of humility and obedience and acts as the mediator between Nineveh and God. The poet handles such scenes with dignity and restraint; at no point do we sense hints of comedy or of absurdity. In creating in Jonah a character who looks forward to Christ and back to Adam, the poet seems to dramatize the tension between the divine and human wills that was thought present in Christ. Christ's anguished prayer in the Garden of Gethsemane could be seen as an instance of the tension between Christ's two natures. Christ's divine nature willed the Crucifixion, but his human nature shrank at the pain and terror of death. Jonah's abortive flight to Tharsis was thought to foreshadow this scene in the garden. In choosing Jonah, who is both a type and a historic man, the poet in one figure dramatically contrasts the weaknesses of man and the strengths of Christ.

The ways in which the poet manipulates the traditions surrounding the figure of Jonah are, however, his own; ultimately he uses them to focus our attention upon the necessity for penance. There are two aspects of the story of Jonah that suggest such an emphasis. First, the poet's portrayal of Jonah is serious only when the scene involves penance: Jonah's brief confession to the sailors in section 1 (205–212) and the entirety of section 3. These instances of penance, the channel through which God's mercy flows to man, stand in sharp relief to the other events of Jonah's career; given the poet's narrative abilities, interest in organization, and economy of style, he no doubt intended the apparent disjunction to underscore the significance of the events he treats seriously. Second, unlike in his treatment of Sir Gawain, the poet does not describe Jonah changing from one sort of man to another. While we may expect a change in Jonah, a movement perhaps from Adam to Christ, the Book of Jonah recounts no change, and the poet invents none. The Biblical account ends with the voice of God chastising Jonah for his shortsightedness, a speech the poet paraphrases in lines 490–523. *Patience*, however, does not end here, but continues through two more stanzas in which the narrator sums up the lessons of his tale. For Jonah to affirm the efficacy of the sacrament of penance would be anachronistic, but the narrator draws such a New Law lesson from Jonah's story.

Only when we appreciate the role the narrator plays in *Patience* can we understand to what purpose the poet uses Jonah. The narrator establishes our point of view from the beginning, and it is his voice—a voice from the contemporary Church—that gives form to the poem's various elements so that, together, they proclaim the message of penance. The linear development that it is natural to expect to see in Jonah is, in fact, apparent only when we take the poem as a unified whole, not as a story of Jonah framed by an introduction and a conclusion. It is the narrator who alerts us to the process of spiritual change, for the emphasis he places upon certain aspects of Jonah's career underscores the theme of penance, the means by which he intends to draw us toward Christ and his perfect patience.

The Narrator's Use of the Story of Jonah

The narrator places his account of Jonah within a specific frame of reference by providing a prologue to his account of the prophet. This prologue falls into three parts. First, the narrator offers us a preliminary definition of patience linking patience with endurance. Second, the narrator recounts the Beatitudes, placing particular emphasis upon the first and the last, humility and patience. Third, the narrator applies the need for patience to his own relationship to his liege lord, intimating a connection between patience and good stewardship. Throughout his account of Jonah, the narrator comments upon and emphasizes elements of Jonah's career that point up the links between patience and stewardship.

Though Jonah is clearly not a good steward and though the narrator hints at his own difficulties in that area, the narrator's shaping of the story suggests the possibilities of attaining perfect stewardship or perfect patience. By exploring Jonah's trials, the narrator suggests an attitude toward patience that transcends simple endurance of adversity, for he shifts the emphasis from passive endurance to the creative suffering a man may find in penance. The poet's conception of the virtue of patience reflects its importance as the final virtue of the Beatitudes.

The Beatitudes, especially the first and the last, and their lesson of spiritual growth provide a focus for the story of Jonah by suggesting what elements of his career are most important for the themes of the poem. The narrator introduces the Beatitudes by setting them within a liturgical context: "I herde on a halyday, at a hyȝe masse" (9). Ordelle Hill has linked this reference to the New Testament lesson for the Feast of All Saints, a day commemorating the achievements of those who have progressed beyond the limitations of the human will.[19] The Beatitudes, with their eight rewards for eight spiritual states, sketch a movement toward perfection and would have prepared the audience for a poem dealing with radical spiritual change. The narrator makes it clear that, though he focuses upon only two of them, he intends us to keep the entire progression in mind. Thus, after paraphrasing each Beatitude, he goes back and gives each a name— *Dame* Poverty, *Dame* Pity, and so on. He then isolates two, the first and the last, noting the resemblance in the wording of these two, "For in þe tyxte þere þyse two arn in teme layde, / Hit arn fettled in on forme, þe forme and þe laste" (37–38). Dame Poverty and Dame Patience are linked because each of them promises the kingdom of heaven as a reward.

For the Middle Ages, the first Beatitude, poverty of spirit, and the last, patience in suffering, were intimately related virtues; so the poet's emphasis on these two follows medieval convention. Saint Augustine saw these two Beatitudes as embodying the entire wisdom of the Sermon on the Mount.[20] For Augustine, the Sermon on the Mount represented the perfect model for the Christlike life. The first and last Beatitude summarize the lessons of the Beatitudes, sketching the movement toward the true perfection of Christ. The first Beatitude concerns humility, with which the process of spiritual refinement begins. Accordingly, this Beatitude was linked with Proverbs 1:7, "The fear of the Lord is the beginning of wisdom" (cf. Ps. 110:10; Ecclus. 1:16), and to the seven steps from fear to wisdom outlined by Saint Augustine in *On Christian Doctrine* 2.8. Beginning in humility or fear, the progression ends in patience, a perfectly Christlike virtue. Thus the eighth Beatitude signified resurrection, release from the Old Law, and the New Man. Saint Augustine connected the number eight with the Circumcision, Resurrection, and the day of Pentecost, feast days which celebrate the triumph of the New Law and the New Man.

The narrator's translation of the Beatitudes reflects the emphasis that was placed on the last Beatitude. Whereas the text of Matthew 5:10 reads, "Blessed are they that suffer persecution for justice' sake," the poem reads, "Þay ar happen also þat con her hert stere" (They are blessed who can govern their hearts, 27). Rather than endurance, the narrator stresses achievement, perhaps echoing "In patience you shall possess your souls" (Luke 21:19), the verse that most frequently occurs in medieval discussions of patience.[21] In *Patience*, this last Beatitude stands out from the rest because it appears to be a measure of spiritual ability, the attainment of the sort of wisdom that provides for good spiritual governance. However, the links between patience and governance that this verse conveys are less apparent in the narrator's early efforts to define the virtue.

The narrator, in the prologue of the poem, provides us with a preliminary definition of patience, a description of the virtue expanded by the narrative of Jonah. On its most basic level, patience is related to long-suffering, so the narrator begins:

Pacience is a poynt, þaӡ hit displese ofte.
When heuy herttes ben hurt wyth heþyng oþer elles,

Suffraunce may aswagen hem and þe swelme leþe,
For ho quelles vche a qued and quenches malyce.

(1–4)

In using "suffraunce" as a synonym for patience, the poet links patience with suffering. According to the *OED*, *suffraunce* means patience, endurance, forebearance, and long-suffering, a series of associations that depend upon whatever is to be suffered or endured. The poet goes on to say that "suffraunce" assuages or quenches malice, a remedy for malice also advanced by Chaucer's Parson, who says: "Pacience, that is another remedie agayns Ire, is a vertu that suffreth swetely every mannes goodnesse, and is nat wrooth for noon harm that is doon to hym. / . . . This vertu maketh a man lyk to God, and maketh hym Goddes owene deere child, as seith Crist." [22] Chaucer, too, associates patience with suffering; furthermore, his use of "swete" implies an attitude toward suffering that is active rather than passive. After pointing out the relationship between patience and endurance, the narrator of *Patience* goes on to apply the need for patience to his own feudal obligations and to explore the links between patience and suffering in his account of Jonah. Both his personal observations and his retelling of the Biblical story make it clear that suffering may be of two sorts. An individual may respond to adversity with grudging endurance or with positive acceptance. Only the latter attitude toward suffering releases a man from the constrictions of self.

The narrator, after recounting the Beatitudes and the different phrasing of the last Beatitude, goes on to apply the idea of patience as endurance to his own situation, using himself, as he later uses Jonah, as an example:

Ȝif me be dyȝt a destyne due to haue,
What dowes me þe dedayn oþer dispit make?
Oþer ȝif my lege lorde lyst on lyue me to bidde
Oþer to ryde oþer to renne to Rome in his ernde,
What grayþed me þe grychchyng bot grame more seche?
Much ȝif he me ne made, maugref my chekes,

And þenne þrat moste I þole and vnþonk to mede,
Þe had bowed to his bode bongre my hyure.

(49–56)

The narrator describes himself as a steward, as a man ow-
ing certain duties to a "lege lorde." He appears to see these
duties as inevitable, and, therefore, he has no right to grumble.
Instead, he notes that he must endure certain unpleasant
aspects of stewardship. Moreover, he uses two expressions,
"to mede" and "hyure," that have a special relation to the
ideals of stewardship. The phrase "to mede," which here
refers to the reward a disobedient vassal receives for grum-
bling, when used in conjunction with "hyure" anticipates
the maiden's recasting of the Parable of the Vineyard in *Pearl*
and her lesson in good stewardship. Although the narrator
links the concepts of stewardship and patience, he does so
in a negative manner, stressing the necessity for endurance,
rather than governance. His message is clear, but not com-
pelling: in order to be a good steward, a man must cultivate
humility and patience, or he will reap the rewards of a bad
steward. This approach to stewardship recalls the opening
line of *Patience*, "Pacience is a poynt, þaȝ hit desplese ofte."
The negative rewards of justice are far less compelling as
spurs to virtue than the benefits of mercy. Moreover, as the
narrator implies about his own situation and as the story of
Jonah indicates, suffering borne grudgingly is passive rather
than active and does little to assuage malice or anger.

For the most part, Jonah suffers because he is afraid of
adversity, and so his suffering is a reaction to his attitude
toward the world. First, he is afraid to go to Nineveh because
he is afraid to suffer bodily harm (73–84, 113). Later, he is
forced to experience both fear and suffering on the sea voyage
and in the whale's belly. When the woodbine is destroyed,
Jonah suffers over his loss and wishes to die. In these inci-
dents, the narrator suggests the effects of rejecting suffering
and the difficulties involved in enduring adversity. However,
at one notable point in his career, Jonah chooses the suffer-
ing of penance and the prospect of harm in Nineveh. By his

act of penitential suffering, Jonah is delivered from the whale to become the instrument of Nineveh's salvation. By choosing to suffer, Jonah moves away from passive reaction to creative action.

In his "De prophetia alia Balaam," Origen discusses the nature of fear in a way that illuminates Jonah's experience. Origen is here concerned with spiritual refinement as it relates to the prophetic role, and he links the figures of Balaam and Jonah in his discussion of fear. Origen stresses the beneficial, or catalytic, nature of fear because a man may, in fearing God, become an instrument of heavenly love. God thus teaches man to fear him, rather than the world, and can terrify a man in order to refine him. Origen suggests that fear precedes grace as a crucial first step in the process of spiritual change.[23] Hence, Jonah's suffering proceeds first from his fears of the world; only when he fears God more than the world does he agree to go to Nineveh. His fear of God results in obedient action, the fulfillment of his typological role. By his penance, he reaps mercy for himself and for the Ninevites.

Whereas Jonah's initial fears result in justice, the citizens of Nineveh, upon hearing Jonah, fear God. By choosing the physical deprivation and spiritual anguish of penance, they become deserving of mercy. The narrator thus implies that suffering can be creative, a point underscored by God's response to Nineveh's penance: "Þe sor of such a swete place burde synk to my hert, / So many malicious mon as mourneȝ þer-inne" (507–508). Man can, through penitential suffering, deflect justice and be rewarded by mercy. Patience need not be passive endurance but can be an active virtue, chosen freely. Patience, like good stewardship, requires an act of will inspired by the rewards a good steward receives.

By linking the idea of perfect patience to that of stewardship, the narrator implies a similarity between himself and Jonah. Both men have liege lords and hence responsibilities to them. Thus Jonah reacts to God's command to go to Nineveh in words similar to those the narrator uses to describe his own situation, " 'if I bowe to his bode . . . '" (75). To Jonah,

God seems capricious, but Jonah nonetheless describes God in terms of authority, as father, "syre," the maker of men. Jonah's lesson in stewardship culminates in the lesson of the woodbine. Jonah's assumptions in this section are those of the overlord rather than of the steward. He refers to the plant as his, taking its destruction personally. God's speech to Jonah after its disappearance alerts us to the spiritual duties of man—man is always a steward in relation to God, the maker of men. God points out the crucial difference between them: Jonah did not own the vine, never planted it, and never tended it, whereas God planted and tended Nineveh. God's sorrow over Nineveh, his decision to destroy it, and his acceptance of Nineveh's penance are justified because he is its maker. Jonah, the whale, Nineveh, and the woodbine were all created by God, for God: Jonah's wrath is therefore both foolish and presumptuous.

The crucial element of good stewardship added by the story of Jonah and underlined by the narrator's final words is penance. The narrator's initial definition of patience as suffrance is correct but incomplete. The narrator next adds another dimension to our understanding of patience by placing it within the context of the Beatitudes which were thought to sketch a progression toward Christlike perfection. The narrator's recasting of the eighth Beatitude makes it clear that patience is an active, rather than a passive, virtue and that it has to do with the ability to govern. However, the narrator's early application of patience to his own situation and the story of Jonah points up the difficulties involved in endurance. Neither the narrator's personal references nor his account of Jonah describes perfectly patient men, and simple endurance of adversity is not always possible. But the poet is realistic about human nature; without God's grace, man will fail to endure. Through penance, he may repent his failures and substitute mercy for justice.

By linking patience with penance, the narrator's definition of patience in the final lines of the poem transcends his earlier definition; for patience is described as both positive and possible:

For-þy when pouerte me enprecez and paynez in-noȝe,
Ful softly with suffraunce saȝttel me bihouez;
For-þy penaunce and payne to-preue hit in syȝt
Þat pacience is a nobel poynt, þaȝ hit displese ofte.

(528–531)

The narrator balances the first clause, which states that patience allows him to endure pain and poverty, by the last clause, which states that penance and pain prove the nobility of patience. This final clause alerts us to the possibilities of creative suffering, for, through penance, a man chooses to suffer. To return to an earlier point, by choosing penitential suffering, a man indeed governs his soul. Penance is, of course, the channel through which grace acts on man, releasing him from the limitations of the human will. By associating penance with patience, the narrator implies that perfect patience is a gift of grace, an idea also stressed by Saint Augustine.[24] Thus, by penance a man may achieve patience, through grace, the perfection of Christ. Although Jonah himself never steps outside the confines of Old Testament history to affirm either suffering or patience, the narrator deduces these New Law lessons from his story.

Within the framework of typology, the narrator stands as the third figure in a progression that begins in the Old Testament, is fulfilled in the New Testament, and is reflected in the contemporary Church.[25] Thus Jonah looks forward to Christ, and the narrator imitates Christ. Although the poet's account of Jonah, like the Biblical account, ends with the voice of God chastising Jonah for his lack of mercy, commentaries on the Book of Jonah end with discussions of salvation and of the continuing life of the Church. Fittingly, the poet ends the poem with a voice from that Church, a voice that deduces the New Law lessons of penance and mercy from an Old Law narrative. It is through the narrator that the poet manifests the possibilities of spiritual change; for it is the narrator who first advances an attitude toward patience, then recounts and comments upon the story of Jonah, and finally testifies to an understanding of patience that is both positive and possible. The narrator explains the spiritual lessons of Jonah's career and thereby tells the audience how to imitate, not Jonah, but Christ, the figure who gives Jonah his typological reality. Most notably, the narrator intrudes upon his own story, pointing out Jonah's human weaknesses. His emphasis upon Jonah's inadequacies is most apparent in section 1, where Jonah tries to flee from the sight of God. Rather than merely relate the action, like the author of the Book of Jonah, the narrator of *Patience* steps in to note that Jonah is a "wytles wrechche" who will not suffer (113), underlining the lesson of suffering as it relates to obedience. In line 114, he further empahsizes Jonah's folly by placing his flight within a larger perspective, "Now hatʒ he put hym in plyt of peril wel more." His melodramatic comment sets the narrator and the audience at a distance from Jonah, whose actions are made to appear foolish in light of the greater peril of the sea.

The narrator's comments on Jonah's flight culminate in a quotation from Psalm 93, an insert that does not appear in the Book of Jonah:

"O foleʒ in folk, feleʒ oþer-whyle
And vnderstondes vmbe-stounde, þaʒ ʒe be stape fole.
Hope ʒe þat he heres not þat eres alle made?
Hit may not be þat he is blynde þat bigged vche yʒe."

(121–124)

The poet identifies the quotation, saying that the lines are a reference to one of David's psalms, clearly intending us to note that his use of the verses is his interpolation. His reasons for having the narrator quote Psalm 93, especially that part of it that questions human folly, the foolishness that can imagine that God who made man's ears and eyes might be deaf and blind to human disobedience, become more clear when we look at commentaries on the psalm. The issues that are addressed in commentaries on Psalm 93 are those that are central to *Patience*.

Psalm 93 was thought to consider the issues of patience, refinement by suffering, obedience to the will of God, and Christian stewardship. Furthermore, Psalm 93 was specifically linked to the eighth Beatitude.[26] It is, of course, impossible to know if the poet expected the audience to be familiar with the allegorical lessons of Psalm 93 and equally impossible to know in what way the poet intended the quotation from the psalm to comment upon the poem. But clearly the narrator quotes the verses in an effort to point up Jonah's blindness and folly; and the context suggests that the true lesson of *Patience* rests in the complex relationship between the narrator's understanding of patience and his perspective on the story of Jonah.

There are numerous other examples of the narrator's efforts to guide our understanding of Jonah. The narrator's effective use of "þenne" to underline the relationship between Jonah's good and bad actions and their consequences points to the providential nature of events in Jonah's life. His use of adjectives such as "joyles" and "janglande" to describe Jonah, of similes comparing the whale's belly to Hell, his descriptions of Jonah's sleep ("sadly," "sloumbeselepe"), and his emphasis on Jonah's physical delight in the shade of the woodbine influence the way in which we see Jonah. The narrator distances us from Jonah by glossing his actions, forcing us to see human self-absorption objectively and preventing us from an overly empathetic response to Jonah's fears and angers. In short, he forces us to observe ourselves, a recognition that should turn our eyes to Christ and to his perfect response to pain and fear. The narrator describes Jonah in order that we may see Christ foreshadowed in the events of Jonah's life, and in order that we may turn from the imperfect and toward the perfect.

Conclusion

The poet uses the figure of Jonah to point up some basic lessons about the human experience. He creates a thoroughly human protagonist who wants his own way, his own comfort, and his own stable universe. To this extent, Jonah is everyman writ large.[27] That he is comic says a good deal about human expectations and frustrations; it also says a good deal about the higher, sometimes incomprehensible, ways of Providence. However, Jonah is more than a bad example. The poet might have used any number of protagonists to illustrate the moral lessons of this poem. He uses a type of Christ and underlines Jonah's typological role in section 3 where Jonah's actions and demeanor look forward to Christ.

The poet, in fact, uses Jonah as a type of both Christ and everyman. Throughout his account of the prophet's career, he underlines those details that were interpreted typologically. Section 3 is the section that most clearly reflects these associations, but, even in his anger and duplicity, Jonah foreshadows a more perfect response to pain and fear. Those moments when Jonah's typological role is obvious are followed by moments of human folly. The poet is able to manipulate Jonah in such a way because he is a type and can thereby illuminate the pattern of Christ and the problems of everyman. Jonah is both typological and tropological.

By providing a narrator who interprets and tells the story of Jonah after a discussion of the Beatitudes, the poet places the Old Testament narrative within a particular series of considerations. By stating that he will "play with" (36) both poverty and patience, the narrator implies that the story of Jonah will expand upon these two lessons of humility and patience, the first and last steps in the progression the Beatitudes were thought to sketch. In his handling of the episode of the whale, the narrator emphasizes the virtue of humility; and in his treatment of the woodbine, he focuses upon the nature of the eighth Beatitude, patience.[28]

The first lesson of humility was linked with fear. While the fear of the Lord may be the beginning of wisdom, Jonah begins by fearing bodily harm. His initial fear for his life ironically demonstrates the sterile nature of this type of fear, a fear that, for Jonah, ends in a stay in "Hell." Later, his fear of God, the true humility captured in his second prayer from the deep, results in obedient action and the salvation of Nineveh. In both cases, Jonah is afraid, but only the second fear is creative.

The incident of the woodbine illustrates the truly beneficial nature of patience, which is the culmination of the Christlike life. Jonah is angry over the death of the woodbine and wishes to die; God advances patience, rather than despair, as a remedy for anger. Jonah's anger here is as sterile as his earlier fear, a sterility that is implied also by Prudentius in the *Psychomachia* where Anger kills herself after an encounter with Patience. Anger, like fear, can be turned into something else, or it can remain self-absorbed and become despair. The fact that God's final speech connects patience with mercy moves the poem, and the lesson of Jonah, beyond justice to grace, grace that, for everyman, operates through penance.

The shape of Jonah's story in *Patience* reflects the shape of the Beatitudes and the movement they adumbrate from fear to Christlike perfection. Thematically, the poet intimates two types of movement, one comically described by Jonah's role as everyman, the other implied in the typological overtones of his actions and in the use the narrator makes of Jonah's story. The relationship between Jonah and Christ, Jonah and the narrator, and the narrator and Christ suggests that man may choose himself and move from fear to anger to despair; or he may choose Christ and move from fear to penance to patience. Though neither Jonah nor the narrator can be described as undergoing a spiritual change, the idea of change is the dominant theme of the poem. The sort of spiritual movement each of the poem's elements—the Beatitudes, the story of Jonah, the narrator's use of the story—suggests is that of radical spiritual conversion, a movement the poet and his audience would have associated with penance. The poet uses the narrator to guide us toward this recognition, for, throughout, his handling of his materials implies such an emphasis. In the final stanza, the narrator affirms his choice of penance as a bridge between fear and anger, anger and patience, and justice and mercy, thus exhorting his audience to penance. His most striking act of affirmation is, however, the poem itself, for through it the narrator signifies his choice of the new life by retelling a story, or by using his "speche" as a good steward.

Two

Sir Gawain
and the
Green Knight

Sir Gawain and the Green Knight recounts an adventure of
the best of Arthur's knights. Gawain journeys north to keep
a bargain he makes on New Year's Day with a green knight
who offers any member of Arthur's court the opportunity to
cut off his head if the Green Knight may have the same
opportunity the next year. Sir Gawain goes in search of the
Green Knight on November 2. While he is in the north,
Gawain spends the days from Christmas Eve to the morning
of New Year's Day in a strange castle, Hautdesert, as the
guest of its lord, Bercilak, and his lovely wife. During his
stay, Gawain makes yet another bargain, this time with his
host, to exchange the winnings from three days' hunts. Ber-
cilak hunts abroad, Gawain in the castle, and, at the end of
the first two days, Gawain exchanges for the host's deer and
boar kisses won from his hostess. On the third day, Gawain
fails to mention a green girdle the wife gives him, a girdle
that is supposed to preserve him from harm. When, on New
Year's Day, he meets the Green Knight, Gawain learns that
the nick in his neck he receives is a punishment for the
broken bargain with Bercilak; for Bercilak and the Green

Knight are the same. Gawain acknowledges his failure and returns to Camelot, wearing the girdle as a token of his untruth.

Literally, the poem is an account of failure, and, in this, *Sir Gawain* and *Patience* have much in common. In both poems, the poet focuses upon protagonists who embody certain ideals. Jonah, as an Old Testament type, suggests the ideal of Christlike perfection because he foreshadows Christ. Gawain, whose shield is a token of the ideals of chivalry, embodies the virtues of strength, intelligence, faith, and truth. Yet both men fail to live up to these standards of perfection and reveal characteristics that are not always either noble or praiseworthy. In both poems, the poet concerns himself with more than the problems of a single, historic man, for both protagonists have traits that link them with everyman. Although the poet treats Jonah with a good deal more humor than he treats Sir Gawain, both figures suggest the comic insufficiencies of man when faced with dangerous, perhaps impossible, situations. Thus, both figures suggest ideals larger than themselves while pointing up the weaknesses and struggles of man in general. Ultimately, both figures lead us to consider the means by which man can triumph over himself.

Through Sir Gawain, the poet explores themes pertaining to the individual; in his handling of Arthur's court and of English myth, he addresses himself to England. In this sense *Sir Gawain* is a national poem, for it is directed at England's awareness of itself as a nation with a special history and hence a special set of ideals.[1] The poet alludes to these ideals by prefacing his account of Sir Gawain with a sketch of England's mythic genealogy. Furthermore, though the poem recounts a tale of the past, the poet makes no effort to describe the customs, clothing, architecture, and food of an earlier England. He describes Arthur's court as if it were a contemporary court. This technique, similar to that of the mystery plays in its apparent anachronisms, allows him to underline the relationship between England's past and its present and to scrutinize contemporary issues by placing them within the framework of an earlier era. The very real concerns of England for the standards of chivalry and of nationhood provide the poem with its general theme. The poet's handling of the themes both of individual and of national reform suggests the possibilities of renewal. In linking the two, the poet demonstrates a conventional medieval awareness that national reform is inextricably bound up with individual reform, for it is impossible to separate individual morality from national morality.

The poet underlines the urgency of his message by setting both Gawain and Arthur's court within various sequences of time. The poet's careful, and sometimes complex, use of time in this poem has been virtually unexplored; but the subject of time is a crucial one.[2] The poet provides us with three ways of telling time in *Sir Gawain:* cyclic, degenerative, and regenerative.

In the first two stanzas of the poem and in the last, he offers one way of looking at time by placing Camelot, implicitly contemporary England, within a cyclic framework. He describes the destruction of Troy, Aeneas's flight, the founding of Rome under Romulus, and Brutus's discovery of and founding of Britain. He thereby introduces into the poem the ideals of the English national myth and the warning that myth was thought to convey. His use of cyclic history is designed to stress the lessons of the past, the ways in which the present might learn from both the successes and the failures of earlier national cycles.

The poet also suggests the degenerative nature of time by intimating its diminishing possibilities for nations and individuals. The mutability that rules men's lives also rules the lives of nations. The change from an age of gold to one of iron; the decline from the grandeur of the past to the paler imitations of the present; the progression from youth, with its seemingly endless potential, to the realities of age; and the movement from spring's anticipatory life to autumn's actual harvest all suggest the debilitating effects of time. The poet describes a young Camelot, a Camelot at the height of its fame, wealth, and beauty. But the myth of Camelot, like the myth of Troy, includes more than glory; the fame of both cities entails their destruction.

The poet's use of both cyclic and degenerative time depends upon an awareness of flux and, while pointing up the lessons of the past and the dangers of ignoring time, does not provide contemporary man with a way to transcend time. To this end, the poet places the action of the poem against the framework of the liturgical calendar. This calendar transcends time because its revolutions are built around the life of Christ and the eternal life of the Church. The poet, by building into the poem a calendar that proclaims regeneration rather than decay, suggests time's redemption for nations and for individuals through those truths impervious to the mutability which otherwise restricts human efforts.

Time and Its Shape

Cyclic Time. The first two stanzas of *Sir Gawain*, which link England with Rome and Troy, would have evoked England's most important national myth. British accounts of history, from the prose chronicle of Geoffrey of Monmouth to Spenser's *Faerie Queene* and afterward, trace the founding of Britain to Brutus and his band of rescued Trojans. English institutions were thought to reflect the glories of Trojan civilization, and Englishmen saw in their own nation a successor to the noble world of Troy.[3] Because of this sense of national lineage, the study of history was considered an inquiry into national failures and successes that could shed light on contemporary problems. Both the strengths and the weaknesses of lost civilizations were scrutinized and related to those of present civilizations. The most notable example of this sort of historical inquiry is, of course, Saint Augustine's *City of God*, the first half of which explores the reasons behind the fall of Rome, once a pagan but then a Christian city. Similarly, other writers explored the glories of Troy and the weaknesses that brought about its destruction. Both Troy and Rome were inspirations to English medieval institutions: in both civilizations, Englishmen found authority for their own chivalric ideals. In tracing its lineage back to Troy, England could participate in the most notable cycles of national glory.

For medieval Europe, the Trojans were the real heroes of the ancient world and stood as testimony to the verities of chivalric institutions. Caxton's later translation of the *Aeneid* reveals the extent to which Troy furnished a noble example of victory in defeat. Caxton notes that, although Troy was assailed, it was "coragyously and volyauntly defended," going on to say that his translation is intended "for to enstructe smale and grete, for euerych in his ryght / to kepe & defende. For a thynge more noble is to dye / than vylanously to be subdued."[4] Troy reaped all the glory inherent in a lost cause and became a powerful example of the nobility of hopeless valor.

England also traced its conception of knighthood to the pagan world, specifically to the Romans. The medieval respect for the discipline and bravery of Roman knights is apparent in John of Salisbury's *Policraticus*, which adopts Roman standards of military discipline as spurs to contemporary standards. The medieval reverence for Vegetius bears further testimony to the respect for the Roman military past.[5] In the fourteenth century, Thomas Brinton, in defining the word *knight*, links English chivalry to its Roman origins. He goes on to say that the word denotes both honor and labor; knightly honor thus derives from the Roman origins of the institution of knighthood.[6] Thus, in both Troy and Rome, England found an ideal of glory and courage that could inspire the chivalry of the present.

In his handling of British myth, the *Gawain*-poet demonstrates that he was well aware of the lessons of history. He suggests these lessons by stressing the wealth, glory, and courage of England's mythic ancestors. In the first two stanzas of the poem, which describe a series of national cycles, he links Arthur's achievements to those of his mythic forebears by emphasizing the valor and wealth of each successive nation. He stresses the fact that Aeneas, after his flight from Troy, regained many times over the lost wealth of the past: Þat siþen depreced prouinces, and patrounes bicome / Welneʒe of al þe wele in þe west iles" (6–7). Following in Aeneas's footsteps is "riche Romulus," who founded an equally rich Rome, and Felix Brutus, who founded Britain "wyth wynne" (joy, 15). Arthur, like his ancestors, rules a wealthy kingdom whose knights and ladies enjoy unsurpassed meat, drink, and fame. The picture of all three civilizations is one of wealth, of empire, and of civilized nobility. Through its high degree of wealth, fame, and nobility, Camelot shares in the glories of an older classical world. For medieval Englishmen, England thus participated in the glories of the past and could trace its valor and prosperity to those of an earlier age.

For medieval Britain, its mythic links to Troy and Rome added glory to the present, but they also served as reminders of the fall of cities. In *The Fall of Princes* (book I), for example, Lydgate uses the figure of Priam, king of Troy, as a means of undercutting a sense of worldly security. He notes that Priam was "most renommed off richesse and tresours."[7] Despite his wealth and power, Priam's success fell to Fortune. In reference to Priam, Lydgate concentrates upon the realities of change, linking Fortune with time as threats to worldly success. After describing Priam's fall from happiness, he didactically reiterates the necessity for vigilance against the world: "And onwar chaunge[e], which no man may knowe, / The hour whan Fortune will make him loute lowe."[8] But Lydgate by no means casts Priam as passive in the grip of change, for, in book IV, he maintains that Priam lost all for sustaining "fals avoutrye" (181). Lydgate is, however, concerned with the ultimate limitations of worldly prosperity and, like other medieval writers, uses the example of Troy as a warning to his contemporaries about the dangers of trusting to the world.

Neither is the *Gawain*-poet's account of the past entirely positive. In emphasizing the chaos of earlier civilizations, he implies what Lydgate overtly states. In the first two stanzas, the *Gawain*-poet adumbrates the power of change without slipping into didacticism. Thus, the poet begins by chronicling the ravages of time, the destruction that is an inevitable aspect of new national ventures. The opening stanza contains a series of words pertaining to war: "sege," "assaut," "brent," and "brittened" (referring to Troy); "depreced" (referring to Aeneas's conquest of the West). The series culminates in line 16 with words describing Brutus's England: "werre" and "wrake" and "wonder," the final word by no means altering the stress on the first two, for "wonder" suggests the possibility of instability or chance. In short, the first stanza is not only a history of the founding of Britain, but also a history of destruction and of chaos. It begins with the destruction of Troy and moves to Britain, which is characterized by the same national chaos as its mythic parent state. The extraordinary rapidity with which the poet recounts these events highlights the chaotic aspects of history. His concern is not with the peace that preceded the war, or with the beauties of Troy, Rome, or Britain, but with the themes of conquest and empire. His emphasis upon war suggests the instability of national efforts and thus the cyclical nature of human history. He sketches the progress of time in a way that underlines the brief glory of man's attempts to create orderly civilizations, for man's cities are always at the mercy of man's tendency to wage war.

In the second stanza, the poet arrives at the figure of King Arthur, like Brutus a noble king and a builder of cities and, like his mythic predecessors, an inspiration to contemporary Britain.[9] By using Arthur's court as the setting for his poem, the poet adds one more layer to his cycle of British history, for, from the thirteenth century onward, the legend of Arthur began to play a significant role in British ideology.

The use of Arthur for either national or propagandistic purposes of course predates the thirteenth century, but the occurrence of Round Table tournaments at this time affords a popular use of the legend. The Arthurian legend flourished under Richard Coeur de Lion, who gave Arthur's sword Caliburnus to Tancred of Sicily. In 1252 there was a famous Round Table at Walden which Matthew Paris described as a primarily social occasion accompanied by various games, among them jousting with blunted instruments. In the reign of Henry III, there were only two, in 1252 and 1257, and only three in the reign of his son, in 1279, 1281, and 1284. Edward I, in fact, had had Arthur's tomb at Glastonbury opened in 1289,[10] a circumstance that Trevisa records as effectively shattering the notion that Arthur would reappear in England.[11] However, the Mortimer family seems to have been as interested as the crown in the legend, for the Round Table of 1279 celebrated Edward I's knighting of the three sons of Roger de Mortimer at Kenilworth. In honor of this occasion, the baron of Wigmore entertained one hundred knights and one hundred ladies for three days with this tournament. In 1284, Edward I held a Round Table of his own to honor the newly found relics of ancient kings, one of which, the crown of Arthur, was presented to Edward I at the time.[12] The Mortimer claim to descent from Arthur and Brutus gave impetus to a later Round Table held in 1328 at Bedford in which the knights played the parts of Arthur and his court.[13]

The fourteenth century, with the victories of Sluys and Crécy, Poitiers and Najera, was a period of particular national pride and, consequently, of increased popularity for the myth of Arthur. In light of the striking popularity and visual force of the Plantagenets, a resurgence of the Arthurian legend is not surprising. With the return of Edward III to England wearing the victories of Crécy and Calais, and with the establishment of the Order of the Garter in 1348, it seems only natural that Englishmen should recall the glories of their Arthurian past. Thus, perhaps prompted by the increased interest in tournaments under Edward III, the great tournament of the Round Table in 1344 was distinguished by the construction of a huge round table for the knights and by the beginning of a great round tower to enclose it. At this tournament, the king vowed to restore the glory of the Round Table to England and swore in a certain number of barons and knights as companions of the Round Table. Regulations for observances of the brotherhood stipulated an annual feast at Whitsuntide. On St. George's Day, 1358, the most splendid of Round Tables was held, reflected in a ewer in the king's treasury, enameled *ove les chivalers de la rounde table*.[14] Moreover, around 1356, the figures of Arthurian romance began to appear in carvings, tapestries, and frescoes.

The lessons Camelot had for England during the fourteenth century, like those of Troy and Rome, also suggested a warning, for the history that recorded Camelot's glory also recorded its fall. The reasons for Camelot's fall are both explicit and implicit in medieval accounts of the Arthurian myth. Adultery and treason were the obvious causes for its fall, but the luxury, worldliness, and laxity of Camelot were constant components of descriptions of Arthur's court from Geoffrey of Monmouth onward. In many ways it is ironic that the period that saw a revitalization of the ideals associated with King Arthur should also have, in the older Edward III, a man who devoted far too much time and money to his mistress, Alice Perrers, and, in the young Richard II, a ruler who was careless, weak, and self-indulgent. Historical parallels aside, the medieval Englishman's use of the legend of Arthur's court was as two-sided as his use of the histories of Troy and Rome.[15]

The Camelot of *Sir Gawain*, like Troy, is a city whose brilliance and glory, though real, rest upon shaky foundations. The poet's description of Camelot at its Christmas festivities in the third stanza depicts a court whose allegiance is to the world. The stanza abounds with superlatives: "mony luflych lorde," "þe best," "gentyle kniʒtes," "most kyd knyʒtez" (most famous knights), "louelokkest ladies," "fayre folk." The first impression of the court is dazzling. However, the poet undercuts his picture of a court composed of the best, most famous, and most handsome by his description of their attitude toward the Christmas season. They celebrate with "rych reuel oryʒt and rechles merþes" (40), with food, with "dere dyn vpon day, daunsyng on nyʒtes" (47). They keep the fifteen-day feast with "all the mirth that men could devise" (45) and "live with all delight of the world" (50). Juxtaposed with the first two stanzas of the poem and their sketch of significant historical cycles, Camelot's delight in the world appears, at the least, naive. The poet's emphasis here upon beauty, strength, wealth, and delight suggests Camelot's vulnerability to time by describing those things that time can destroy.

The first three stanzas of *Sir Gawain* underline the theme of mutability. By rapidly sketching the fall of Troy, rise of Rome, rise of Britain, and the emergence of Camelot, the poet nods to the glories of the past while intimating its weaknesses. Cities are built by men and thereby reflect men's ideals and their failures to sustain these ideals. The message inherent in cyclic history, or in the rise and fall of significant nations, is double. First, for medieval Englishmen, the ideals of the cities of the past were inspirations to contemporary valor. However, lest history repeat itself, the failures of the past should be recognized and understood. England, like Troy and Rome, might find itself an example of another failed attempt to create order from chaos.[16]

Degenerative Time. For the Middle Ages, history was at once a source of knowledge and a way of understanding the present. Cyclically, England participated in the past, reflecting its glories and trying to avoid its mistakes. However, the men of the Middle Ages were also aware that their world was perhaps less grand than former worlds and saw time as a diminishing spiral. Medieval thinkers were therefore able to apply the study of history to themselves by measuring the present against the past. Frequently, an awareness of time's diminishing glory resulted in a vision of a lost world, of lost possibilities, for either a nation or an individual. Nationally, England could be seen to reflect but dimly the glories of the past; individually, a man could squander his youthful potential and find his "winter" far less satisfying than his "spring." A concept of degenerative time is thus inextricably linked with the theme of mutability or decay.

The theme of decay came to the Middle Ages by two routes—classical and Biblical. The most important classical source for the theme of mutability was Ovid, who begins his poem of change with an account of decay. The first hundred fifty lines of the *Metamorphoses* describe the ages of the world, beginning with gold and ending with iron. For Ovid, human history begins in a pastoral, nonmercantile world and ends in a world of profit, greed, industry, and war.[17] In Christian myth, the story of Adam's expulsion from Eden marks a similar decline in human history. Adam leaves the pastoral world of Eden for a world where he will live by the sweat of his brow and where all human relationships will be accompanied by varying degrees of disorder.[18] That the poet was aware of this concept of time as a diminishing thing is clear from his description in *Purity* of the descendants of Adam. The early members of the human race, unlike men after the Flood, were possessed of extraordinary beauty, strength, and longevity and were subject to no masters or laws other than the laws of nature. His account of the early members of the human race reflects both the Ovidian description of earlier, most blest ages and the Christian conception of the negative effects of sin upon man.

For the Middle Ages, decay was a continuous process, so medieval men not only saw around them an age of iron but felt that the age steadily declined. John of Salisbury in the *Policraticus* mourns the debased nature of his own age: "Our age has run out, and is reduced almost to nought, is puffed up with empty honors but ignorant of the degrees of honor, delights in the vanity of words and names, but despises the true and fruitful substance of realities."[19] Here, John of Salisbury focuses upon the debased nature of language wherein words no longer reflect higher meanings; they reflect only the vanity of worldly glory. Froissart, Chaucer, and Christine de Pisan all voice a similar concern for the decline in true value.[20] The author of *Piers Plowman* and Gower likewise describe a world of greed and of lost potential, a world that has slipped from its own ideal standards.

For the historian, history became a way of keeping those ideals fresh through education. In his translation of the *Polychronicon*, Trevisa mourns that men are not what they were, for now the liberal arts have declined. He justifies his translation precisely because it is a record, concluding, "but þe mercy of God had i-ordyned vs of lettres in remedie of vnparfiȝtnesse of mankynde."[21] Learning, or an understanding of history, might slow down the process of decay and allow a nation or an individual to gain, at least, self-knowledge. The *Gawain*-poet reflects this vision of diminishing time, particularly in his portrait of Camelot. He is able to intimate the decay inherent in time, in part because he writes about a city whose fame includes its destruction. Not only does he focus upon Camelot; he focuses upon a young Camelot, still without the treachery that was to precipitate its fall. However, for each member of his audience and probably for each modern reader, the beauties of Camelot remain colored by the awareness that it did fall. Although the poet never mentions its destruction, he frames the portrait of Camelot by linking it with other fallen cities, reminding us that Camelot, too, is circumscribed by time. In addition, he provides other hints of Camelot's vulnerability to time by suggesting its callowness and its superficiality. The implications of Camelot's heedless enjoyment of youth and good fortune become ominously clear in his description of the yearly rotation from spring to winter.

Camelot's potential for decay is implicit in the description in the third stanza of its Christmas festivities. In a stanza in which he records the wealth, fame, and beauty of the court, he says, "For al watz þis fayre folk in her first age, / on sille" (54–55). The word "age" is itself suggestive because it denotes a distinct and specified period of time. By modifying "age" with "first," the poet sets this age apart as special and still, in a sense, blessed. The phrase "first age" implies a second and a third, and, for Camelot, our awareness of its first age is also a recognition of its last. Camelot in its first age may be carefree and lovely; but, in its fall, that first age will seem naive. The phrase also evokes the idea of a golden age, also lost, which was characterized by youth, harmony, and contentment. That idyll also ended, and the world decayed to an iron age. The phrase "on sille" (in the hall) tells us where that first age occurs and underlines Camelot's vulnerability because the hall itself will disappear with the civil war that ends Arthur's reign. The poet heightens our awareness of time's effects by noting in the last two lines of the wheel that it would now be hard to find so "hardy a here (castle) on hille." Not only have the glories of Camelot disappeared; there are fewer possibilities for such glory in present time.

Camelot, young and glorious, reflects its king, whom the poet describes as restless and eager for adventure. In the second stanza of the poem, the poet introduces the idea of instability into his portrait of Arthur's England by using five synonyms for marvels to describe the land: "ferlyes," "aunter," "selly," "outtrage awenture," "wonderez." All of these words denote strange or untoward happenings linked to Arthur's love of risk: "He watz so joly of his joyfnes, and sumquat childgered: / His lif liked hym lyȝt, he louied þe lasse / Auþer to longe lye or to longe sitte, / So bisied him his ȝonge blod and his brayn wylde" (86–89). Though the lines appear to praise Arthur's good spirits, they cast some doubt upon Arthur as a figure of stable rule. The word "childgered" is not laudatory: it connotes childishness and thoughtlessness and would not have been applied to a king as a form of praise.[22] The phrase "ȝonge blod" loses its neutral cast when coupled with "brayn wylde."

The poet also suggests that Arthur himself is somehow responsible for the appearance and challenge of the Green Knight. After the Green Knight has departed, carrying his head and leaving behind a shaken Sir Gawain, the poet remarks, "This hanselle hatz Arthur of auenturus on fyrst / In ȝonge ȝer, for he ȝerned ȝelpyng to here" (491–492). The adventure has, in fact, fallen to Sir Gawain, but the poet ascribes it to Arthur. Arthur's youth and restlessness appear foolish. He has created a court as young as he is, and the court's fame has spread. It is exactly this fame that draws the Green Knight.

Camelot's weaknesses remain implicit until the appearance of the Green Knight. He makes them apparent by challenging the true nature of Camelot's fame, taunting the court with its own reputation: "'Where is now your sourquydrye and your conquestes, / Your gryndellayk and your greme, and your grete wordes?'" (311–312). His challenge may not be clear to the court, but his meaning must have been apparent to the poet's audience. He wishes to know if fame is only an empty word, a false rumor, or if the men in Camelot deserve their name. He challenges, not Camelot's physical strength, but its very nature. Although Sir Gawain finally accepts the challenge, he fails to perceive the nature of the test, a failure that reflects Camelot's own heedless delight in appearance.

Sir Gawain's, or Camelot's, deadly innocence is made even more explicit by his failure to understand either Bercilak, his host in the north, or the nature of his castle. Not only is the host gracious and the castle comfortable, but the dinner table is "Clad wyth a clene cloþe þat cler quyt schewed, / Sanap, and salure, and syluerin sponez" (885–886). Gawain seems never to realize that a castle boasting a clean table-cloth and silver spoons might be dangerous. Later, when Gawain reveals his identity, the guests are pleased to meet a knight of such fame, "'Now schal we semlych se sleʒtez of þewez / And þe teccheles termes of talkyng noble'" (916–917). Gawain never questions the fact that, in Hautdesert, chivalry is reduced to good manners and smooth talking. He is blinded by his own preconceptions. Hautdesert looks like Camelot, talks like Camelot; so Gawain, a representative of Camelot, does not stop to look beyond beauty, youth, manners, and excitement.

Camelot's heedlessness is finally placed in perspective by the poet's description of the process of time in lines 498–535. These lines form one of the most famous and beautiful seasonal descriptions in medieval literature, but their implications are sobering because they define time as a process of decay. A year itself is a neutral quantity of time, and a description of a year can evince any theme a poet might wish. The *Gawain*-poet underlines the urgency of time, its limits, and its diminishing possibilities by allowing winter to dominate the yearly cycle.[23] He also underlines the constrictions of time by placing his description of the seasons between the Green Knight's appearance and Gawain's embarkation on his journey. The passage telescopes the events of a year much as the first two stanzas telescope British history. The rapid pace of both accounts suggests how brief an age, or a year, or a century can be in the life of a nation or a man. Gawain's year is especially brief and gives us evidence of how illusory spring or youth may be. The year begins with Lent, when the flesh fasts, but then spring contends with winter and releases the flesh to new life. In describing spring and summer, the poet uses soft sounds that capture the languor of the seasons: "Schyre schedez þe rayn in schowrez ful warme" (506); "solace of þe softe somer" (510); "After þe sesoun of somer wyth þe soft wyndez" (516). The tone becomes less languid and more urgent with the advent of autumn: "Bot þen hyȝes heruest, and hardenes hym sone, / Warnez hym for þe wynter to wax ful rype" (521–522). Not only are the sounds harsher, but the pace of these lines is more rapid. The lines themselves describe autumn as a season of warning and reflect a sense of impending judgment. Winter itself will judge each living thing, and autumn is the last point in the yearly cycle for the gathering of the year's fruit.

With the advent of winter comes another struggle, of winds, or of strengths:

> Wroþe wynde of þe welkyn wrastelez with þe sunne,
> Þe leuez lancen fro þe lynde and lyȝten on þe grounde,
> And al grayes þe gres þat grene watz ere;
> Þenne al rypez and rotez þat ros vpon fyrst,
> And þus ȝirnez þe ȝere in ȝisterdayez mony,
> And wynter wyndez aȝayn, as þe worlde askez,
>   no fage . . .
>   (525–531).

The wind of winter "wrastelez" with the sunlight of fall, sending the leaves to the ground; what was green becomes gray; and what flourished in spring now "rypez and rotez." Time itself becomes a series of yesterdays. The description ends with winter's triumph ("wynter wyndez aȝayn"), placing every other season and every other living thing in relation to the threat of winter.

Though the description of the seasons is rooted in nature, the realities of birth and death, of fruit and harvest, are ominous in relation to Arthur's court. The seasonal cycle serves as a reminder that Camelot exists within a world characterized by change, not in a golden age of eternal spring, and must either use time or be destroyed by it. The court's present heedless enjoyment of the world, its delight in all those qualities that time devours, make it a particularly powerful emblem of decay. Unlike herbs and bushes, which awaken and flourish every spring, man and Camelot exist within the framework of a single cycle.

Regenerative Time. Both a vision of history as a series of cycles and a vision of history as a process of dissolution underline the effects of time and thus the theme of mutability. In both cases, man is a prisoner of time, and human history may perhaps teach only certain lessons about the art of living in time. In his efforts to cope with time, man is alone. The universe and the earth undergo a similar process of change, but only man knows he changes and knows his time is limited. In *The Cosmographia*, Bernard Silvestris distinguishes between man and nature in their relations to time:

> The nature of the universe outlives itself, for it flows back into itself, and so survives and is nourished by its very flowing away. For whatever is lost only merges again with the sum of things, and that it may die perpetually, never dies wholly. But man, ever liable to affliction by forces far less harmonious, passes wholly out of existence with the failure of his body. Unable to sustain himself, and wanting nourishment from without, he exhausts his life, and a day reduces him to nothing.[24]

Man, unlike nature, perceives time's limits and is therefore forced to use time or to escape it. An awareness of change need not, however, end with a simple recognition of mutability. For the Middle Ages, the Bible described the end of time itself in apocalypse. Decay could therefore become a providential process, ushering in a new golden age without the strictures of time, as Gower affirms:

> And seide how that is goddes myht,
> Which whan men wene most upryht
> To stonde, schal hem overcaste.
> And that is of this world the laste,
> And thanne a newe schal beginne,
> Fro which a man schal nevere twinne;
> Or al to peine or al to pes
> That world schal lasten endeles.[25]

For Gower, as for other medieval writers, change is a natural process, and man's insecurity in a universe of change should align him with infinite and changeless principles. This process of reorientation is, of course, the lesson Lady Philosophy teaches Boethius and the lesson deduced by numerous medieval and Renaissance personae who contemplate the process of time. Change exists, but it need not threaten man.

The liturgical calendar thus offered another way of ordering time. Like the natural cycle, the liturgical cycle describes a circular motion, but it revolves from spring (March 25) to spring, not from winter to winter.[26] This year begins and ends in new life and has as seasons central events in the life of the Church. The liturgical calendar allows an individual to transcend time by participating in moments that transcend time. He can thus celebrate the eternal truths figured by Church festivals and escape time's limits by figuratively aligning himself with those truths.

Although *Sir Gawain* addresses itself to the ethical lessons of time and history, the poet also provides us with a cycle of regenerative time. The poet's careful references to certain significant dates in the life of the Church serve to remind his audience of the lessons of another way of reckoning time. While we recognize the lessons of history implicit in *Sir Gawain*, and the reality of decay, we also see Sir

Sir Gawain's Year

Date	Liturgical Date	Liturgical Significance of the Day	Event in Poem
January 1	Feast of the Circumcision		
November 1	Feast of All Saints		Green Knight's appearance; Gawain celebrates at Camelot
November 2	Feast of All Souls; Advent	"Christi est duplex in Scriptura, scilicet Adventus in carnem, & Adventus ad judicium. Primus fuit amorosus, sed secundus rigorosus; primus fuit clementiae, sed secundus justitiae; primus fuit pietatis, sed secundus severitatis."	Gawain leaves Camelot; Gawain journeys north
December 24	Eve of the Nativity		Gawain prays to Mary; he arrives at Hautdesert
December 25	Feast of the Nativity	"Primus fuit nativitatis ex matre Virgine, in quo notatur constantiae stabilitas . . ."	Feasting at Hautdesert
December 26	Feast of St. Stephen, Protomartyr	"in quo notatur constantiae stabilitas . . ."	Feasting at Hautdesert
December 27	Feast of St. John the Evangelist	". . . qui comparatur Aquilae, in quo notatur contemplationis sublimitas . . ."	Feasting at Hautdesert

Date	Feast	Latin quotation	
December 28	Feast of the Holy Innocents	"...in quo notatur innocentiae synceritas...."	Unaccounted for
December 29	Feast of St. Thomas à Beckett	"...qui fuit audacissimus martyr; in quo notatur spiritualis audaciae virilitas...."	Hind-hunt; temptation of lust
December 30		"...a nullo denominatur, quo notatur ipsius mirabilis humilitas..."	Boar-hunt; temptation of pride
December 31	Feast of St. Sylvester (receiver of the Donation of Constantine)	"qui fuit sanctissimus Episcopus, in quo notatur suae praelationis auctoritas. (Et iste assimulatur veneri seu lucifero, qui sc. Episcopi lucem scientiae & honestatis prae caeteris debent habere.)"	Fox-hunt; temptation of avarice: Gawain's failure in truth
January 1	Feast of the Circumcision	Octave of Christmas, denoting resurrection, or the New Man	Beheading scene

NOTE Latin quotations from Petrus Berchorius, *Dictionarium morale*, in *Opera* (Colona, 1730), s.v. "Adventus," "Circumciso."

Gawain and Camelot against the framework of another sort of year whose lessons concern spiritual renewal, eternal life, and the duties of the Christian warrior in the battle of life.

Every event in the poem occurs on a meaningful date in the liturgical calendar. *Sir Gawain* begins on New Year's Day, the Feast of the Circumcision, and moves quickly through the seasonal cycle to begin again on the Feast of All Saints, November 1, the day Gawain prepares to leave Camelot. Gawain's adventure occurs between November 2, All Souls' Day, and the Feast of the Circumcision, the next New Year's Day. The poet's references to the liturgical calendar are particularly important because the lessons of the Church year are reflected in the action of the poem. As the chart illustrates, the poet uses the framework of the liturgical calendar to suggest Gawain's spiritual progression from ignorance to knowledge and thus the possibilities of man's regeneration in time.[27]

The Feast of All Saints, the last full day Gawain spends at Camelot, is an especially auspicious day for his preparation for what will be a test of inner chivalry. The poet notes that the day is a feast day (536–537) and is celebrated at Camelot by "reuel and ryche of þe Rounde Table" (538). The Beatitudes are the assigned Gospel reading for All Saints' Day.[28] As we have seen in relation to *Patience*, the Beatitudes outline the steps from fear to wisdom that culminate in recreation of spirit. All Saints' Day celebrates this process of perfection by commemorating the physical and spiritual struggles of those who have achieved this standard. In his translation of *The Golden Legend* Caxton stresses the importance of this festival, which should be celebrated as a recognition of "the debt of interchanging neighborhood": "For the angels of God and the holy souls have joy and make feast in heaven of a sinner that doth penance, and therefore it is right when they make of us feast in heaven, that we make feast of them in earth."[29] Furthermore, on this day, death becomes a sign of triumphant change: "What thing is more precious than death, by which sins be pardoned and merits increased?"[30]

The despair of the Round Table over Gawain's proposed

journey sharply contrasts to the Church's affirmation of death and change:

> Þere watz much derue doel driuen in þe sale
> Þat so worthé as Wawan schulde wende on þat ernde,
> To dryȝe a delful dynt, and dele no more
> wyth bronde.
>
> (558–561)

Whereas the Church celebrates the everlasting life of the saints of God, Camelot mourns Gawain's death in a way that underlines Arthur's court's dependence upon the world, or mortal life. The fact that, after he keeps his bargain with the Green Knight, Gawain shall no longer fight with a sword seems to be Camelot's only way of confronting Gawain's departure.

In both *Sir Gawain* and *The Golden Legend*, we may find an emphasis upon the theme of chivalry in relation to the Feast of All Saints. The *Golden Legend* exhorts those now living to emulate the spiritual discipline of the saints by evoking the ideals of military discipline in the figure of the Christian warrior:

> . . . whereof S. John Chrysostom saith to us: Thou, christian man, art a knight delicate if thou ween to have victory without fighting and triumph without battle. Exercise thy strength mightily, and fight thou cruelly in this battle. Consider the covenant, understand the condition, know the noble chivalry, know the covenant that thou hast made and promised, the condition that thou hast taken, the chivalry to whom thou hast given the name. For by that covenant all men fight, and by that condition have all vanquished, and by that chivalry.[31]

The scene in Camelot at this point in the poem includes a knight who has made an agreement, or a covenant, with the Green Knight and who is pledged to battle. But the *Golden*

Legend refers to the battle of life, while Camelot and Gawain appear to recognize only a test of physical endurance. Camelot's limited perception is especially striking because the Green Knight challenges not strength but fame, and, from the beginning, the test is clearly spiritual rather than physical. Gawain arms, attends Mass, and leaves Camelot on November 2, the Feast of All Souls. The prayers and responses for All Souls' Day celebrate the deaths of the faithful, affirming that their souls live eternally and sleep only to rise at the Second Coming. The Epistle is 1 Thessalonians 4:13–18, part of which reads: "For if we believe that Jesus died, and rose again; even so them who have slept through Jesus, will God bring with him."[32] The Gospel reading is the story of the raising of Lazarus. In spite of the penitential awareness that permeates the day, the Feast of All Souls teaches the lesson of rebirth through grace.[33]

The court's response to Gawain's departure leaves no room for hope, and, in fact, marks Gawain's departure with extraordinary sorrow:

. . . "Bi Kryst, hit is scaþe
Þat þou, leude, schal be lost, þat art of lyf noble!
To fynde hys fere vpon folde, in fayth, is not eþe.
Warloker to haf wroȝt had more wyt bene,
And haf dyȝt ȝonder dere a duk to haue worþed;
A lowande leder of ledez in londe hym wel semez,
And so had better haf ben þen britned to noȝt,
Hadet wyth an aluisch mon, for angardez pryde."
(674–681)

These lines are, in part, a eulogy for Gawain, whose nobility will be ignobly destroyed by an "elvish" man. Not only does the court expect Gawain to die, but it laments his death in a way that suggests the finality of death. Once more, the attitude of the court contrasts to that of the Church, for the Church similarly recognizes death but relieves death of its power by calling it sleep and by reaffirming eternal life. Camelot mourns death as the end of all fair things, as a mysterious process of destruction. However, the poet has noted the reality of death, or winter, in his description of the seasonal cycle with which he opens the second section. There, death is neither mysterious nor ignoble; it simply exists. In fact, winter most threatens things without fruit for harvest. In relation to the year's cycle of growth and decay, Camelot, in its spring, appears dangerously inadequate to the demands of fall and winter. Winter and death exist in nature, and Camelot only mourns their existence without seeming to prepare for their coming.

Gawain journeys north during Advent, a season devoted to penance and preparation. Because Advent precedes Christmas, it was, in the Middle Ages, a time of fasting and of self-examination when men were exhorted to prepare themselves for the message of mercy figured in the Feast of the Nativity. For example, in a sermon on Advent, Hugh of St. Victor discusses what should be men's attitude toward the season:

> In hoc itaque tam sacro tempore debemus in bone propensius exerceri, ut per ejus gratiam mereamur abundantius visitari. Certe si rex dignaretur ad nos venire, et nobiscum facere mansionem, diligenter et nos, et nostra in ejus susceptionem praepararemus. [Therefore, in this so sacred time, we should more willingly be employed in the good, in order that through his grace we may deserve to be visited more abundantly. Certainly, if the king deems it worthy to come to us, and to make us a mansion, diligently likewise we should prepare ourselves in advance for his undertaking.][34]

The emphasis upon preparation and worthiness is likewise apparent in the figure of Saint John the Baptist who presides over this season. Saint John was considered the last prophet of Israel, and his cry, "Prepare the way of the Lord," was thought to be directed to the human heart during Advent. As Saint John's strict life in the desert and spiritual preparation led him to recognize Christ, so each man should emulate John and move toward the message of human redemption through penance.

Gawain's journey through a wilderness mirrors the theological concerns of the season in which he travels. Both the land and the battles he fights are reminders of hardship and of the constant battle against temptation characteristic of the season.[35] The landscape itself is bare and inhospitable to man and beast: "With mony bryddez vnblyþe vpon bare twyges, / Þat pitosly þer piped for pyne of þe colde" (746–747). Gawain himself suffers from the cold and the loneliness:

Ner slayn wyth þe slete he sleped in his yrnes
Mo nyȝtez þen innoghe in naked rokkez,
Þer as claterande fro þe crest þe colde borne rennez,
And henged heȝe ouer his hede in hard iisse-ikkles.

(729–732)

The poet's description of privation, harsh weather, and struggle is similar to the descriptions in the mystery plays of the shepherds' hard life at the moment just before the angels announce the Incarnation. The world is dark and cold and unsympathetic to man. Whereas the shepherds of the mystery plays move directly from darkness and privation to the light stable and God's bounty, Gawain moves to a castle that only appears bright and safe. His worst trials occur after the hardships of his physical journey end on December 24, in Hautdesert.

The fact that Gawain's worst trials occur after the more obvious struggles of Advent is less surprising when we consider the warnings many writers expressed about the dangers inherent in the Christmas season. Whereas Advent is a time of vigilance and spiritual preparation, Christmas is a season given over to rejoicing. The sudden shift from privation to plenitude has its own dangers; for it was thought all too easy to relax during the Christmas season, to forget the reality of human sin that inspired the Incarnation. Writers focused on the temptations of luxury: abundant meat and drink and too much thoughtless merrymaking can provide an ideal occasion for certain types of sin.[36] Gawain's own situation at Hautdesert during Christmas captures in many ways what were considered the temptations of the Christmas season. Gawain moves abruptly from harsh weather and loneliness to luxury and hospitality, and, once in Hautdesert, he lets down his guard and relaxes the vigilance that sustained him in the wilderness.

The poet heightens our sense of Gawain's spiritual lassitude by emphasizing the secular tone of Hautdesert's Christmas celebrations. Though the court observes the literal requirement that Christmas Eve continue the fast of Advent, Hautdesert's fast involves little hardship:

Seggez hym serued semly innoȝe
Wyth sere sewes and sete, sesounde of þe best,
Double-felde, as hit fallez, and fele kyn fischez,
Summe baken in bred, summe brad on þe gledez,
Summe soþen, summe in sewe sauered with spyces,
And ay sawes so sleȝe þat þe segge lyked.

(888–893)

The poet follows up this description of fish cooked in a variety of ways with Bercilak's remarking to Gawain, "'Þis penaunce now ȝe take, / And eft hit schal amende'" (897–898). The words "penance" and "amend" serve several purposes here. First, they alert us to the nature of the meal the court is about to eat: the "fast" should remind men of man's spiritual want that is satisfied by the central event of Christ's nativity. The penance man observes during Advent prepares him for Christ's coming and, hence, for his own amendment. Second, the words alert us to Bercilak's irony, an irony Gawain appears not to fathom. Bercilak has neither penance nor amendment to offer Gawain, or any member of Arthur's court, but Gawain accepts the merely literal nature of the fast and prepares to enjoy his meal. Bercilak's remark may also have been intended to awaken a more literary awareness of the nature of Hautdesert. For example, G. R. Owst cites

John Bromyard's detailed account of the Devil's Castle, where "Gluttony holds the office of Master of the Kitchen." Conversely, in the *Abbey of the Holy Ghost*, the cook is Penance.[37]

Gawain's inability to perceive the dangers of prosperity is his major weakness in the poem, and his misapprehension reflects the inherent spiritual weaknesses of Camelot. Gawain comes from a court that celebrates the Christmas season in much the same way, as illustrated by the poet's description of Camelot's own festivities earlier in the poem. Thus Gawain's ignorance, though not excusable, is understandable. Faced with a court that mirrors Camelot, Gawain ignores the fact that temptations may be concealed in the pleasures of noble living. It is worth remarking, at this point, that the two courts are similar in many ways: both contain a charismatic leader, a lovely lady, a magician, and all the trappings of wealth in clean linen, silver spoons, fine apparel, and elaborate preparations for the dinner table. Gawain finds himself tempted in terms of Camelot's values, which are its weaknesses.

The period from Advent to the Feast of the Circumcision was thought to describe a progression from ignorance and darkness to knowledge and light. The week between Christmas and Circumcision, which Gawain spends at Hautdesert, contains important feasts that celebrate the saints, or spiritual warriors, of the Church.[38] Gawain, a temporal warrior, fails his own struggle on December 31, the Feast of St. Sylvester.[39] On the Feast of the Circumcision, Gawain is punished for his failure, receiving a nick in the neck as payment. The lessons of the Feast of the Circumcision centered upon the virtue of humility which signified the resurrection of the *novus homo*, born again in knowledge and grace. Curiously, Berchorius's remedy for what he considers the proud sins of January is a more humble inclination of the head, ". . . contra Januarium, humilitatem in capitis inclinatione, quia inclinato capite emiset spiritum, id est, superbiam."[40] For Berchorius and others, the Feast of the Circumcision should teach us the humility that releases us from the justice otherwise rendered human pride.

The medieval celebration of the Feast of the Circumcision was a celebration of Christ's circumcision, for by his act Christ fulfilled the requirements of the Law, offering man a new covenant of mercy. The actual circumcision recorded in the Old Testament was considered a sign of the old covenant made between God and Israel by which Israel pledged faithful worship and obedience and God pledged his care for Israel's safety. As a sign of this covenant, circumcision was seen as ineffectual, for the bargain was inevitably and frequently broken by Israel. Israel's act of circumcision may have signified its good intentions, but, given human nature, it was also a reminder of human failure. In terms of Old Testament history, failure was met with punishment, and thus, for medieval Christians, circumcision became a sign of justice.[41]

By his obedience to the Law, Christ was thought to have released man from the necessity of circumcision; instead, he offered man a sacrament of mercy. Baptism was usually discussed as the sacrament signifying man's acceptance of this new covenant. Rather than the punishment afforded disobedience, Christ offered man the opportunity for renewal through baptism and for continuous renewal through humility and penance. Circumcision was discussed as a figure for spiritual circumcision, an operation that cut away the old man and that released the new man to life. In a sermon on this feast, Hugh of St. Victor captures the emphasis upon renewal: "Renovemur in novo homine per novam circumcisionem, in hoc novo ano in hoc mundo, ut in ipso renovari mereamur in coelo."[42] The word *novo* provides him with the basis for his argument and with the basis for his vocabulary. He speaks of renewal, the new man, the new circumcision, the new year, all fitting considerations for a feast celebrated on New Year's Day.

Warnings against temptations were often a part of sermons on the Circumcision. If the feast concerns, as Saint Bernard says, the cutting away of nonessentials, the nonessentials are those things that tempt man away from his own renewal, such as the lures of worldly adulation ("alii adulationibus in vanam gloriam").[43] In juxtaposition with the false light of worldly glitter and glory, Saint Bernard places the true light of discretion.[44] Man, then, must determine what parts of himself need cutting away; he can do this through the act of penance. Taken figuratively, circumcision offered man an escape from his own inadequacy; for, by recognizing temptation for what it is and by turning from lesser goods, he might move toward God in humility and penance. Taken literally, circumcision remained a bargain between man and God that could be made only once although it could be broken many times. As such, circumcision was a sign of the justice man receives for broken bargains. However, as a spiritual operation, man could, each New Year's Day, remind himself of those things he might cut away that kept him from true faith and obedience.

In *Sir Gawain*, the poet describes the events of two New Year's Days in a way that evokes the lessons of the Feast of the Circumcision. On the first New Year's Day, Gawain makes a bargain; on the second, he appears to fulfill his promise but receives a wound for a bargain he has broken with the same man. Significantly, Gawain is wounded in the name of justice—because he has broken faith with his host. The themes of true and false renewal are also central to the poet's description of the two days: the Green Knight's physical renewal after his beheading in Arthur's court anticipates Gawain's true spiritual renewal at the Green Chapel. The Green Knight comes to Camelot to test it. He first tests the court's bravery by calling for a Christmas game; later, in Hautdesert, he tests the nature of its fame and chivalry by testing Gawain's good faith. Gawain, like man, fails in perfect truth but redeems his loss through penance. Finally, Gawain returns to Camelot having "cut away" those aspects of himself that are superfluous and that hinder his spiritual growth. Thematically, then, the poet evokes both the ineffectual bargain of good faith and the truly valuable bargain man can make and remake with God through penance. The cut Gawain receives, while a sign of his inadequacy, is the mark of his rebirth into humility. The events of the second New Year's Day supersede those of the first; for, on the first day, we are reminded of the realities of justice as they apply to human weaknesses.

The poet's description of the first New Year's Day suggests the ideas of justice associated with circumcision under the aegis of the Law. First, the Green Knight enters the hall carrying an ax in one hand and a holly branch in the other. As a Christmas decoration, holly was a symbol for renewal because it remains green all year. The ax, used by headsmen and by warriors, appears to be an instrument of justice.[45] The poet emphasizes the ax, rather than the holly bough, devoting nine lines to a description of its size, sharpness, color, and design. The ax directly threatens Camelot, for it is the instrument the Green Knight has chosen for his test of the court's fame. The Green Knight states that Camelot's reputation for prowess and courtesy have brought him ("wayned me hider," 264), and that he now wishes to play a Christmas game: he will exchange one stroke for another. The game itself recalls the idea of justice; for a stroke is given for a stroke just as, for the Middle Ages, the old covenant was frequently compressed into "an eye for an eye." When we consider the picture the poet has just painted of Camelot's youth, ignorance, and self-absorption, the ax appears doubly ominous, "For now the axe is laid to the root of the trees. Every tree therefore that doth not yield good fruit, shall be cut down, and cast into the fire" (Matt. 3:10). These are Saint John the Baptist's words to a Jerusalem he considered corrupt and unprepared for the coming of the Messiah; they are words frequently used as warnings in medieval discussions of national weakness. The Green Knight's ax is certainly laid at the roots of Camelot, for he comes to judge the nature of its "fruit"—its fame.

The language the Green Knight uses to describe his proposal even more strongly recalls the idea of justice. First, he states the terms of the game he wishes to play to the court in general. His language is legalistic, for "quit-clayme" (293), "barlay" (296), "respite" (297), and "a twelmonyth and a day" (298) were commonly used in situations involving legal agreements.[46] He restates the terms once Sir Gawain accepts

the challenge. Once more, the Green Knight's tone is legal-
istic, for he begins by saying to Sir Gawain, "'Refourme we
oure forwardes, er we fyrre passe'" (Let us restate our agree-
ments before we proceed, 378). A few lines later, the Green
Knight refers to their agreement as a "couenaunt" (393).
Finally, upon leaving the court with his head under his arm,
the Green Knight reiterates the terms of his bargain with Sir
Gawain:

> "Loke, Gawan, þou be grayþe to go as þou hettez,
> And layte as lelly til þou me, lude, fynde,
> As þou hatz hette in þis halle, herande þise knyȝtes;
> To þe grene chapel þou chose, I charge þe, to fotte
> Such a dunt as þou hatz dalt—disserued þou habbez
> To be ȝederly ȝolden on New ȝeres morn."
>
> (448–453)

The Green Knight's tone here is imperative; he commands
Sir Gawain to appear at the Green Chapel to receive the blow
he deserves. Furthermore, the Green Knight stresses the le-
gal nature of the agreement between them by alluding to the
fact that Gawain promised before witnesses to meet him on
the next New Year's morning.

The events of this first New Year's Day also suggest the
theme of renewal. After Gawain has taken the challenge and
chopped off the Green Knight's head, the Green Knight leaps
up with an unearthly vitality:

> And nawþer faltered ne fel þe freke neuer þe helder,
> Bot styþly he start forth vpon styf schonkes,
> And runyschly he raȝt out, þere as renkkez stoden,
> Laȝt to his lufly hed, and lyft hit vp sone . . .
>
> (430–433)

In a sense, the Green Knight's physical renewal parodies the
spiritual renewal celebrated in the feast. More important,
the Green Knight's renewal has no effect on Camelot's per-
ception of itself. After the knight has left the hall, the court

returns to the feast: "Wyth alle maner of mete and mynstral-
cie boþe, / Wyth wele walt þay þat day, til worþed an ende /
in londe" (484–486). The Green Knight threatens the court
when he first appears; he should doubly threaten them now.
They, however, keep their manners and their feast. Came-
lot's sophistication is made to seem foolish in the line fol-
lowing—"Now þenk wel, Sir Gawan"—for the poet inter-
poses the voice of the narrator as a means of underlining the
necessity for thought, given what has just happened.

The second New Year's Day is the day of Gawain's re-
newal, but his renewal is neither as simple nor as quick as
that of the Green Knight. First, at the hands of the Green
Knight, he receives two mock blows, before receiving a third,
which only nicks him. After the third blow, Gawain experi-
ences a physical renewal: "Neuer syn þat he watz burne borne
of his moder / Watz he neuer in þis worlde wyȝe half so
blyþe" (2320–2321). These lines echo Christ's words to Nic-
odemus on being born again (John 3:3), and the poet height-
ens their effect in line 2328 when Gawain announces that
the "couenaunt" has been fulfilled. However, only the literal
covenant has been fulfilled, for Gawain then learns that the
ax has rendered spiritual judgment: "'At þe þrid þou fayled
þore, / And þerfor þat tappe ta þe'" (2356–2357). Had Gawain
not deceived his host, the ax would not have touched him:
it punishes broken bargains. Only at this point does Gawain
begin to experience true renewal, a model for the process of
spiritual rebirth.

He begins the process with contrition and confession, fi-
nally moving to satisfaction.[47] The first New Year's Day, Ga-
wain accepts the Green Knight's challenge, using the empty
language of social politeness: "'I am þe wakkest, I wot, and
of wyt feblest, / And lest lur of my lyf, quo laytes þe soþe'"
(354–355). A year later, he confesses to spiritual inadequacy:
"Now am I fawty and falce, and ferde haf ben euer / Of
trecherye and vntrawþe: boþe bityde sorȝe / and care!'" (2382–
2384). There is a real difference between a polite murmur
about physical weakness and intelligence and an anguished
cry acknowledging treachery and untruth. The first defines

humility in terms of the court and is relevant only to the social microcosm of Camelot. The second defines humility in human, mythic terms. Like Adam in the York Cycle, who cries "'Allas! for sorowe and care! oure handis may we wryng,'"[48] Gawain mourns the result of his own broken oath. Gawain then goes on to compare himself to Adam and Solomon who also gave in to the weaknesses of the flesh.

Gawain ignores the Green Knight's levity about the seriousness of his sin and moves beyond confession to satisfaction: he wishes to keep the girdle as a symbol of his weakness:

> Bot in syngne of my surfet I schal se hit ofte,
> When I ride in renoun, remorde to myseluen
> Þe faut and þe fayntyse of þe flesche crabbed,
> How tender hit is to entyse teches of fylþe;
> And þus, quen pryde schal me pryk for prowes of armes,
> Þe loke to þis luf-lace schal leþe my hert.
>
> (2433–2438)

He wears the girdle in humility, and with his humility he is a different man who can return to court and admit his failure. Gawain's spiritual progression in this sequence is a paradigm of what should be everyman's movement away from self. Gawain has cut away those nonessentials, such as the pride he takes in his reputation and worldly glory. At the end of the poem, he can humbly confess to being a man.

The poem's liturgical framework suggests a cycle of renewal. The poem begins with reminders of justice and mercy, hints of the choices man must make in time. The poet then focuses on the period from November 1 to January 1, a time that contains central feasts in the life of the Church. The lessons of All Saints' Day concern issues central to Sir Gawain's coming adventure—the movement from humility to wisdom suggested by the Beatitudes, a reminder that man should consider himself a Christian warrior, sworn to a spiritual covenant. On the Feast of All Souls, Gawain leaves Camelot. While the court mourns his death, a sign of its superficial spiritual understanding, the Church celebrates the resurrection of the faithful in Christ. Gawain's journey north embodies the privation of Advent. The week from Christmas to New Year's, the week Gawain relaxes at Haut-desert, is a sequence that celebrates spiritual heroes who have triumphed over temptation. Gawain's activities at Hautdesert—eating, sleeping late, talking to his hostess—provide a sharp contrast to those of the saints celebrated for their discipline and devotion. The final day of this sequence brings us back to the Feast of the Circumcision, a day of justice for Gawain; for he receives his reward for a broken covenant. However, on this day, he gains both humility through failure and renewal through penance and thus evades spiritual death.

The poem, like its liturgical frame, describes the move-ment from worldliness, pride, and thoughtlessness to spiri-tual knighthood, humility, and self-awareness. The concept of time the poet adumbrates in his references to the liturgi-cal calendar, unlike natural and cyclic time, offers tran-scendence because it lifts man above the limits of winter, death, and justice. Thus the poet suggests that time can offer man more than worldly fame and more than dissolution; used properly, it can offer him regeneration.

The Representative Man in Time

If the general message of *Sir Gawain* is directed to England and its sense of itself as a nation, the particular message of the poem is directed to the individual and his efforts to live heroically in time. Sir Gawain is the poet's vehicle for a message of individual renewal; for, in Sir Gawain, the poet describes an individual who is both a hero and a failure. The ambiguities of Sir Gawain's heroic position reflect those of other medieval heroes. Medieval writers and thinkers found heroes in both classical and Biblical sources and also created heroes of their own, such as Beowulf and Roland. While figures like Hercules, Hector, David, and Samson were in-deed seen as examples of special bravery or wisdom, they were also frequently seen as examples of moral laxity.[49] The *Gawain*-poet depicts a hero who is certainly heroic, but who, at the same time, displays a number of weaknesses. However, we also see in Gawain a figure who goes beyond failure to achieve self-knowledge. The acquisition of self-knowledge was intimately connected with the theme of heroism for the Middle Ages. For this reason, Hercules was considered the classical figure who stood as an example of the true hero.[50] Hercules, who was seen as a pagan type of Christ, and whose labors and failures resulted in success and wisdom, illustrated what a hero should be. Ideally, a hero is not simply a champion fighter or a conqueror; he is a man who has also attained wisdom. Thus, the heroic life was frequently seen as a progression or a pilgrimage, in both cases a movement away from one state and toward another. In the process, a hero learns to govern himself and thus can begin to exert control over the chaotic elements that surround him. The process includes failure because failure is an integral part of growth.

The poet prepares us for a realistic appraisal of the heroic man in the opening stanzas of *Sir Gawain*, where he describes the heroes of England's mythic past. Aeneas, hero of Troy and the embodiment of Roman ideals, was both a true man and a traitor: "Þe tulk þat þe trammes of tresoun þer wroȝt / Watz tried for his tricherie, þe trewest on erthe" (3–4). Romulus is noble, but Romulus is also proud: "Fro riche Romulus to Rome ricchis hym swyþe, / With gret bobbaunce þat burȝe he biges vpon fyrst" (8–9). Brutus is also a noble warrior, but his knights love fighting, "Bolde bredden þerinne, baret þat lofden" (21). Arthur shares nobility with his forebears, but Arthur is also "childgered." In each hero, the poet describes a man who is brave, noble, and capable; but a man who is also flawed.

The poet's first representative hero is Aeneas, whose career was seen as a pilgrimage from folly to wisdom. Vergil's account of Aeneas's flight from Troy, dalliance with Dido in Carthage, journey to Italy, descent into the underworld, and unification of Italy was thought to capture the progression from youth to maturity. The first six books of the *Aeneid* received particular attention; each of the six was linked with one of the six stages of human life.[51] The fact that Aeneas is on ship in search of his new homeland for much of the time in these books underlined the connections between Aeneas's voyage and the pilgrimage of human life.[52] Aeneas's journey culminates in his ascent from the underworld, a figure for resurrection, and hence for the attainment of self-knowledge. Aeneas thus was thought to have learned the art of ruling himself; he is then worthy to rule others. He becomes a hero. The career of Aeneas became a paradigm of man's painful journey toward mastery over and knowledge of the self.

Aeneas's journey from Troy to Italy may lie behind Gawain's journey to the north and his experiences there. Gawain, like Aeneas, is forced to leave his own city and finds himself lost in unfamiliar territory. Each hero finds shelter and hospitality in a strange court which is similar to the court he has left. Both men are tempted in conjunction with hunting and give in to temptation. Aeneas flees Carthage and journeys to the underworld, carrying his passport, the golden bough. His return was seen as a symbolic rebirth. Gawain also experiences a sort of death at the hands of the Green Knight, followed by a spiritual renewal. The green girdle that Gawain first wears to save his life and later wears as a token of untruth is, like the golden bough, a symbol of self-knowledge. Both poems contain a female who manipulates the action: Morgan, like Juno, stands behind Gawain's ordeal, for she wishes to destroy Camelot as Juno wishes to halt the founding of Rome. Moreover, both heroes are associated with national myths, and their careers were thought to embody certain national ideals. The affinities between the two poems are, in any event, worth noting, primarily because they illuminate the issue of heroism. For the Middle Ages, Aeneas was a hero, despite his reputation as a traitor.

In line 4, the poet links what appear to be two mutually exclusive qualities, treachery and truth, and thereby evokes the legend of Aeneas's double treachery. Aeneas and Antenor, in an effort to end the Trojan War, were thought to have plotted with the Greeks to destroy Troy. According to the *"Gest Hystoriale" of the Destruction of Troy* (book XXIX) they urge Priam to accept the wooden horse, knowing all the while what it contains. It refers to them as "great traytouris" and to Aeneas as "the traytor with tene, vntristy Eneas."[53] Hecuba persuades Aeneas to hide Polixena, and when the Greeks discover this, they try and banish him for treason. Throughout the Middle Ages, this interpretation was fairly common and became a standard addition to the history of Aeneas. Aeneas's treachery is twofold: the treachery to Priam which brings about the destruction of Troy, and the treachery to his Greek conspirators. Gawain's self-accusation of "trecherye and vntrawþe" in line 2383 reflects the charge of treason against Aeneas in line 3 and links Gawain more closely to this particular mythic hero.

In addition to treason, Aeneas was thought guilty of moral weakness in Carthage. His experience in Carthage—his seduction of Dido, life of luxury, and temporary willingness to ignore his destiny as the founder of a new nation—was seen as manifesting the dangers and the delights of luxurious living. In the *Policraticus*, John of Salisbury, while discussing Aeneas as a heroic model (book VIII), also accuses Aeneas and all Romans of vainglory, greed, and a love of flattery (books II:15, III:10). In book VI:22, he elaborates upon Aeneas's folly in Carthage, outlining the dangers inherent in noble talk and luxurious surroundings:

> And so, smooth words led to the introduction of the man into the city, seductive flattery won for him the favor of hospitality, the captivated attentiveness of all spread an elaborate banquet, the banquet was followed by marvelous tales and accompanied by the frivolity of a hunt and various other wanton delights. These things brought forth fruit in fornication, in the burning down of the city and the desolation of its citizens, and bequeathed to future generations the seeds of undying enmity.

John of Salisbury here lays the blame on Aeneas's ability to speak fluently. While I am not suggesting that the *Gawain-*

poet is directly indebted to the *Policraticus* for his portrait of Sir Gawain, it is nonetheless true that Gawain, like Aeneas, has a reputation for smooth words and a tendency to relax in luxurious surroundings. Aeneas's treachery and his moral laxity in Carthage do not detract from his heroism, but the combination of strength and weakness sets a pattern for subsequent descriptions of heroes.

As Robert Hanning has suggested, the traditional story of Brutus is patterned on that of Aeneas.[54] Brutus is driven by fate from his homeland, liberates a band of Trojans from their Greek captors, and finally journeys to a new land, Britain, to found a new nation. England, like Rome, thus rested on Trojan foundations and, like Rome, thought itself to possess a special destiny. The *Gawain*-poet's description of Brutus is as brief as his portrait of Aeneas; he also shades Brutus's character with less than ideal traits. In particular, he associates Brutus with greatness and war. Under Brutus, the nobles were fractious, and England became a land of "blysse" and "blunder."

The poet's sketch of British heroes culminates in the figure of Arthur, a man who was also seen as less than perfect. The legend of King Arthur is probably as well known today as it was in the Middle Ages, with the exception that a modern audience may be more idealistic about Arthur. The poet describes Arthur as "childgered," as given to adventure, as being physically always in motion. None of these characteristics would have been found attractive in a king. The poet is not, however, creating a new portrait of Arthur, for there is ample evidence within medieval tradition for a shaded portrait of England's most famous king. Particularly in ecclesiastical writings, Arthur is called cruel, tyrannical, greedy, lecherous, arrogant, and chaotic.[55] The poet does not apply any of these epithets to Arthur, but he does imply that Arthur is a less than perfect king, implicitly linking him with other flawed heroic figures.

The poet's descriptions of representative men prepare us for an imperfect hero. The description of the court in the third stanza further prepares us for a realistic portrayal of men and societies, for the court we see celebrating the

Christmas season hardly looks ready for a visitor as strange and as rude as the Green Knight. Initially, Gawain shares the weaknesses of his city: his concern for his reputation, his politeness, his manners, and his dress identify him as Arthur's knight. Like Camelot, he is vulnerable, particularly when his chivalric reputation is involved.

However imperfect, Gawain was nonetheless a figure associated with a special type of heroic journey. As Larry Benson has noted, both the possible sources for *Sir Gawain* and the legend of Sir Gawain point toward a theme of self-discovery, for Sir Gawain was traditionally linked with the journey to self-knowledge, which is like the experience of rebirth.[56] Before Malory, Gawain was the hero of most Arthurian romances. He was depicted as brave and courteous and rode the same horse, Gringolet, that he rides in *Sir Gawain*. More important, stories about Sir Gawain usually recounted a journey to the "other world," ending with a sort of rebirth.[57] These stories frequently contained two characters who tested Sir Gawain—a lady of supernatural origins and a magician, usually lord of the castle in which Gawain finds himself tested. According to one version, retold by Petrus Berchorius, Gawain is carried away to a castle under water where he encounters a man's head affixed to a lance and a giant before he escapes to safety.[58] The tale is similar to others about Sir Gawain, and the strange castle, the beheaded man, the dangerous giant, and Gawain's escape from the chaos beneath the water combine to suggest the theme of rebirth when the hero emerges from the depths.

However, the *Gawain*-poet, though he seems to have drawn upon medieval legend and tradition, uses the fantastic elements of his story to point up a specifically fourteenth-century lesson. For his audience, the message of renewal was a Christian message. Although Gawain acts out a classic and mythic pattern of descent and ascent, or of death and rebirth, that pattern, for the Middle Ages, was established by Christ.[59] It is the pattern that lies behind Jonah's descent into the whale in *Patience*. The poet relates this process to the concerns of his audience by choosing to describe the experiences of an

English heroic figure, a paradigm of chivalry. Gawain's ideals and failures consequently reflect the concerns of fourteenth-century chivalry, and his renewal is Christian. This treatment of Gawain allows the poet to address both social and spiritual concerns. Gawain fails in precisely those areas that were considered important to the institution of chivalry; his failures and his ultimate success also provide a model for the spiritual journey available to everyman, the metaphoric Christian warrior.

The ideals of military chivalry were both temporal and spiritual. Literally, the armed knight was seen as an arm of the orderly state, as its instrument of defense, of peace, and of justice. The knight's relationship to the harmony of the state made military discipline a necessity; and, for ideas about military discipline, medieval writers turned to Roman writers. However, medieval writers incorporated into Roman theories of military discipline those of Christian spiritual discipline. A medieval knight was not simply a soldier of the temporal state; he was a representative of the nontemporal empire of God. The Biblical source for knighthood's figurative dimension was Ephesians 6:10–20, Saint Paul's description of the spiritual warrior. Just as it was impossible to separate the duties of the temporal knight from his spiritual duties, it was equally impossible to separate inner strength from outer fame or might. Medieval writers stressed the relationship between the strength of the spirit and the strength of the fighting arm.[60]

The hero of *Sir Gawain* is a medieval knight, and the poet, through Gawain, explores the ideals of chivalry by exploring its temptations. As the representative of Camelot's fame, Gawain's chivalry is subjected to trial. Because the basis for medieval thought is primarily Christian and Platonic, outward appearance is ultimately guaranteed by inward qualities. Chivalry, like other medieval ideas, was not simply a name for manners or for class, but denoted an inner chivalry. For chivalry to be "real," it must be based upon a certain strength of mind and upon an inner purpose. The contrast Chaucer draws between the Knight and the Squire suggests the distinction between true chivalry and a chivalric appearance. It is for this reason the poet recounts a story of spiritual temptation and growth, rather than a story of physical adventure. Sir Gawain's adventures occur in Hautdesert, at the dinner table or in the bedroom; and in order to understand how he fails and what he learns, we must turn to the unseen, spiritual duties of the medieval knight.

The armed knight, though an actual part of medieval society, also embodied the ideals of spiritual warfare. Saint Paul's assertion in Ephesians 6 that life is a process of war against an unseen foe and his careful allegory of the armor of the knight added a figurative dimension to knighthood. The fact that the enemy was not a physical one underlined the nature of Christian warfare: "For our wrestling is not against flesh and blood; but against principalities and powers, against the rulers of the world of this darkness, against the spirits of wickedness in the high places" (Eph. 6:12). The nature of the enemy necessitated spiritual strengths: fortitude, honor, vigilance, and perception. The last, perception, is crucial because a knight must know the enemy in order to fight him. Medieval writers emphasized the fact that Satan could transform himself into an "angel of light" (see 2 Cor. 11:14), depending upon human misapprehension for his power.[61] Innocence could be deadly if it masked ignorance; so the knight must be able to discriminate between the nature of a situation and its appearance.

The ceremony of medieval knighthood reflected the awareness of a knight's double duties. Both the state and the Church presided over the making of a knight, and the arms he would carry in defense of his overlord rested on the altar of the church as a sign of his dual commitment. In the *Policraticus*, John of Salisbury remarks that a knight does not signify his commitment in writing, but with the arms that are the signs of his calling (book VI:10): the covenant between the knight and his temporal and spiritual overlords was ratified by the arms of actual knighthood.

The relationship between the inner and outer knight became more explicit in the fourteenth century when the shield became even more symbolic. As shields began to play a lesser part in warfare, they began to be used as decorative devices which said something about the men who carried them. Decorative shields began appearing on architecture, in illuminated manuscripts, and on tombs as symbols, rather than as actual armor.[62] The shield Sir Gawain carries is such a symbol. Of the 102 lines describing the arming of Sir Gawain, 46 are devoted to the shield. We do not see Sir Gawain ever use his shield, and it disappears in the final section of the poem. Rather than an actual shield, dented and battered, the poet gives Gawain a shield that outlines the ideals of chivalry Gawain is supposed to embody.[63]

The ideals figured on the shield are those of both temporal and spiritual chivalry. The poet introduces the shield by noting that it is a symbol. He calls it a sign or a token: "Hit is a syngne þat Salamon set sumquyle / In bytoknyng of trawþe, bi tytle þat hit habbez" (625–626). He traces its pentangular form to Solomon, who, according to medieval tradition, possessed mysterious wisdom and esoteric knowledge.[64] After stating that the shield "betokens" truth, the poet describes the components of truth. Each of the five points of the pentangle stands for a set of five ideals. Gawain is faultless in his five senses, has never failed in his five fingers, places his trust in the five wounds of Christ, derives his fortitude from the five joys of Mary, and possesses the five virtues of franchise (magnanimity), fellowship, purity, courtesy, and mercy. The pentangle itself is an interlocked form, suggesting the impossibility of separating any of the virtues and underlining the oneness of truth.[65] On its reverse, the shield bears a picture of Mary, patroness of chivalry and friend to penitent sinners. The poet stresses the shield's reality as a symbol of those ideals Gawain carries north. The ideals on the shield do not fail, but Gawain fails to achieve the standards he is supposed to embody.

The shield blazons Gawain's five wits, faith, five fingers, and his fellowship, courtesy, and franchise; yet he fails to apprehend the nature of the Green Knight, his northern host, or Hautdesert itself. Whereas Sir Gawain can detect the dangers of an ogre, a giant, or of harsh weather, he has no ability to see the dangers of good food, good wine, and a roaring fire. The poet establishes Gawain's credulousness near the end of his journey north. Trapped by bad weather on Christmas Eve and filled with fear and misery, Gawain prays to Mary for a place to hear Mass. The castle that Gawain suddenly sees ahead of him appears to be an answer to his prayer: the poet devotes four stanzas to a description of the castle, its architecture, apparent prosperity, and its sumptuous interior and the appearance of its master. Gawain calls Hautdesert a "bone hostel" (776); he observes its massive and beautiful structure; he accepts the welcome of its servants; and he apparently leaves his five wits at the castle gate. Once inside, he evaluates solely by appearance.

Gawain's view of Bercilak is especially striking because it is based on assumptions, rather than perceptions:

> And þuȝt hit a bolde burne þat þe burȝ aȝte,
> A hoge haþel for þe nonez, and of hyghe eldee;
> Brode, bryȝt, watz his berde, and al beuer-hwed;
> Sturne, stif on þe stryþþe on stalworth schonkez,
> Felle face as þe fyre, and fre of hys speche;
> And wel hym semed, for soþe, as þe segge þuȝt,
> To lede a lortschyp in lee of leudez ful gode.
>
> (843–849)

Gawain sees that Bercilak is physically attractive—large and strongly built. He notices his age, his coloring, his complexion, and his ease of speech. His first, and manifestly superficial, impressions conclude abruptly with Gawain's judgment that the man seems like a leader. The fact that Gawain has no real basis for his conclusion is suggested by the poet's use of "semed" and "þuȝt," words that convey ambiguity. Gawain never questions the assumptions he draws from his host's physical appearance, nor does he entertain the possibility that Bercilak might be dangerous to him.

Gawain's faulty judgment becomes even more pronounced in his conversations with his host. In a manner similar to that of the Yeoman in Chaucer's Friar's Tale, Bercilak tells the truth, but tells it in such a way that it can be misconstrued by the unwary. For example, after the second day's hunt, Bercilak tells Gawain that he is testing Gawain's good faith and that the third test will prove the first two: "'For I haf fraysted þe twys, and faythful I fynde þe. / Now "prid tyme þrowe best" þenk on þe morne'" (1679–1680). His final admonition to "þenk on þe morne" should alert Gawain to his peril. The host then follows up what is an explicit warning with "'Make we mery quyl we may and mynne vpon joye, / For þe lur may mon lach when-so mon lykez'" (1681–1682). "Make merry while we may" is hardly the sort of advice with which to face bad fortune, and Bercilak's words ominously echo the advice to "eat, drink, and be merry, for tomorrow we may die."

Bercilak, in fact, has a number of traits that would alert an audience to the ambiguities of Gawain's position in Hautdesert. First, he is a hunter, an avocation likewise shared by the Yeoman in the Friar's Tale. Within the context of medieval literature, hunting is not always either innocuous or positive, for, under the guise of hunting animals, a hunter might hunt souls.[66] The poet conveys the possibility that Bercilak may be hunting more than animal game by linking Bercilak's success in the field to Gawain's in the castle through the bargain they make and, finally, near the end of the poem, by linking Bercilak's test of Gawain to Morgan le Fay:

"Þurȝ myȝt of Morgne la Faye, þat in my hous lenges,
And koyntyse of clergye, bi craftes wel lerned,
Þe maystrés of Merlyn mony hatz taken—
For ho hatz dalt drwry ful dere symtyme
With þat conable klerk, þat knowes alle your knyȝtez
        at hame . . . "
                                                        (2446–2451)

Bercilak couches his description of Morgan and her association with Merlin in decidedly equivocal language. On the surface, he describes merely a relationship between pupil and teacher. However, the fact that other medieval accounts of Arthur and his court link the two figures sexually and the striking use Bercilak makes of the poet's own alliterative line pattern ("koyntyse of clergye," "maystrés of Merlyn" and "conable klerk") combine to imply something more than pedagogy. According to the *Middle English Dictionary,* "koyntyse," "maystrés," and "conable" are innocent enough; in this context, however, and given Bercilak's tone, we may be reminded of the similar-*sounding* "queinte" and the all too apt words "mistress" ("maistres") and "cunning" ("conning"). As at other points in the poem, Bercilak here suggests more than he says. Through innuendo, he seems to dig slyly at the now "reborn" Sir Gawain, tempting him to see Camelot and its ideals through Bercilak's eyes. Rather than succumb to the temptation, thus opening ourselves up to anger and ridicule or to disillusionment and cynicism, we—like Gawain—should retrace our steps, not to Hautdesert, but to Camelot.

Through Bercilak's descriptions of Morgan, the poet at once reiterates the spiritual nature of Gawain's trial and suggests a bond between the two courts. Since Morgan wishes to employ Bercilak as a means of shaming Arthur, Guinivere, and the knights of the Round Table, thereby exposing Camelot's spiritual, rather than its physical, weaknesses, the proper weapons against her are those of inner chivalry, those qualities depicted on Gawain's shield. Morgan's success depends upon her quarry's fear and lack of perception. The poet's reference to Morgan also reminds us of one more link between the two courts of Camelot and Hautdesert: not only does each contain a magician, but Morgan learned her magic from Merlin, who "knowes alle your knyʒtez / at hame." The Middle Ages, which distrusted the practice of the magic arts, found authority for their distrust in the New Testament references to Simon Magus. There were a number of stories about Simon Magus, his attempts to buy the powers of the apostles, and his efforts to deceive others into thinking him filled with the power of the Holy Spirit. There is one curious story about Simon's illusive beheading, staged by him to deceive others into thinking him immortal.[67] By establishing the fact that both Camelot and Hautdesert contain a figure versed in magic, the poet intimates once more the subtle affinities between the two courts.

The hints about Bercilak's intent toward Gawain, the nature of the test, and the dangerous similarities between Camelot and Hautdesert alert the audience to Gawain's peril and to his ignorance. What is merely a first impression in the introductory stanzas of the poem of Camelot's youth, glitter, and deadly innocence is borne out by Gawain's experiences in Hautdesert. The poet thus provides his audience with information allowing it to learn about the often deceptive nature of temptation as it watches Gawain skate over what is clearly very thin ice.

Bercilak's temptation of Gawain is threefold: he tests Gawain's chastity, humility, and selflessness. It is now recognized that Bercilak's hunts and Bercilak's lady's hunts parallel each other: the barren hind of the first day reflects the temptation of lechery, the boar suggests the temptation to pride, and the fox avarice. These three sins of the flesh, the devil, and the world were, as Donald Howard has suggested, a convenient way of organizing the subject of sin for both preachers and poets.[68] Through Gawain, the poet addresses himself—as he does in *Purity*—to the nature of man and his efforts to triumph over the classic weaknesses of the sons of Adam. The poet's use of these categories of sin directly relates to Gawain's position as both a figure for everyman and a figure for heroic chivalric ideals. For, just as Adam and all men after him are susceptible to these temptations, so, for medieval writers, were those who had taken the vows of temporal knighthood. Contemporary discussions of the perils a knight might face focus on the need for inner chivalry as a defense against the triple dangers of luxurious food, of pride in position, and of avarice.

Discussions of the dangers inherent in luxury center on the issue of luxurious living, of good food in particular. Geoffroi de Charney in his *Book of Chivalry* at once conveys the pleasures of and warns against the dangers of gourmet delights: "Si ne doit-on avoir à telx délices nulle grant plaissance, ne ne t'entremette trop de savoir deviser bonnes viandes, ne bonnes saulces, ne lesquelx des vins valent le miex, ne n'i mets trop ta cure."[69] His emphasis upon good food, good wine, and rich sauces is not unlike other discussions of luxury in relation to chivalry, for luxurious living was thought to lead to lechery all too often. Finally, soft living was thought to erode the strictures of military discipline and result in a knight unmanned by his fleshly instincts. For the Middle Ages, the picture Vergil paints of an oiled, well-groomed, relaxed Aeneas in Carthage is perhaps the classic depiction of a hero detained by his own attraction to luxury; and the many treatments of Venus's deleterious effects on Mars's vigor were meant to convey the same warning. In *Sir Gawain*, the poet described both luxury and its effect; his emphasis upon luxury culminates in the events of the first day's hunt.

Hautdesert is certainly luxurious. The poet devotes many lines to describing the huge fires, elegant appointments, and gustatory delights of Hautdesert. In fact, the poet strikes the note of wealth and luxury with Gawain's first sight of the castle and continues to play upon the theme as he describes the interior and the sumptuous Advent fare of the meal served on Christmas Eve. Hautdesert's celebration of Christmas is even more splendid:

> On þe morne, as vch mon mynez þat tyme
> Þat Dryȝtyn for oure destyné to deȝe watz borne,
> Wele waxez in vche a won in worlde for his sake;
> So did hit þere on þat day þurȝ dayntés mony:
> Boþe at mes and at mele messes ful quaynt
> Derf men vpon dece drest of þe best.
>
> (995–1000)

This sentence falls into two parts. The first part states the meaning of the celebration, and the poet underlines the eternal truth celebrated on Christmas Day by saying, "On the morning that God was born to die for *our* destiny." The second part of the sentence describes Hautdesert's celebration and is connected to the first by the conclusive "so." The sense that the poet is drawing a distinction between what is being celebrated and how it is being celebrated is strengthened by his use of alliteration and stress. The second, fourth, and sixth lines should be read in relation to one another. All three lines contain similar patterns of stresses and all are dominated by the *d* sound. Thus, *Dryȝtyn, destyné, deȝe, day, dayntés, derf, dece,* and *drest* comment upon one another: implicitly, there is a contrast between the God born to die for men and the men dressed of the best in the hall.

The description of Hautdesert's festivities is doubly striking because it hardly differs from the description of Camelot's New Year's festivities:

> Dayntés dryuen þerwyth of ful dere metes,
> Foysoun of þe fresche, and on so fele disches
> Þat pine to fynde þe place þe peple biforne
> For to sette þe sylueren þat sere sewes halden
>   on clothe.
> Iche lede as he loued hymselue
> Þer laght withouten loþe;
> Ay two had disches twelue,
> Good ber and bryȝt wyn boþe.
>
> (121–129)

The lines describe a groaning board: there is hardly room to put all the dishes, for each pair has twelve dishes, in addition to both beer and wine. Both Camelot and Hautdesert offer a variety of good foods, ample drink, and elegant service. It is then hardly surprising that Gawain fails to detect any danger lurking in the castle of Hautdesert: it is too like his own court.

The poet suggests the effects of luxury in his account of the first day's hunt. First, Bercilak suggests an exchange of winnings by urging Gawain to lie in bed in the morning while he hunts abroad. Bercilak phrases his proposal in terms of luxury and of ease, "ȝe schal lenge in your lofte, and lyȝe in your ese" (1096). The *l* sounds and the drawn-out vowels combine with the meaning of the line to convey a sensual and languorous effect. Gawain accepts what is from the first a strange bargain, and the poet moves toward a comic climax that says a good deal about the emasculating effects of luxurious living. Before describing Gawain "lying in his ease," the poet devotes three stanzas to Bercilak's early-morning preparations for the hunt. The sense of vigor and masculine energy of these stanzas sharply contrasts to the description of Sir Gawain who "in gay bed lygez" (1179), "vnder couertour ful clere" (1181). Enjoying the pleasures of a good bed, Gawain hears a noise, only to discover his hostess in his room. What follows is a purely comic rendering of a knight trapped in his bed by a lovely lady who wishes to engage him in amorous conversation. His weapons for this particular hunt are those of the quarry, rather than the hunter, since he must apply his courtesy, his five wits, and his franchise to the task of evading her advances. Gawain preserves his chastity, but his situation in bed strongly suggests the effects of of luxury. The poet describes, not an armed and valorous knight, but a man without his clothes, trapped under the covers while the lady ranges abroad.

For medieval writers, the offense of inordinate chivalric pride was linked to excessive conversation. For example, Geoffroi de Charney warns knights against talking too much because too much talking can lead to foolish behavior. A knight may enjoy the sound of his own voice recounting his own achievements so much that he may forget that his prowess is a gift from God who made him.[70] Gawain faces a similar trial. First, Bercilak's court admires his fame, wishes to hear of his chivalric might, and desires to learn of him the art of "love talking." On the morning of the second day's hunt, his hostess also encourages him to talk about himself and thus to take pride in himself:

"I woled wyt at yow, wyȝe," þat worþy þer sayde,
"And yow wrathed not þerwyth, what were þe skylle
Þat so ȝong and so ȝepe as ȝe at þis tyme,

So cortayse, so knyȝtyly, as ȝe ar knowen oute—
And of alle cheualry to chose, þe chef þyng alosed
Is þe lel layk of luf, þe lettrure of armes . . . "

(1508–1513)

While the lady continues the amorous advances of the pre-
vious morning, she appeals to Gawain's chivalric pride, ask-
ing him how one so young, so bold, so famous, and so cour-
teous could be so devoted to knighthood. Gawain turns the
conversation away from himself, escapes with a kiss, and
evades the snare of too much talking.

Gawain avoids obvious sins, but he does not avoid the
occasion for sin and finally falls prey to man's greatest fear.
His fears for his life at the hands of the Green Knight lead
him to accept a girdle from his hostess, for the man who
wears it "'myȝt not be slayn for slyȝt vpon erþe'" (1854). He
does not tell the host of his "winning" and thus compounds
his crime with untruth. Later, at the Green Chapel, Gawain
correctly diagnoses his crimes, accusing himself of "falssyng,"
"cowardyse," and "couetyse" (2378–2380). To these sins, he
counterposes largesse and loyalty, the proper antidotes for
avarice and untruth, as Chaucer's Parson also notes. In re-
lation to the institution of knighthood, the offenses of ava-
rice, cowardice, and untruth are serious, especially as Ga-
wain's shield betokens truth and depicts franchise and bravery
as components of Gawain's fivefold perfection in truth.[71]

Discussions of avarice figure prominently in considera-
tions of chivalric offenses. Geoffroi de Charney links coward-
ice and covetousness as particularly noxious to the stan-
dards of chivalry.[72] Throughout the *Policraticus*, John of
Salisbury warns that avarice is deadly to chivalric integrity.
Thomas Brinton in one sermon addresses himself to the
problem of avarice in fourteenth-century England, with par-
ticular reference to the king and those surrounding him.[73]
Chaucer, of course, castigates the love of luxury and conse-
quent avarice that appear to pervade his time, as does the
author of *Piers Plowman*. Finally, John of Hanville in the
Architrenius links the figure of Sir Gawain with a discussion

of avarice and knighthood. Book VI, chapter 1, bears the title, "De Arturo, Ramofrigio, Walgano in Avariciam dimicantibus." In the first part of the chapter, Gawain is the mouthpiece for a diatribe against avarice.[74]

In discussing avarice, medieval writers treated it in two ways. First, they focused, as do the preceding comments, on what we can call simple avarice—a desire for temporal goods. In terms of the civil state, avarice and justice do not mix well, for avarice introduces the evil of self-interest into what should be a dispassionate attention to the order of the commonweal. However, the men of the Middle Ages were aware that the term *avaritia* could cover a broad range of desires— the desire for goods, for people, for sensation (as it does in *Purity*), and, finally, for life itself.[75] The *Gawain*-poet suggests a more complex desire than simply the desire for goods on Gawain's part by having him reject the ring the lady first offers before he accepts the girdle. He falls to a desire for life, an *avaritia* that reflects the temptations of spiritual chivalry. Whereas Gawain's failure to overcome the temptation of avarice suggests many of the concerns of fourteenth-century writers, his failure alerts us to the even more subtle temptation the world offers the knight pledged to the covenant of faith.

The poet suggests the relationship between temporal and spiritual chivalry by describing both of Gawain's agreements with the Green Knight as "covenants." Gawain makes his first covenant on New Year's Day in Camelot; he makes his second in Hautdesert, promising to exchange the winnings of each day's hunt with his host, Bercilak (see 393, 1123, 1384, 1408, 1642, 2242, 2328, 2340). The word itself is suggestive because it can refer to both legal and spiritual bargains. Legally, as M. H. Keen notes, "such a contractual agreement was binding on all men, regardless of allegiance because the sanctity of all voluntary pacts was a principle of the *jus gentium* which no prince could alter."[76] Gawain makes two such voluntary pacts, and his failure to exchange the girdle he receives for the fox the host kills alerts us to what is, in effect, a broken covenant.

The term "covenant" might also apply to a spiritual bond contracted between God and man. In this, Gawain, as a Christian and a knight, has contracted a bond of faith, a bond also stipulated on his shield. His decision to take the girdle breaks that bond of faith, for his act signifies that his care for his life outweighs either his faith in God's providence or his sense of personal honor. Thus, while avarice and untruth are sins against temporal knighthood, they are also sins against the faith and discipline of spiritual knighthood. As a specifically fourteenth-century figure of chivalry, Gawain points up the vulnerabilities of the fourteenth century as they were recognized by writers and preachers; as a figure for everyman, his experience points up the vulnerabilities of man in general.

The poet's interest in using Sir Gawain's experience to highlight a general lesson of spiritual chivalry is apparent in his handling of the Green Chapel. As the poet describes it, the chapel has three main characteristics. First, the churl who guides Gawain to the site says that it is dominated by the presence of the Green Knight, who tests anyone who passes by: "'For be hit chorle oþer chaplayn þat bi þe chapel rydes, / Monk oþer masseprest, oþer any mon elles, / Hym þynk as queme hym to quelle as quyk go hymseluen'" (2107–2109). The chapel is anyman's chapel, for any man may find himself challenged by the Green Knight. Second, the chapel is located in a desolate spot and is surrounded by water. Third, it resembles a cave, or a grave, rather than an actual chapel:

Hit hade a hole on þe ende and on ayþer syde,
And ouergrowen with gresse in glodes aywhere,
And al watz holȝ inwith, nobot an olde caue,
Or a creuisse of an olde cragge . . .

(2180–2183)

On seeing it, Gawain calls it a "chapel of meschaunce" (2195).

Although this chapel has never been identified, the poet possibly took its characteristics from accounts of a legendary site in medieval Lincoln, counted among England's geographic marvels. In the *Reductorium Morale*, Berchorius discusses England's geographic marvels shortly after discussing its literary "marvel," Sir Gawain. As Berchorius describes this site in Lincoln, it features a great brook and an open grave close to it, a grave open to all estates and sizes of men ("ad omnem plenae aetatis hominem"). He follows this description with an account of a Cluniac monastery that contains a *lavatorium*, a place for the washing of corpses, likewise suitable for all sizes and estates ("sive magnus fuerit sive parvus"). Berchorius links these two descriptions by focusing upon the equality of death and the equally democratic resurrection of each Christian soul. Berchorius is not the only writer who describes such a location. In the *Polychronicon*, Ranulph Higden describes a similar hole in the ground surrounded by water, again underlining its "democratic" appeal.[77] The two accounts explicitly and implicitly suggest the idea of death, for just such a hole in the ground awaits everyman, regardless of rank or size.

If the poet, as he seems to be, is hinting at an association between the Green Chapel and the idea of death, he is not necessarily instructing us to face death as Sir Gawain faces it.[78] In fact, the poet's handling of the Green Chapel is intended only gradually to suggest the sort of death Gawain will find there. First, we see through the eyes of Sir Gawain, who, here as elsewhere, sees badly. Gawain does not at first see anything he recognizes as a chapel: "And seȝe no syngne of resette bisydez nowhere" (2164); "And ofte chaunged his cher þe chapel to seche: / He seȝ non suche in no syde, and selly hym þoȝt" (2169–2170). Gawain finally concludes it is a devil's chapel: "'Here myȝt aboute mydnyȝt / Þe dele his matynnes telle!'" (2187–2188). Whereas Gawain sees only a fit landscape for his own demise, the chapel that looks like a cave becomes the site for his spiritual renewal. He does not understand that the chapel and all it portends is dangerous only if the man who goes there has placed himself in jeopardy. Gawain has indeed placed himself in jeopardy, for he wears around him the girdle that is supposed to save his life. That the girdle earns him a wound is only one of the ironies of Gawain's experience at the Green Chapel; for the girdle, rather than saving his life, allows him to begin to lose it and to concentrate on saving his soul.

The girdle, as Howard has noted, displaces the shield as the poem's dominant symbol.[79] The poet uses the girdle to signify Gawain's spiritual movement from Arthur's knight to God's knight. As a symbol, the girdle might have had various associations for the poet's audience, some of which shed light on the poet's use of it. In medieval iconography, girdles could signify knighthood, avarice, temperance, chastity, and penance. This last is particularly important because both Elias and Saint John the Baptist wore girdles as signs of their spiritual isolation from the world. Of Saint John the Baptist's girdle, Bede notes that it protects the living from death.[80] Gawain, of course, first wears his girdle to save his mortal body; later, he wears it to save his soul:

> Bot in syngne of my surfet I schal se hit ofte,
> When I ride in renoun, remorde to myseluen
> Þe faut and þe fayntyse of þe flesche crabbed,
> How tender hit is to entyse teches of fylþe;
> And þus, quen pryde schal me pryk for prowes of armes,
> Þe loke to þis luf-lace schal leþe my hert.
>
> (2433–2438)

Gawain here draws a distinction between his identity as a man and as a knight. Rather than a shield which betokens the ideals of chivalry, he now wears a girdle which betokens the weaknesses of the flesh. He defines himself, now, as a man and signifies his acceptance of the remedy for the human condition, penance, by wearing what is a memorial token of his failure. For Gawain, the girdle has changed its meaning, from a girdle of magic properties to a girdle of true life; for it is now a girdle of spiritual restraint, restraining his sense of personal chivalric pride. By Gawain's new attitude toward the green girdle, the poet suggests that Gawain has moved beyond the literal—and, hence, superficial—code of temporal chivalry to a recognition of his position within the framework of spiritual chivalry.

It is only when Gawain returns to Camelot that the nature of the poet's concern with chivalry becomes explicit. In the northern country, we see a Gawain who is clearly alone and in dangerous surroundings and have no difficulties in identifying with the forces of Camelot as opposed to those of Hautdesert. Once Gawain returns to Camelot, it becomes apparent that Gawain and his city no longer stand for the same ideals. Camelot is the repository for the ideals of chivalry, but Camelot's chivalry is literal or one-dimensional, while Gawain's is a chivalry of the inner man. The poet highlights the distance between Gawain and Arthur's court by depicting what are decidedly different opinions about the meaning of the girdle.

The sequence in Camelot follows much the same pattern as the sequence at the Green Chapel after Gawain has received his wound. Gawain first confesses to the court:

> "Lo! lorde," quoþ þe leude, and þe lace hondeled,
> "Þis is þe bende of þis blame I bere in my nek,
> Þis is þe laþe and þe losse þat I laȝt haue
> Of couardise and couetyse þat I haf caȝt þare;
> Þis is þe token of vntrawþe þat I am tan inne . . . "
>
> (2505–2509)

This is an admission of chivalric failure, for Gawain admits to crimes inimical to the ideals of knighthood, especially as they are proclaimed on his shield, which is a token of truth. The girdle is a token of untruth.

Rather than recognize the serious implications of Gawain's confession, the court, like Bercilak and like so many light-hearted confessors in medieval literature—Chaucer's Friar, his Pardoner, the bad priests of *Piers Plowman*—laughs: "Þe kyng comfortez þe knyȝt, and alle þe court als / Laȝen loude þerat, and luflyly acorden" (2513–2514).[81] They then decide to adopt the girdle as a "sign" of the "renoun of þe Rounde Table": "Vche burne of þe broþerhede, a bauderyk schulde haue, / A bende abelef hym aboute of a bryȝt grene,

/ And þat, for sake of þat segge, in swete to were" (2516–2518). The girdle is indeed a symbol of brotherhood, but not the sort of brotherhood Camelot intends. Gawain wears his girdle as a symbol of self-recognition; Camelot wears it as a fashion, for Camelot has not taken Gawain's journey to death and new life. Many critics have seen this final scene as a reassertion of harmony and as an affirmation of fellowship, but the poet stresses the two sharply distinct sets of attitudes toward the green girdle.[82] In that distinction, captured by the court's laughter, is the sound of Camelot's fall. The poet underlines Camelot's vulnerabilities by describing a court that is as carefree, frivolous, and "innocent" as it is at the beginning of Sir Gawain's adventure. Camelot has remained static, fixed in a chivalry of manners and fashion; Gawain, in confronting his human frailties, manifests the realities of true chivalry in the girdle he wears as a sign of his "death." In ignoring Gawain's confession, Camelot implicitly chooses the sort of death that turns the "renoun" of nations into double-edged lessons for the living.

In regard to the temporal institution of chivalry, Gawain's experience points up the dangers of allowing an ideal to degenerate into a code. The fact that Gawain can neither detect the ambiguities of his situation at Hautedesert nor withstand the temptation of his hostess illuminates the weaknesses of Arthur's court. If chivalry is merely a code of manners, it may save a man from lusting after his hostess, or from boasting about himself, but it cannot save him from so elemental a reaction as the unwillingness to die a lonely and ignominious death.[83] In his scrutiny of the ideals of knighthood, the Gawain-poet reflects the concern of his own time that chivalry was being replaced by fine clothes, fine manners, and empty fame. Lest the rot spread, many writers counseled a return to older standards, frequently harkening back to the early period of Edward III's reign. As a figure for temporal knighthood, Gawain reminds his audience that fame, manners, youth, and strength are worthless unless they are rooted in more lasting spiritual attributes.

As a figure for everyman, Gawain undergoes an experience

modeled along classic lines. Gawain fails where Adam fails, transcending his failure through penance, an act of self-recognition. He thus takes his place with other significant medieval figures for the heroic life as an example of earned heroism—he becomes more than he was. The girdle, rather than the shield, becomes his sign; and in that shift the poet adumbrates the shift from an awareness of individual reputation to an awareness of general humanity. The shift, however, does not imply that those things betokened on the shield are empty. Instead, the shield blazons what man may become; the girdle signifies what he is. Gawain, in replacing a shield of perfect knighthood with a girdle of penance, points the way to true perfection through penance. The picture the poet paints of Gawain on his return to Camelot contains ample room for perfection; for, in failure, Gawain learns of the flesh's frailties and thus of its potential for success through grace.

Conclusion

Sir Gawain and the Green Knight teaches the two lessons of "blysse" and "blunder." These lessons are addressed to England through the poet's use of Camelot and to individual Englishmen through the poet's use of Sir Gawain. By placing nations and heroes in relation to time—cyclic, degenerative, and regenerative—the poet dramatizes the effects of ignoring time and suggests the remedy for man's existence in time. Adding his voice to others of the late fourteenth century, the poet writes a poem of warning and renewal.

In the sense that *Sir Gawain* is a warning, it is a "fall of Britain" poem, describing the fall of cities in time.[84] Though the court of Arthur is the major city of the poem, the poet begins by sketching the rise and fall of significant cities and ends by recapitulating the theme:

Þus in Arthurus day þis aunter bitidde,
Þe Brutus bokez þerof beres wyttenesse;

Syþen Brutus, þe bolde burne, boȝed hider fyrst,
After þe segge and þe asaute watz sesed at Troye,
   iwysse . . .

                          (2522–2526)

These lines do more than bring the poem full circle: they replay the theme of the fall of Troy, rise of Britain, with which the poet began. The reference to Troy ends the poem with an allusion to Troy's fall, implicitly a reminder of the effects of time. Time, as "democratic" as the Green Knight, presides over human efforts; and Troy and Camelot are now only names. By underlining the multiple effects of time, the poet suggests the lessons of time.

The various ways of reckoning time in *Sir Gawain* ultimately suggest the different uses of time. Cyclic time contained two important lessons for a nation that believed itself heir to past cycles. First, a cyclic view of history provided inspiration. England's myth of its Trojan lineage evoked the ideals of a feudal civilization—nobility, chivalry, national prosperity. However, medieval Englishmen did not see their myth as containing only a message of inspiration: Troy and Rome both crumbled from within before being overrun from without. Indulgence, luxury, lax standards, and false worship were weaknesses commonly ascribed to both cities; and the lessons of the fall of cities provided medieval writers with a theme from Gildas to Caxton. England, perceiving itself as an heir to the past, must learn from both of the lessons of history. The *Gawain*-poet underlines this double lesson by placing Camelot within such a cycle and by describing Camelot as glorious and potentially unstable. His portrait of Camelot is ultimately directed to his own time, and his portrait is both an inspiration and a warning.

The lesson enclosed in a sense of degenerative time is not a particularly comforting one. Time declines and man in time declines. Troy disappeared; Camelot disappeared; however, those glories would be hard to find in the present age. The description of the seasonal cycle is the poet's most powerful evocation of decay, and it alerts us to time's diminishing possibilities by describing what each man can see for himself—the sure movement of the year. Every man and every nation exists within a world of change, and the reality of harvest is far more threatening for man than for plants and trees. Man's awareness of mutability is perhaps his most haunting problem, and the poet dramatically vivifies that problem by juxtaposing the young court, young king, and, implicitly, each one of us, with the inexorable rotation of the year.

Camelot is the poet's major vehicle for warning. In Arthur and in Gawain, the poet demonstrates how vulnerable the court in fact is. Arthur's desire for a marvel before his New Year's dinner and Gawain's behavior in Hautdesert are equally naive. Arthur's anticipation of marvels is naive because he has no expectation of disaster from an act of chance. In this, he is certainly childlike. The Green Knight's appearance, his rude vitality, his ability to carry his head away with him are truly horrible. The poet heightens our sense of the court's danger by comically emphasizing its incomprehension: the court returns to feasting as if nothing had happened, and it spends its year as quickly as the seasons succeed one another. A great deal has happened, but Arthur and his court simply bid Gawain to hang up his ax and return to the feast. The court's behavior allows the audience to distance itself from Camelot because the audience can, if it wishes, understand the nature of the Green Knight's challenge.

Gawain in Hautdesert is also naively comic. The poet provides his audience with enough clues to the dangers of Hautdesert—Bercilak's ambiguous appearance, his laughter, his admonition to eat, drink, and be merry, his hints of a double hunt—for the audience to observe Sir Gawain's incomprehension. Sir Gawain remains oblivious. He is agreeable, well-mannered, entertaining, but not perceptive. He never questions, partly because he is trapped by his own code of courtly conduct, a code that is almost an inversion of the values depicted on his shield. His courtesy, fellowship, franchise, and fame are those attributes that keep him in Hautdesert, keep him in bed talking to the lady, and that provide an occasion for his acceptance of the girdle. His blindness is Camelot's, and the fact that Camelot remains blind while Gawain learns to see suggests the importance of knowledge. Knowledge is the crucial factor in penance. Unless a man knows, he cannot repent. Thus the emphasis of Chaucer's Parson's Tale is on knowledge, the ability to identify or diagnose a sin and to assign it a remedy. If *Sir Gawain* contains a warning of the fall of cities in time, it also contains a remedy for time in its message of penitential recreation. The season that the poet chooses is most notably connected with this theme. Gawain's adventure takes place in the period between All Souls' Day and New Year's Day. He journeys north during Advent, a season of fasting and of penitential preparation for the birth of Christ. The lessons of Advent revolve around the figure of Saint John the Baptist, the voice crying in the wilderness; and sermons were likely to concern the themes of national reform, or of civic evil, of penance, and of spiritual struggle, and to focus on the duties of the armed Christian knight.[85] The details of Gawain's journey— the weather, his battles, his loneliness, the wilderness through which he moves—reflect many of the themes of Advent. However, Advent ends with Christmas, and a week later comes the Feast of the Circumcision. The entire period of time was thought to suggest the movement from darkness to light, from ignorance to knowledge, from the Old Law to the New, from death to life. In particular, the final date in this sequence, the Feast of the Circumcision, was associated with the process of spiritual renewal and hence with penance. For the Middle Ages, this feast celebrated Christ's circumcision and thus man's release from the requirements of justice if he availed himself of the spiritual circumcision of penance. The movement the poet suggests by his use of significant dates in the liturgical calendar is given focus and reality in the experience of Sir Gawain.

Gawain takes what is a journey of spiritual growth as a hero, as a representative man, and as a Christian knight. He moves through privation to the glitter of Hautdesert. Fearing to die, he does a number of very human things: he lies; he tries to cheat death by magic; he flinches from the Green Knight's ax; he blames someone else for his mistake. Only when he admits the responsibility for his sin, calls it by name, and accepts the girdle as a token of humility does he experience rebirth. His rebirth occurs, fittingly, on New Year's Day, and Gawain's experience is a model for the process of spiritual growth which begins in acknowledged failure and humility. The nick he receives for justice' sake is a reminder of the harsher judgment due him under the law. By choosing humility and penance, he exchanges mercy for justice and evades the debt he otherwise must pay for broken covenants. For the poet and his audience, Gawain's way is the only way to elude time and its effects. Nations and heroes may choose either to fall in time through ignorance, self-interest, and luxury; or to escape time through self-knowledge, penance, and new life. Gawain's journey, like the mythic journey of Aeneas, like the spiritual journey of the medieval Christian, opens up possibilities for nations that otherwise will remain delimited by the power of time.

Three

Purity

Purity is perhaps the least-beloved poem in the *Pearl* manuscript, and probably the least read. There are several reasons for its relative lack of popularity. First, it is the most discursive of the four poems, exploring the consequences of impurity and the rewards for purity within a Biblical framework. In order to reinforce his exhortation to purity, the poet narrates the stories of Noah and the Flood; of Abraham, Lot, and the destruction of Sodom; and of the capture of Zedekiah's Jerusalem and Balthazar's feast. Along the way, he touches on the fall of Lucifer and of Adam and discusses the relationship between purity and penance. The poet initiates his consideration of purity and of these incidents from Old Testament history by referring to the sixth Beatitude ("Blessed are the clean at heart: for they shall see God") and by narrating the New Testament Parable of the Wedding Feast. Second, and perhaps more important, *Purity* is the most moral and didactic of the four poems. The poet guides our response to each of these sections by expressing explicit disapproval for impurity and approval for purity. The poem therefore demands an intellectual, rather than an empathetic, response and a knowledge of, if not a sympathy for, ways in which a medieval audience might have understood its retelling of Old Testament history.

Purity has been scrutinized for its descriptive passages, for its imagery, for its content, and for its structural unity.[1] Despite the critical attention it has received, the poet's method of organization in *Purity* is still not entirely clear. Thus, although it is clear that *Purity* is about purity or "clannesse," it is less clear what the poet means by the term, why he selects these particular Old Testament stories as illustrations of purity or impurity, and why he chooses to introduce his account of Old Testament history with the New Testament Parable of the Wedding Feast. However, it is with this parable that we should begin, for the parable provides the poet with his "text" and hence with his organizing principle.

The parable in *Purity* is a conflation of two Biblical parables and is thus an artistic creation rather than a mere translation. Drawing upon Matthew 22:1–14 and Luke 14:15–24, the poet explores the positive rewards for purity, the punishments for impurity, and the need for penance, all of which receive more fulsome treatment in the Old Testament narratives that follow the parable in *Purity*. The parable has two significant structural components: the account of the three excuses of the three guests who are originally invited to the wedding feast, drawn from Luke, and the story of the man who attends the feast wearing foul clothes and who is cast out for his filth, drawn from Matthew. Like the poet's version of the parable, his account of Old Testament history has a threefold structure, in which each story contains both a group of characters who refuse to become pure and a figure who, knowing the punishment for impurity, insists upon his own way and turns back from virtue into vice.[2]

The poet's conflation of the parables is equally significant, for each of the parables probably had fairly standard associations for a medieval audience. The three excuses of the three guests were traditionally linked with the triad of lust, avarice, and pride, a triad that lies behind the temptation of Adam and figured in a wide variety of medieval considerations of temptation, including *Sir Gawain and the Green Knight*. The incident of the man in foul clothes was thought to teach the necessity for penance by illustrating the punishment for impenitence. The poet's conflation of these two parables suggests the meaning both parables were thought to have, and his Old Testament stories expand upon the na-

ture of the three classic vices—lust of the flesh, lust of the
eyes, and the pride of life. The figure in each tale who "turns
back" reiterates the hortatory message of each of the stories.
The raven turns back to flesh and is cursed by Noah; Lot's
wife turns back to satisfy her curiosity and becomes a pillar
of salt; Balthazar turns away from the message of judgment,
and his pride finds its reward in an ignoble death. Thus, by
combining two parables, each of which had fairly common
interpretations, the poet adumbrates the themes and the or-
ganizing principle of the poem. Like a mystery play, or a
sermon, or a series of pictures, *Purity* is organized around
the tenets of its introductory play or text. As we proceed
through the poem, we are intended to keep in mind the
message of the initial parable, a message that has both neg-
ative and positive components.

The Parable of the Wedding Feast

The two New Testament parables of the wedding feast both
recount the story of a rich man who prepares a feast, a feast
that is ignored or scorned by the invited guests. Matthew's
version contains a description of the preparations for the
feast, the rich man's invitations to those who will not attend
his feast, and the man's decision to invite anyone and every-
one to this marriage feast which is "like the kingdom of
heaven" (Matt. 22:2). The parable ends with the story of the
man who accepts this general invitation, but who does not
wear a wedding garment:

> And the king went in to see the guests: and he saw there
> a man who had not on a wedding garment. And he saith
> to him: Friend, how camest thou in hither not having on
> a wedding garment? But he was silent. Then the king
> said to the waiters: Bind his hands and feet, and cast him
> into the exterior darkness: there shall be weeping and
> gnashing of teeth. For many are called, but few are cho-
> sen. (Matt. 22:11–14)

Luke's version of this parable recounts the excuses of the invited guests and ends with the rich man's decision to make his invitation an open one:

A certain man made a great supper, and invited many. And he sent his servant at the hour of supper to say to them that were invited, that they should come, for now all things are ready. And they began all at once to make excuse. The first said to him: I have bought a farm, and I must needs go out and see it: I pray thee, hold me excused. And another said: I have bought five yoke of oxen, and I go to try them: I pray thee, hold me excused. And another said: I have married a wife, and therefore I cannot come. And the servant returning, told these things to his lord. Then the master of the house, being angry, said to his servant: Go out quickly into the streets and lanes of the city, and bring in hither the poor, and the feeble, and the blind, and the lame. And the servant said: Lord, it is done as thou hast commanded, and yet there is room. And the Lord said to the servant: Go out into the highways and hedges, and compel them to come in, that my house may be filled. But I say unto you, that none of those men that were invited, shall taste of my supper. (Luke 14:16–24)

The poet's combination of these two parables is seamless. He underlines the thematic unity of his own version in line 51 by acknowledging only one source for the parable, Matthew. His ten lines of preliminary description are a paraphrase of Matthew 22:1–4; lines 61–72 recount the story of the three excuses from Luke 14; lines 73–76, which describe the wealthy man's disdain for the refusals of his invited guests, occur in neither Matthew nor Luke. The long description of the man's second invitation to the poor and the needy (77–132) is an expansion of both Matthew and Luke. The episode of the man in foul clothes and his punishment is an elaboration of Matthew 22:11–14. The parable in *Purity* ends with the expulsion of this man (160), after which the poet discusses the necessity for purity and stresses the similarity between the wedding feast of the parable and the kingdom of heaven. He brings his commentary on the parable to a close by alluding to the sixth Beatitude and the reward promised to the pure in heart, "Þenne may þou se þy Savior and his sete ryche" (176). The poet's decision to make one parable of two is not only a narrative success; by combining them, he points up the lessons both were thought to teach.

The parable of the three excuses in Luke 14 was seen as embodying a warning against the three classic vices of lust, avarice, and pride. Saint Augustine and others after him associated the first man's excuse, "I have married a wife," with concupiscence of the flesh; the second excuse, "I have bought five yoke of oxen," with concupiscence of the eyes; and the third excuse, "I have bought a farm," with the ambition of the world.[3] The farm was thought to signify the desire to possess or to dominate other men. The five yoke of oxen were thought to refer to the five senses and thereby to denote the dangers of curiosity. Curiosity about the world could, as Saint Augustine notes, end in a preoccupation with the flesh or with sensual cognition: what appears to be simple lust could, in fact, be symptomatic of the more serious crime of avarice. The excuse of the new wife thus was thought to suggest an excessive, but simple, sensuality. Within the context of the parable, these three vices are dangerous because a preoccupation with any of them might lead a man to refuse an invitation to the great wedding feast of the kingdom of heaven. In themselves, the three are simply the classic temptations of human life; when a man agrees to and persists in one of them, he jeopardizes his chance for delight or fulfillment.

The poet's treatment of this parable reflects the conventional understanding of these excuses. The account of the first man's excuse suggests its associations with pride: "On hade boȝt hym a borȝ, he sayde, by hys trawþe, / 'Now t[ur]ne I þeder als tyd, þe toun to byholde'" (63–64). The poet translates the Latin villam (estate or farm) as "borȝ," which may mean either estate or city; in line 64 he uses "toun" as a synonym for "borȝ." The poet's substitution of two words denoting cities for the word for estate looks forward to his scrutiny of the two classic cities of Jerusalem and Babylon, for his use of language here hints at the theme of domination that is explored in his third Old Testament tale. In that tale, he focuses upon civic pride and the evils that can arise when King Zedekiah ignores God and encourages his people in false worship. The issues of pride in possession and of domination are even more pronounced in the poet's treatment of Balthazar, who dominates the city of Babylon, delighting in the fact that he "owns" everything and everyone in it.

The wording of the second excuse hints at its association with avarice or curiosity. The invited guest states: "'I haf ȝerned and ȝat ȝokkez of oxen, / And for my hyȝez hem boȝt; to bowe haf I mester, / To see hem pulle in þe plow aproche me byhovez'" (66–68). First, the poet underlines the man's subjugation to a greater power by using "to bowe" and "me byhovez." He intimates the nature of the man's "ruler" in "ȝerned," "ȝat," "boȝt," "see." The sequence of verbs begins with desire ("ȝerned") and proceeds from purchase, or fulfillment of the initial desire, to another desire to prove the worth of the oxen, to *see* them pull in a plow. The poet shifts the conventional emphasis upon the five senses (figured in the five yoke of oxen) to an emphasis upon only one sense and one yoke of oxen. The man's desire to see, or to prove by sight, looks forward to the narrative of Lot and Sodom, in which the poet emphasizes the Sodomites' preoccupation with sight and Lot's wife's desire to see Sodom as she leaves it.

The final excuse in *Purity* is as simple as in Luke's version ("'And I haf wedded a wyf,'" 69). The association between this excuse and concupiscence of the flesh is suggested in the poet's account of Noah and the Flood. Noah, unlike his neighbors, does not commit fleshly crimes, and is therefore saved. The raven returns to the old crimes of the antediluvian world by abandoning the ark for carrion flesh.

The theme of reversion is suggested by the second element of the parable, Matthew's story of the man without a wed-

ding garment. Because of this parable and exegetical treat-
ments of the incident, the state of a man's clothing became
a figure for the state of his soul.[4] Hence the incident was
frequently used as an exhortation to penance, an association
familiar to students of medieval literature through Hawkyn
in *Piers Plowman* (B-text, XIII), who soils his baptismal gar-
ments and cannot find a way to clean them. Hawkyn's clothes
are an outward sign of his inward impurity; only the laundry
of penance may clean his clothes, or his soul. The poet sug-
gests the meaning the incident has for the poem by changing
the Biblical account: whereas Matthew states that the man
appears without a wedding garment, the poet says that he
wears a dirty one. In fact, he stresses the filthy condition of
the man's clothes: "Ne no festival frok, bot fyled with werk-
kez;/Þe gome watz ungarnyst wyth god men to dele" (136–
137). A few lines later, he describes the man as wearing "wedez
so fowle" (140), implicitly contrasting this man to the citi-
zens of heaven who wear "wedez ful bryȝt" (20). If the inci-
dent illustrates the punishment for impenitence, it also sug-
gests a way of understanding other characters who appear in
Purity. The raven, Lot's wife, and Balthazar all receive warn-
ings about impurity because each of them witnesses the
punishment for vice. The raven sees what happened to an
old, carnal world; Lot's wife what happened to Sodom; and
Balthazar what happened to Jerusalem. Yet each ignores the
warning, rejects the opportunity for reform, and is conse-
quently punished.

The poet's handling of the two parables does not, however,
point up only the themes of vice and impenitence. Following
the "spirit" of the two parables, he places the greatest em-
phasis upon the feast itself, an emphasis consistent with the
associations that were made between the two Biblical feasts
and the Church or paradise.[5] The poet suggests these asso-
ciations by describing a feast that is at once lavish and or-
derly, terms that might well apply to the description of heaven
in *Pearl*. First, the host, who prepares the feast for invited
guests, does not alter the nature of the celebration when he

extends his invitation to men at large. Indeed, the poet's description of his hospitality underlines the extraordinary fulfillment each guest finds at the banquet table:

> And ȝet þe symplest in þat sale watz served to þe fulle,
> Boþe with menske and wyth mete and mynstrasy noble,
> And alle þe laykez þat a lorde aȝt in londe schewe.
> And þay bigonne to be glad þat god drink haden,
> And uch mon wyth his mach made hym at ese.
>
> (120–124)

The poet conveys the pleasures of this feast by describing it in terms of gustatory satisfaction: even the least of the guests has good food, good drink, and "ese" at the lord's table. The fact that he chooses the language of physical delight to describe a banquet that was associated with spiritual fulfillment is not surprising in light of medieval treatments of such texts as the Song of Songs. As Saint Gregory notes in his introduction to his commentary on the Song of Songs, we may more easily understand the true satisfaction of spiritual joys in light of the comparatively lesser satisfactions of physical joys.

By establishing an analogy with a contemporary feast, the poet suggests the orderly nature of the joys the New Testament feast affords. Thus, the guests sit on benches in a "brode halle" (129) according to rank (see 114–117). Like the citizens of heaven in *Pearl*, the guests at this feast are equal in delight but different in degree, or, in this case, in seating.[6] The sense of decorum extends to the responsibilities of the guests, for they do not come as they are, but wear proper clothing to the banquet: "Wheþer þay wern worþy oþer wers, wel wern þay stowed, / Ay þe best byfore and bryȝtest atyred" (113–114). It is therefore more serious when the host comes in to greet his guests and finds a man wearing dirty clothing to such a splendid feast. The fact that this feast resembles an earthly one strengthens our awareness of order as a principle of the banquet, in that it makes the duties of a guest implicit because familiar. For this reason, the poet introduces his account of the parable by comparing an earthly feast to the heavenly feast and by saying that if a man in dirty clothes is unacceptable to a worldly prince, he is doubly unacceptable to the king of heaven (see 33–50, especially 49–50). The feast then, though open to all, demands certain things from its guests; and guests should be aware of the nature of the feast and dress for the occasion.

The emphasis upon the decorum and hospitality of the wedding feast should color our understanding of the exemplary tales that follow the parable. By stressing the pleasures of the feast, the poet indicates what the original guests missed and what the man in foul clothes forgoes. Similarly, the antediluvian population, the inhabitants of Sodom, and the citizens of Jerusalem miss a grand celebration by refusing their invitations. Others miss the banquet by ignoring the responsibilities of guests, or by refusing to put on clean garments. The poet expands upon the principle of order or decorum in his portraits of Noah, Abraham, and Daniel, for these figures are all marked by orderly behavior, and, through them, the poet suggests the associations between order and purity.

Finally, the feast is both democratic and selective. At the end of his account of the two parables, the poet notes the democratic nature of the feast by quoting Matthew 22:14: "To þis frelych feste þat fele arn to called" (162). His statement however implies more than open hospitality because he translates only the first half of the verse ("For many are called") but omits the last half ("But few are chosen"). His description of the feast implies a principle of selection that depends upon the volition of the guests. The feast exists; one need only wear a clean garment. The state of the garment is a matter of personal choice. Just so, in each of the Old Testament stories that follow the parable, the poet emphasizes the element of choice or free will in human history. Those who are punished are punished because each of them chooses something other than God.[7] In the language of the parable, each of them chooses not to attend his own banquet.

The Old Testament Exempla

The fact that *Purity* has a New Testament text and Old Testament exempla is not particularly surprising in light of the medieval habit of interpreting the Old Law with the New; however, the poet's decision to recount the tales he does demands scrutiny. All of the tales were familiar ones, but his reasons for grouping them together remain somewhat of a puzzle. One possible source of authority is exegetical. In his homily on the Parable of the Wedding Feast in Matthew 22, Saint Gregory discusses the process of spiritual election as it is recorded in Old Testament history. Gregory uses Saint Augustine's metaphor of the city of God and the city of man as his standard for election; in so doing, he refers to Noah, Abraham, and Lot as citizens of the city of God, or the Church, living righteous lives among unrighteous neighbors.[8] Although Gregory mentions two out of the three examples the poet uses in *Purity*, he does not mention the old Jerusalem, Balthazar, or Daniel. However, the figures of Noah and Daniel were frequently linked together as examples of upright men, with Job added to the sequence (see Ezek. 14:14).

In addition to Gregory's homily, there are three passages from the Bible that contain sequences similar to the one in *Purity*. All three passages concern the process of election and the issue of truth, righteousness, or purity. 2 Peter 2 and Luke 17:20–37 are primarily apocalyptic and focus upon the evils of the Last Days. On the other hand, Wisdom 10 describes a more positive panorama of history, focusing upon the men whom Wisdom rescued from danger.

2 Peter 2 is a warning against false teachers, those who are corrupt and who corrupt those around them. The epistle warns by enumerating the figures whom God has punished for unrighteousness and by referring to the men who were saved. The list of the unrighteous includes the rebel angels, the antediluvian world, and the citizens of Sodom and Gomorrah; the righteous are Noah and Lot. The chapter then notes that the unrighteous exhibit certain traits: they are dissipated, carousing at all hours; they entice unsteady souls;

they are greedy; and, like the dog returning to his vomit, they shun their knowledge of the truth and return to their old ways. Although Peter does not name Balthazar, he describes Balthazar's habits, even saying that these men are the followers of Baal. Furthermore, in his commentary on this chapter, Bede notes that such men are distinguished by proud and hyperbolic speech, hearts inflated by impurity, and a devotion to carnal luxuries.[9]

Like 2 Peter 2, Luke 17:20–37 is an apocalyptic warning to the unrighteous. The warning is occasioned by the Pharisees who ask Christ when he will return and the world come to an end. Christ replies that he will come like lightning and at a point in human history when most men will have forgotten the prophecy. He compares this future date to the days just before the destruction of the five cities. He goes on to link Noah's generation with carnal preoccupations, specifically with marriage, and Lot's with eating, drinking, buying, selling, planting, and building. Finally, Christ refers to Lot's wife who looks back at the things of the world.[10]

Both of these New Testament passages have certain affinities to the scheme of *Purity*. In both passages, righteousness or purity is an issue, and figures like Noah and Lot are distinguished from their unrighteous neighbors. Both warn against impurity by alluding to the punishments of the past and teach by using historical examples of purity and salvation. Both apply the teachings of the new covenant to the historical record of the old. Finally, both passages are ultimately directed at the process of spiritual election, a process completed by the events of Judgment Day, and thus have a certain sternness of tone.

In contrast, Wisdom 10 presents a more positive vision of history, describing the historical process of salvation in a way that illuminates the positive features of *Purity*. The company of the saved, protected by Wisdom, includes Adam, Noah, Abraham, and Lot. Wisdom 10 mentions the dangers surrounding each figure but places the emphasis on the man's salvation by countering the first part of the verse with the ultimate victory of Wisdom. For example, in reference to man's wickedness in the days before the Flood, Wisdom 10 underlines, not the power of evil, but the triumph of good: ". . . when water destroyed the earth, wisdom healed it again, directing the course of the just by contemptible wood" (Wisd. 10:4). In addition to recounting the providential course of human history from Adam's creation to Joseph's delivery from prison, Wisdom 10 uses the Dead Sea and the incident of Lot's wife as examples of the evil that has been overcome through the intervention of Wisdom. The cities of the plain, once fertile and beautiful, became a wasteland where fruits do not ripen; Lot's wife became a pillar of salt, or a monument to nonbelief. Both the Dead Sea and the pillar of salt stand as emblems, or warnings for present time. It is, of course, impossible to tell if the poet had Wisdom 10 in mind when describing the trees around the Dead Sea that bear fruit that turns to ashes in the mouth, but both the poet and Wisdom 10 use the trees in a way that suggests their symbolic value for the contemporary reader.[11] The entire passage in Wisdom has other affinities with *Purity* because it was seen as demonstrating the salvation of the New Law, embodied in the figure of Wisdom, who was traditionally linked with Christ.[12] Perhaps also of significance to *Purity* and the final incident of Balthazar and the temple vessels are chapters 13, 14, and 15 of Wisdom, which chastise false worship and the dangers of idolatry.

The exemplary power of certain events in Old Testament history is also underlined by the fourteenth-century preacher and bishop Thomas Brinton. In one of his sermons he says that many impute natural misfortunes to the influence of planets, such as Saturn. Denying this, he links natural misfortunes with human wickedness such as was manifest before the Flood, before the destruction of Sodom and Gomorrah, and before the Roman dispersion of the Jews. Quoting the sixth Beatitude, he stresses the need for purity of heart. Brinton ends by exhorting his audience to penance and to purity.[13]

Finally, the poet's choice of these three events from Old Testament history as exemplary of the punishment meted

out to the wicked has certain elements in common with
Nicholas Trivet's discussion of vice as it appears in his gloss
on Boethius's *Consolation of Philosophy* (I m. 4):

> First of all it is to be observed that the persecution of the
> wicked is designated in three ways, that is, by the rage
> of the sea, by the eruption of a certain mountain, and by
> the stroke of lightning. The reason for this is that the
> proud are found in three species according to the three
> types of sin which occupy the world as in 1 John 2.16:
> "For all that is in the world is concupiscence of the flesh,
> and the concupiscence of the eyes, and the pride of life."
> Certain of the wicked are therefore lecherous, whose per-
> secution is designated by the raging of the sea. . . . Oth-
> ers, indeed, are the avaricious whose persecution is desig-
> nated by the fire from Mount Vesuvius. . . . Others are
> the proud whose persecution is designated by the flash of
> lightning.[14]

Trivet discusses wickedness in general by dividing it into
the sins of lust, avarice, and pride. In each case, the punish-
ment suits the crime. The carnal are carried away by the
raging and hence moving sea, becoming emblems of the dan-
gers inherent in carnality. The avaricious are rewarded by
fire, and the proud receive a reward as swift as a stroke of
lightning.

None of these passages can with certainty be called a source
for *Purity.* Nor can we be sure that the poet did not find a
precedent for his exemplary scheme in a vernacular sermon
or in a pictorial sequence. It is, however, clear that he used
a conventional enough grouping of Old Testament events to
point up the New Testament lesson of purity. Each of these
passages is concerned with the process of salvation and the
reality of punishment as they appear in history, and each of
these passages directs men to purity which, for the Middle
Ages, was possible only through penance. The sequence it-
self and the ways in which it was used complement the in-
troductory parable, or text, of the wedding feast. Both the

parable and the sketch of Old Testament history demon-
strate the selective process of the New Law as it is worked
out by each man for himself.

The poet's account of Old Testament history at first ap-
pears somewhat random. Although he tells the stories of
Noah and the Flood, Abraham and Lot, and the destruction
of Jerusalem and Balthazar's feast, he also touches on the
stories of Lucifer's fall and Adam's fall. The tripartite scheme
becomes more apparent in the last lines of the poem, where
the poet notes that he has demonstrated the rewards for pu-
rity and the punishments for impurity in three ways: "Þus
upon þrynne wyses I haf yow þro schewed, / Þat unclannes
tocleves in corage dere / Of þat wynnelych Lorde þat wonyes
in heven" (1805–1807).[15] This statement alerts the audience
to an ordering principle that it had perhaps missed. What
appear to be five examples of impurity are, in fact, only three,
since the poet clearly distinguishes the first two accounts
from the last three. The accounts of Lucifer's and Adam's
falls, rather than providing further examples of the impurity
that "tocleves" God's heart, prepare us for a consideration of
intentional impurity and impenitence by suggesting the proper
response to God's bounty. These two stories provide us with
a certain perspective on the three major Old Testament nar-
ratives that follow.

The poet first intimates a similarity between the crimes
of Adam and Lucifer and then points out the major differ-
ence between the two figures. Both were intended for bliss,
and both betrayed their sovereign lord. The poet says of Lu-
cifer that "his Soverayn he forsoke" (210), and of Adam that
he "fayled in trawþe" (236). While both betray their natures
in betraying a sovereign and the standards for fidelity and
truth that that sovereign has ordained, and while both are
punished for betrayal, only Adam is saved from the ultimate
consequences of his sin. The difference between the fates of
the two figures underlines the central theme of penance.
Lucifer refuses to repent: "Ne never wolde for wyl[fulnes]
his worþy God knawe, / Ne pray hym for no pite, so proud
watz his wylle" (231–232). Adam, whose crime brought death

into the world, is nonetheless offered the possibility of regained bliss through the Incarnation: "Al in mesure and meþe watz mad þe veng[a]unce, / And efte amended wyth a mayden þat make had never" (247–248). Lucifer's punishment is endless because his spirit is static: his pride obviates the beneficial change inherent in the sacrament of penance. The poet does not describe Adam's contrition, but he provides us with the remedy for human sin in the person of Christ, whose mercy flows through the Church's sacrament of penance. In their different responses to God, Adam and Lucifer provide a standard against which the other figures in the poem are judged. The poet emphasizes the element of choice: those who choose themselves will receive their reward in punishment; those who choose God will receive mercy.

Saint Augustine's discussion of human history is worth considering for what it may tell us about the poet's intentions in *Purity*. In *The City of God* (XIV:xi–xii), Saint Augustine notes that the punishment meted out to Adam is the first instance of justice in human history. Although Adam was indeed guilty, his crime was not a malicious one, for he had no experiential knowledge of either justice or punishment. Augustine continues his discussion of human history by saying that, since Adam, man has a historical precedent for an understanding of justice and is therefore more culpable because he knows.[16] Augustine's words may explain why the poet states that neither Lucifer's crime nor Adam's angered God (230, 247–248), but crimes of impurity do arouse his wrath. Since Adam, man knows and is therefore neither innocent nor ignorant; so his crimes are committed with a knowingly disobedient will. The poet's three exemplary tales hence illustrate the realities of justice and mercy in terms of human choice. The poet, rather than discussing purity and impurity in general terms, organizes his topic by exploring the three classic sins of lust, avarice, and pride.

Noah and the Flood: Lust of the Flesh. The poet's account of Noah and the Flood follows both the spirit and the letter of Genesis 6–9. Traditionally, the Flood was seen as a punishment for widespread carnality, as an event that washed the world of its carnal impurities. Genesis 6:1–4, which states that the sons of God had married the daughters of men and produced giants, was seen as evidence of the crimes of the flesh, crimes that only Noah and his family refused to commit.[17] The ark carrying Noah and seven others was seen as a type of the Church, carrying the elect through the flood waters of judgment. Because of the ark, the Flood, which was death to the impure, was seen as a type of baptism or cleansing for the pure. The safe landing of the ark was thought to foreshadow the safe landing of the soul or of the Church in paradise, a world characterized by spring, new life, order, and harmony.[18] Thus, though the Flood was an instance of divine wrath and punishment for the carnal, it was a means of passage and cleansing for the pure: what destroyed the impurities of the flesh also cleansed and released the spirit, safe within the ark, in preparation for the harmony of a new world.

The description of the antediluvian world in *Purity* stresses the prevailing carnality of its population. The poet first acknowledges the physical beauty of Adam's descendants: "Hit wern þe fayrest of forme and of face als, / Þe most and þe myriest þat maked wern ever, / Þe styfest, þe stalworþest þat stod ever on fete, / And lengest lyf in hem lent of ledez alle oþer" (253–256). Not only are they beautiful and long-lived, but they have no law except natural law: "Þer watz no law to hem layd bot loke to kynde, / And kepe to hit, and alle hit cors clanly fulfylle" (263–264). They live in a sort of golden, or perhaps silver, age; and the death that Adam brought into the world appears to be their only bane. They react, however, to this bounty with ingratitude and foul the flesh that is a part of their glory:

So ferly fowled her flesch þat þe fende loked
How þe deȝter of þe douþe wern derelych fayre,
And fallen in felaȝschyp wyth hem on folken wyse,
And engendered on hem jeauntez wyth her japez ille.
(269–272)

The poet here alters Genesis 6:2 ("the sons of God saw
that the daughters of men were fair, and they took wives for
themselves, as many as they wished") in order to convey the
traditional reading of this verse, which was thought to evince
carnality. His emphasis is upon individual choice: Adam's
descendants attract the "fende" because they have already
fouled their flesh. The giants, who were traditionally linked
to the sin of pride, come into being because of carnality.
God's decision to destroy the world comes only after the
world has corrupted itself: "When he knew uche contre co-
ruppte in hitselven, / And uch freke forloyned fro þe ryȝt
wayez" (281–282). Moreover, the poet notes, both before and
during the Flood, what the water destroys: "'And fleme out
of þe folde al þat flesch werez'" (287): "'þe ende of alle-kynez
flesch þat on urþe mevez'" (303); "'Schal no flesch upon
folde by fonden on lyve'" (356); "By forty dayez wern faren,
on folde no flesch styryed" (403). The poet, in using "flesch"
to denote life, hints at the carnal nature of the crimes that
precipitated the Flood.

By washing the world, the Flood destroys the ability of the
flesh to foul itself. Hence the poet describes the Flood as a
process of cleansing: "'For I schal waken up a water to wasch
alle þe worlde'" (323); "'þat schal wasch alle þe worlde of
werkez of fylþe'" (355). The poet ends his account of the
Flood by once more linking the flesh with sins that require
cleansing:

Forþy war þe now, wyȝe þat worschyp desyres
In his comlych corte þat Kyng is of blysse,
In þe fylþe of þe flesch þat þou be founden never,
Tyl any water in þe worlde to wasche þe fayly.

(545–548)

These lines make explicit what is more implicit in the nar-
rative itself, for the poet warns his audience of the dangers
of fleshly filth, filth that cannot be cleansed by earthly water.
He also links the Flood and the sins of the flesh with the
wedding feast of heaven by warning his audience that each

man must be clean of "flyþe of þe flesch" before coming into the king's court. Whereas the descendants of Adam "refuse" their invitations to the king's court by choosing the flesh, the raven, like the man in foul clothes, attends the feast without changing his habits. According to Genesis 8:6–7, after the floodwaters began to subside, Noah sent a raven to find evidence of dry land for the passengers on the ark. The raven did not return. According to medieval legend, the raven did not return to the ark because it discovered carrion and stayed to feast. Medieval discussions of the raven or crow are, like those of the man in foul clothes, concerned with the dangers of impenitence and rebellion.[19] Similarly, the poet links the raven with treachery and untruth: "Þat watz þe raven so ronk, þat rebel watz ever; / He watz colored as þe cole, corbyal untrwe" (455–456). Not only is the raven untrue, but his appetites, like those of the antediluvian world, are carnal: "He hade þe smelle of þe smach and smoltes þeder sone, / Fallez on þe foule flesch and fyllez his wombe" (461–462). Both the description of Adam's descendants and the account of the raven reflect the pattern adumbrated in the Parable of the Wedding Feast: a guest refuses a banquet because he "has married a wife," and a guest attends unprepared for the feast itself. The poet, however, does more than describe punishment; he describes the splendor, plenitude, and harmony of the wedding banquet.

In his description of those without sins of the flesh, or of the figurative guests at the banquet, the poet focuses upon obedience as it is manifested in action. Whereas he devotes eighteen lines to the sins of Noah's neighbors, he establishes Noah's purity in only four:

Þenne in worlde watz a wyȝe wonyande on lyve,
Ful redy and ful ryȝtwys, and rewled hym fayre;
In þe drede of Dryȝtyn his dayez he usez,
And ay glydande wyth his God his grace watz þe more.
(293–296)

Unlike his neighbors, Noah dreads God—or understands the consequences of willfulness—and rules himself accordingly. Although his neighbors have engendered giants, Noah and his wife have three sons and they three wives (297–300). Just as Noah is described in terms of obedient and orderly action, the dove, the bird that completes the task originally assigned the raven, is also described as perfectly obedient. Noah sends her out to discover dry land, and she returns, bearing the olive branch as a token of the world that now awaits the company of the ark.[20] Noah and the dove are alike because each exists in relation to something other than themselves; the poet emphasizes neither their desires, nor their eating habits, but their obedience to their lords.

The emphasis upon obedient action, conveyed by the description of the decorum and propriety of the wedding feast, informs the poet's description of the landing of the ark. Noah's first act upon landing is one of service: he builds an altar and sacrifices to God. In answer, he receives a promise that God will not again flood the earth:

> He knyt a covenaunde cortaysly wyth monkynde þere,
> In þe mesure of his mode and meþe of his wylle,
> Þat he schulde never, for no syt, smyte al at onez,
> As to quelle alle quykez for qued þat myȝt falle,
> Whyl of þe lenþe of þe londe lastez þe terme.
>
> (564–568)

The words "mesure" and "meþe," which describe the covenant God makes with man, recall the means by which Adam's crime was redressed, likewise in "mesure" and "meþe." Once more, the poet underlines the element of human choice in history. Adam's crime may be wiped out through individual penance, and the new covenant of mercy that God offers man is available to man if he wishes it. In his description of Noah, the poet first describes Noah's purity, a purity that saves him from the consequences of the Flood, then his act of thanks and worship after the ark has landed. God's promise that there will not be another flood is a response to Noah's act of worship. By his obedience, Noah signifies his willingness to listen to God. After the covenant has been established between God and man through Noah, the poet describes the new harmony of this newly washed world. He enumerates the hierarchical and decorous ordering of creation: birds go to the air, fish to the sea, beasts to their proper environments (see 530–540).

The harmony and decorum of this scene come as a sharp contrast to the earlier description of the Flood. In describing the Flood, the poet emphasizes its chaotic effect upon human relationships:

Frendez fellen in fere and faþmed togeder,
To dryȝ her delful deystyne and dyȝen alle samen:
Luf lokez to luf and his leve takez,
For to ende alle at onez and for ever twynne.

(399–402)

By translating the relationships of daily life—friendship and love—into a setting of such horror, the poet vivifies the consequences of impurity. Like the Doomsday Plays of the cycle dramas, *Purity* underscores the terrors of damnation by describing scenes with which an audience can empathize, thereby warning it of the dangers of choosing self rather than God. Neither the fear, the friendship, nor the love of those who were drowning saves them from the Flood: all cry out to God once they find themselves in danger, but "his mercy watz passed" (395).

Like the Parable of the Wedding Feast, the account of the Flood teaches both a positive and a negative lesson. In his description of Noah, the dove, and the landing of the ark, the poet intimates the nature of purity by describing those outwardly harmonious characteristics that are signs, or garments, of the pure. In his account of the descendants of Adam, the poet suggests the lavish preparations God made for his guests—beauty, long life, society without government—and the ingratitude of the guests who abuse this bounty and demonstrate that they prefer carnality to purity. Their choice precipitates justice, a justice similar to that in medieval descriptions of Judgment Day. The raven, like the man in foul clothes, rejects the harmony of the ark; and, like the man in foul clothes, the raven is doubly culpable, for he has been "called" to the ark, or feast, and chooses the dead flesh of an old world rather than the order of a new. But the story of the Flood, like the Parable of the Wedding Feast, is threatening only for those who refuse or who turn back.

Abraham and Lot: Lust of the Eyes. The second exemplary tale in *Purity* recounts the story of Abraham and Lot. In this section, the poet explores purity and impurity as they are manifested in avarice and curiosity, or an appetite for the delights of the world. Just as the poet's account of the guest who refused to attend the wedding feast emphasizes the temptations of sight, or of sensory perception, so his account of Lot and Sodom underlines the temptations of sensual curiosity. Lot's wife turns away from the possibilities of harmony and order, choosing a last sight of her city rather than the safety she has been promised. The story of Abraham and Lot, like others in *Purity*, contains both a positive and a negative lesson; for it contains both destruction and salvation.

The story itself is a familiar one. Abraham provides hospitality to three men who he perceives are angels. After eating, they tell him that he and Sara, though they are old, will bear a son who will produce a great nation. Sara laughs in disbelief. The angels then tell Abraham that God intends to destroy Sodom, Gomorrah, and three other cities for their persistent wickedness. Abraham bargains with the angels for the safety of the cities, finally exacting a promise of Lot's salvation. The angels go to Sodom, warn Lot, and direct him and his family to safety. Lot's wife, though warned against it, looks back at Sodom as she leaves it and is turned into a pillar of salt. The five cities destroyed by fire and brimstone become a wasteland.

Although the story of Abraham and the three angels appears to be simply an overlong preface to the story of Lot, through Abraham the poet underlines the themes of harmonious action, of proper stewardship, and of heavenly plenitude. He suggests these themes by describing Abraham's relationship to God. Abraham, like Noah, is defined by his actions, which are the outward signs of his spiritual devotion. Abraham, figuratively, wears clean clothes to the great wedding feast; and his clothes signal his recognition of the decorous, yet joyful, nature of the feast. Furthermore, in his account of Abraham and the three angels, the poet suggests both the "letter" and the "spirit" of the Biblical story.

The account of Abraham opens with an almost idyllic description of Abraham sitting under a tree in the heat of the day:

> Olde Abraham in erde onez he syttez
> Even byfore his hous-dore, under an oke grene;
> Bryȝt blykked þe bem of þe brode heven,
> In þe hyȝe hete þerof Abraham bidez,
> He watz schunt to þe schadow under schyre levez.
>
> (601–605)

These lines are an expansion of Genesis 18:1, which is comparatively terse: "And the Lord appeared to him in the vale of Mambre as he was sitting at the door of his tent, in the very heat of the day." The tree under which Abraham sits in *Purity* does not appear until verse 4 of the Biblical account when Abraham directs the angels to sit beneath it. In *Purity*, the lines describing Abraham from a picture that links Abraham with the great oak under whose shade he takes shelter from the sun's heat. In his portrait of Abraham, the poet perhaps, substituting an English oak for a fig tree, alludes to Micah's messianic prophecy that in a new and future age, "every man shall sit under his own vine or under his own fig tree, undisturbed" (Mic. 4:4). This verse was thought to look forward to a new age of peace, ushered in by the birth of Christ. Abraham's situation in *Purity* is certainly one of peace and well-being, for he rests, ready to recognize his heavenly visitors, under a tree that many commentators identified with the cross.[21]

The poet also alludes to the figurative meaning of the three angels whom Abraham sees approaching. Genesis 18:2–3 states that Abraham saw three men before him and hailed them as "Lord"; his use of a singular noun was seen as a prefiguration of the Trinity in Old Testament history.[22] The poet's transformation of the Biblical passage underlines its figurative significance: "When he hade of hem syȝt, he hyȝez bylyve, / And as to God þe good mon gos hem agaynez, / And haylsed hem in onhede, and sayde: 'Hende Lorde'" (610–612). Abraham greets the three as one, and the poet points to the trinitarian importance of the verse by underlining Abraham's new perception with "he hyȝez bylyve." He reinforces the basis of Abraham's belief with the prepositional phrase "in onhede."

The feast that Sara and Abraham prepare for the angels (625–644) was also interpreted as a prefiguration of the New Law, a feast celebrating the sacramental life, penance, and Christian doctrine.[23] Thus, the poet's description of Abraham serving the feast emphasizes the feast itself. The figure of Abraham is subordinate to the elements before him:

As sewer in a god assyse he served hem fayre,
Wyth sadde semblaunt and swete, of such as he hade;
And God as a glad gest mad god chere,
Þat watz fayn of his frende, and his fest praysed.
Abraham, al hodlez, wyth armez upfolden,
Mynystred mete byfore þo men þat myȝtes al weldez.

(639–644)

The words "sewer," "served," and "mynystred" illustrate Abraham's function in this tableau, while "sadde semblaunt and swete" and "armez upfolden" describe his attitude toward his role. The scene itself suggests the feast of the Mass and the operative and yet subordinate role of the priest in relation to those elements which he prepares and serves. Like Noah, Abraham serves God. The feast culminates in the prophecy of the birth of Isaac, the promise of futurity for Abraham and his people.[24]

The account of Abraham and the angels is an appropriate preamble to that of Lot and Sodom since Abraham's actions provide a standard for service and devotion. By portraying Abraham as a "server" or steward, by suggesting the New Law understanding of Abraham's encounter with the angels, and by including God's promise to Abraham of an heir, the poet suggests the rewards of purity, the order and harmony of the wedding feast. The account prepares us to note the differences between Abraham and Lot—between their feasts, their wives, and their places of dwelling. Furthermore, the long description (715–780) of Abraham's bargain with God over the fate of the cities underlines their persistent impurity, just as the long description of Adam's descendants clarifies the persistent carnality of the antediluvian population. Abraham's reaction to God's decision is a proper one: he wishes to save those who remain pure. Hence the angels go to warn Lot, whom they invite away from a world dominated by greed.

Traditionally, Sodom is associated with sexual perversion, but medieval commentators also discussed other crimes in relation to Sodom. The *Glossa Ordinaria,* quoting Isidore, says that Sodom means blindness, or a desire for the things of the world, identifying the five cities with the five senses. Richard of St. Victor and Hugh of St. Victor gloss the flight of Lot from Sodom as the soul's escape from *temporalia.* Berchorius identifies the doomed cities with the world, and Thomas Brinton warned fourteenth-century England that leisure time and an abundance of bread led to the fall of Sodom.[25]

The poet's emphasis in this section upon sensual curiosity, possibly avarice, and sexual perversion may also owe something to medieval discussions of the Parable of the Wedding Feast. In commenting on the second guest's excuse, for example, Saint Augustine notes that avarice, or curiosity, may lead to sins of lust, but what appears as simple lust may be more complex and have avarice as its primary impetus.

Hence, the temptations of the world may include those of the flesh but are nonetheless inspired by "lust of the eyes." The poet suggests that the temptations of Sodom are those of the world not only in his description of Sodom and its citizens, but in his account of Lot. The poet points to Lot's involvement with the world and its temptations by referring to Lot's wealth and its origins in the city of Sodom.[26] Lot is a city dweller, and our first sight of Lot links him to his city: "As Loot in a loge-dor lened hym alone, / In a porche of þat place pyȝt to þe ȝates, / Þat watz ryal and ryche—so watz þe renkes selven" (784–786). The picture of Lot contrasts to the previous one of Abraham— "Olde Abraham in erde onez he syttez" (601)—and is an elaboration of Genesis 19:1, "And the two angels came to Sodom in the evening, and Lot was sitting in the gate of the city." The construction of line 786 is noteworthy because it establishes a comparison between Lot and Sodom: the porch, near to the gates, is rich and royal as Lot also is rich. The poet thus associates Lot with his city as the poet previously associated Abraham with the great tree. Each landscape manifests the nature of the man who stands against it. The poet mentions Lot's wealth in two other places: "Þe bolde to his byggyng bryngez hem bylyve, / Þat [watz] ryally arayed, for he watz ryche ever" (811–812); "'Who joyned þe be jostyse oure japez to blame, / Þat com a boy to þis borȝ, þaȝ þou be burne ryche?'" (877–878). In the first citation, the poet uses "ryally" and "ryche" to describe Lot's home and his worldly position, two words that also appear in the initial emblematic portrait of Lot (784–786). Lines 877–878, however, reveal even more about Lot's involvement with Sodom: he came there as a boy and made his fortune there. His wealth is inextricably involved with the doomed city.

The poet's account of Sodom intimates its concern with the senses. For example, Lot admonishes his wife to omit salt or heavy spices from the meal she prepares for the guests (820), a command she scornfully rejects: "'Þis un[s]avere hyne / Lovez no salt in her sauce, ȝet hit no skyl were / Þat oþer burne be boute, þaȝ boþe be nyse'" (822–824). She then creates a highly seasoned meal, thus aligning herself with the sensual preoccupation of her city and prefiguring her transformation into a pillar of salt. The city is described in terms of the senses. In God's warning to Abraham about Sodom, the poet alludes to the city's blindness: "At a stylle stollen steven, unstered wyth syȝt" (706). After the angels create a cloud to protect Lot and his family, there is another allusion to blindness: "Þat þay blustered as blynde as Bayard watz ever" (886). Given his emphasis on vision, it is not surprising that the poet devotes lines 789–793 to a physical description of the angels as they enter the city:

> Bolde burnez were þay boþe, wyth berdles chynnez,
> Royl rollande fax, to raw sylk lyke,
> Of ble as þe brere-flor where so þe bare schew[e]d;
> Ful clene watz þe countenaunce of her cler yȝen;
> Wlonk whit watz her wede and wel hit hem semed.
> (789–793)

The poet's description of the angels' appearance in Sodom contrasts sharply to the earlier depiction of their appearance before Abraham. The poet only briefly refers to Abraham's guests; here, he describes them in detail. Whereas Abraham, "when he hade of hem syȝt" (610), greets the angels as one, Lot perceives them as two distinct figures. Thus, while Lot's hospitality is as effusive as Abraham's, his perceptions are radically different. Lot's vision of the two exquisite figures, which reveals his own emphasis upon riches and luxury, is further expanded and distorted in the eyes of the Sodomites, whom the angels' beauty inspires to lust. As in Genesis 19:8, Lot offers the Sodomites his daughters rather than his guests, but the poet once again expands the Biblical account to emphasize the daughters' physical beauty (866–872)

The final description of Sodom, now the Dead Sea, brings together these references to sensual perception. In lines 1006–1048, the poet describes what Sodom was and what Sodom has become. First, he describes the initial fairness of the location, its resemblance to paradise: "Þat ever hade ben an erde of erþe þe swettest, / As aparaunt to paradis þat plantted þe Dryȝtyn" (1006–1007). Like Lucifer and like Adam's descendants, these cities were once blessed with physical beauty and with plenitude. However, the citizens, like other impure figures in *Purity*, refuse God's bounty. The poet's use in line 1007 of "aparaunt," meaning perceptible, known by sensory perception, hints at the dangers the cities can pose to men dwelling in them. Like writers before and after him, the poet suggests that what looks lovely may not be lovely.[27] The cities, like other worldly gardens, may pose a threat because they appeal first to the eyes, finally to the other senses. The destruction of the cities reveals them for what they are:

> Þer faure citees wern set, nou is a see called,
> Þat ay is drovy and dym, and ded in hit kynde,
> Blo, blubrande, and blak, unblyþe to neȝe,
> As a stynkande stanc þat stryed synne,
> Þat ever of s[mell]e and of smach, smark is to fele.
>
> (1015–1019)

Whereas once Sodom offended only God's senses ("'The grete soun of Sodamas synkkez in myn erez,'" 689), now it offends the eyes and noses of all men.

The poet also heightens our awareness of the treachery of these cities by describing the illusory garden that grows on their former site:

> And þer ar tres by þat terne of traytores,
> And þay borgounez and beres blomez ful fayre,
> And þe fayrest fryt þat may on folde growe,
> As orange and oþer fryt and apple garnade,
> Also red and so ripe and rychely hwed
> As any dom myȝt device of dayntyez oute;
> Bot quen hit is brused, oþer broken, oþer byten in
>   twynne,
> No worldez goud hit wythinne, bot wyndowande askes.
>
> (1041–1048)

In describing the Dead Sea as a "lake of traitors," the poet links the citizens of Sodom to other figures who betrayed their Lord and hence their natures. Lucifer, once fair, betrayed God and became foul. Adam failed in truth and was punished by death. Adam's descendants betrayed their heritage and lost loves and friends to the floodwaters. The fruit of the trees growing by this sea, like the delights of the world, is ashes in the mouth: though the fruit appears fair, it offers no nourishment, no "worldez goud." The once-fair cities have become a lifeless image of foulness, and Lot's wife, in seeking a last glimpse of Sodom before she leaves it, becomes equally fixed in the results of her choice.

By her disobedient acts, Lot's wife is thematically linked with the man in foul clothes and the raven.[28] The poet emphasizes the element of choice that leads to her metamorphosis into a statue of salt. First, she chooses to season the angels' food "agayne þe bone of þe burne þat hit forboden hade" (826). Her second choice, to look back at Sodom before she leaves it, is a continuation of her earlier culinary self-assertion:

> Bot þe balleful burde þat never bode keped,
> Blusched byhynden her bak, þat bale for to herkken.
> Hit watz lusty Lothes wyf þat over he[r] lyfte schulder
> Ones ho bluschet to þe burȝe, bot bod ho no lenger,
> Þat ho nas stadde a stiffe ston, a stalworth image
> Also salt as ani se, and so ho ȝet standez.
>
> (979–984)

Genesis 19:26 says merely: "And his wife looking behind her, was turned into a statue of salt." The poet, however, underscores the theme of disobedience by describing Lot's wife as "the wretched woman who never obeyed a command," and by noting that she looks over her *left* shoulder. Her choice fixes her, and she becomes a "stiffe ston, a stalworth image." Like the Dead Sea, the statue of salt stands as a monument to human willfulness, to a refusal to turn from the old ways and toward God.

Like the account of Noah and the Flood, the account of

Abraham and Lot teaches purity. The narrative is thematically aligned with the Parable of the Wedding Feast through the allusions to sensual perception, or lust of the eyes, the second guest's excuse, and through Lot's wife, who chooses to look back at Sodom just as the raven chooses to return to the carnality of an old, destroyed world. Within the narrative itself, the poet displays a highly developed sense of balance by presenting the two portraits of Abraham and Lot, two feasts, two wives, and two encounters with angels. In this section, perhaps more than in any other part of the poem, he teaches through contrasting pictures, in effect using the senses to dramatize the danger of sensual appetites. Thus, Lot is defined in relation to Abraham, Sodom in relation to Segor; Sara's laughter is measured against the hostile scorn of Lot's wife. In the portrait of Lot, the poet demonstrates the rewards of penance, the act by which a man escapes the dangers of the world. Like the raven, Lot's wife is impenitent, whereas Lot refuses to look back at an old life. Lot abandons his great wealth, rooted in Sodom, and flees its chaos to the order of Segor.

Whereas Lot's decision to heed the angels' warning and abandon Sodom is rewarded with mercy, the Sodomites, like Adam's descendants, are punished by justice. Medieval commentators frequently linked the Flood and the destruction of the cities of the plain, usually discussing the two incidents in apocalyptic terms.[29] The poet also stresses the chaotic aspects of Sodom's destruction ("Such a ȝomerly ȝarm of ȝellyng þer rysed, / Þerof clatered þe cloudes þat Kryst myȝt haf rawþe," 971–972) and observes that the cities and their inhabitants sank into hell (968). In his description of Sodom's destruction, however, he omits the details of everyday life that heighten the terror of his description of the Flood, focusing instead upon Lot and his efforts to escape the city. Consequently, the poet underlines the reality of punishment even as he shifts our attention to the figure of Lot who, like all men, may choose mercy.

Lot, in fact, is the dramatic focus for the story because his is the story of reform. The poet elaborates upon the Biblical account in order to vivify Lot's very human confusion when he hears of Sodom's imminent destruction: Lot does not know what to do; he knows he cannot flee from God's wrath, and he does not know where to go. Only when the angels assure him that Abraham's intervention has guaranteed his safety does Lot timidly suggest Segor as a refuge: "'Þe[r] is a cite herbisyde þat Segor hit hatte, / Here utter on a rounde hil hit hovez hit one, / I wolde, if his wylle wore, to þat won scape'" (926–928).

That the poet intends us to recognize the importance of the arrival in Segor is clear from the way in which he alters the Biblical account of Lot's flight. According to Genesis 19, Lot and his daughters soon leave Segor for the mountains, but the poet identifies Segor as the end of their journey:

> Tyl þay in Segor wern sette, and sayned our Lorde;
> Wyth lyȝt lovez uplyfte þay loved hym swyþe,
> Þat so his servauntes wolde see and save of such woþe.
> Al watz dampped and don and drowned by þenne;
> Þe ledez of þat lyttel toun wern lopen out for drede
> Into þat malscrande mere, marred bylyve,
> Þat noȝt saved watz bot Segor þat sat on a lawe,
> Þe þre ledez þerin, Loth and his deȝter.
>
> (986–993)

All is destroyed, except Segor, which sits on a "lawe." The poet's reference to Segor perhaps contains a pun: "lawe" means both "law" and "hill," and, in terms of the poem, both laws and hills are places of refuge and order. Noah's ark comes to rest on a mountain, and the arrival is orderly and joyful. Lot and his daughters, likewise, find rest upon a hill in orderly delight. Moreover, like the eight in the ark, Lot and his daughters return thanks to God and, in fact, act out the pattern of harmonious action and service that characterizes the fellowship of the saved in *Purity*.

Exhortation to Purity. In between the story of Abraham and Lot and of the capture of Jerusalem is a section, consisting of a little over a hundred lines, exhorting the audience to purity through penance. This section, like the one that links the story of the Flood to the story of Lot and Sodom, deals explicitly with the tenets of Christian doctrine. These sections allow the poet to sum up the lessons of the preceding tale and prepare us for the next. Thus, the first section (545–600) begins with an allusion to the covenant between God and Noah after the Flood, looks forward to the story of Sodom by considering impurity and its noxious effects on God's senses, and leads into the story of Abraham by noting that God may send a sign of himself to a pure man. The second section begins with a reference to the barren landscape of the Dead Sea, moves to a discussion of clean love, and finishes by exhorting the audience to penance and by warning it of the consequences of impenitence, or of willful impurity. The second section is a more positive exhortation to purity than the first because it emphasizes the delights of purity rather than the consequences of impurity.

The poet introduces what is an exhortation to good love by implicitly comparing the greed of the Sodomites to the greed a soul might have for Christ:

> Alle þyse ar teches and tokenes to trow upon ȝet,
> And wittnesse of þat wykked werk, and þe wrake after
> Þat oure Fader forferde for fylþe of þose ledes.
> Þenne uch wyȝe may wel wyt þat he þe wlonk lovies;
> And if he lovyes clene layk þat is oure Lorde ryche,
> And to be couþe in his corte þou coveytes þenne,
> To se þat Semly in sete and his swete face,
> Clerrer counseyl con I non, bot þat þou clene worþe.
> (1049–1056)

The poet begins by recalling Sodom's love, saying that such things as the Dead Sea and its illusory fruit are "tokenes" that bear witness to the nature of unclean love. However, the emphasis of the passage shifts in the next sentence, which begins with "Þenne," for the poet hints at the type of positive lesson that these "tokenes" can teach. By his use of "wlonk" (pure or fair), the poet suggests that there are degrees of love, degrees that depend upon the object of love and that it is possible to distinguish between love-objects. With his reference to Christ in line 1053, the poet establishes a standard for comparison, following up his reference to Christ by saying that we may covet Christ and his court. The poet's use of "coveytes" looks backward to Sodom's barren trees, its tokens, and forward to a discussion of good covetousness. Whereas the Sodomites covet what they see, the soul should covet in order to see, "to se þat Semly in sete and his swete face" (1055). By emphasizing words like "wlonk," "semly," "swete face," the poet underlines his implicit comparison between good and bad desire, for these words relate to the verb "se" in line 1055. The poet thus suggests that the object of desire determines whether the love is barren or fruitful.

The poet continues his exhortation to spiritual covetousness by paraphrasing the advice Jean de Meun has Friend give Lover in the *Roman de la Rose;* once more, the poet suggests a comparison between carnal and spiritual desire:

> For Clopyngnel in þe compas of his clene Rose,
> Þer he expounez a speche, to hym þat spede wolde,
> Of a lady to be loved: "Loke to hir sone,
> Of wich beryng þat ho be, and wych ho best lovyes,
> And be ryȝt such, in uch a borȝe, of body and of dedes,
> And folȝ þe fet of þat fere þat þou fre haldes;
> And if þou wyrkkes on þis wyse, þaȝ ho wyk were,
> Hir schal lyke þat layk þat lyknes hir tylle."
>
> (1057–1064)

Friend here tells Lover that he may gain the lady's "fair welcome" by copying her tastes and habits, that he may win her by becoming a reflection of her.[30] When we consider the nature of the advice and its source, it is clear that, for the author of *Purity,* the object of one's desire determines the nature of one's love. If the object is a person and the end of desire is physical sensation, then the love is likely to be as limited as the delights of the world—fruit that turns to ashes in the mouth. But, if the object is Christ, "þou coveytes þenne."

The analogy the poet draws between the techniques of carnal and spiritual courtship establishes "clene" love as a standard for comparison. His shift in emphasis, from the punishment of Sodom to the joys of Christ, likewise suggests what the Sodomites denied themselves by coveting the wrong thing. Hence, the poet focuses upon the benefits of mercy in the figures of Mary and Christ. He describes the Nativity in terms of the world's heightened sensual appeal: "And þer watz rose reflayr where rote hatz ben ever, / And þer watz solace and songe wher sorȝ hatz ay cryed" (1079–1080). Like the authors of the Shepherds' Plays in the mystery cycles, the poet captures the meaning of the Nativity by demonstrating its effect upon the natural world: where once earth smelled of decay and cried with sorrow, with the birth of Christ there are sweet odors, solace, and song. The poet's assertion that the fragrance of roses replaced the smell of decay possibly also looks back to the "rose" that Lover wishes to win in the Roman de la Rose. The lover's "rose" may be "clene," but the lover is less interested in its purity than he is in possessing it; the roses that bloom with Christ's birth manifest the eternal and selfless love born on earth for man. The poet then describes Christ as physician ("For what so he towched, also tyd torned to hele," 1099), enumerating the ailments Christ healed during his ministry on earth.

The poet's enumeration of the superior delights of pure love and his description of the health and refuge Christ offers man continue through line 1108, when he asks, perhaps, the central question of the poem:

Þus is he kyryous and clene þat þou his cort askes;
Hou schulde þou com to his kyth bot if þou clene were?
Nou are we sore and synful and souly uch one,
How schulde we se, þen may we say, þat Syre upon
    throne?

(1109–1112)

How can man, who is impure, see God if he must be pure to approach God's court? The poet explicitly poses the question implicitly raised in the Parable of the Wedding Feast: how can a man find the clean clothes a guest must wear to the feast? The remainder of the section answers the question by discussing penance as a process of cleansing.

The poet follows the exhortation to penance with a warning. He outlines the dangers of resoiling what has been washed—a basin, a bowl, a dish, or anything that once *served* God. He thereby foreshadows the events of the third exemplary tale with its harsh lesson of justice. The delights of purity are real, but equally real are the rewards for impurity. Jerusalem under Zedekiah turns from God and is taken into Babylonian captivity; Balthazar willfully and maliciously abuses "vessels" dedicated to God's service and learns that justice indeed comes "like a thief in the night."

The Capture of Jerusalem and Balthazar's Feast: The Ambition of the World. The third exemplary tale narrates the story of Nebuchadnezzar's capture of Jerusalem, the captivity of its citizens in Babylon, and Balthazar's feast, which culminates in the supernatural handwriting on the wall, a warning to the profane king of Babylon. This third example comments upon the sin of pride, introduced in the Parable of the Wedding Feast by the guest who excuses himself because he had just bought an estate. As noted above, exegetical discussions of this excuse consider the attractions of possession and of domination as manifestations of pride. The poet also suggests this way of considering the excuse by having the guest say that he has just bought a "borӡ" or a "toun." The two words, in some measure, foreshadow the appearance of the two opposed cities of Jerusalem and Babylon and the poet's emphasis upon kingship and the duties of rule. Rather than simply oppose Jerusalem and Babylon, however, the poet describes the absorption of one into the other because of Jerusalem's lack of truth, embodied in her faithless king. The citizens of Jerusalem ignore God's bounty and, metaphorically, refuse their invitations to the feast. Nebuchadnezzar, who conquers Jerusalem and takes its citizens into captivity, acts as an agent of divine justice by depriving them of their homeland. Balthazar, like the other figures who ignore previous instances of heavenly justice, chooses himself rather than God and so joins the raven and Lot's wife as a figure of willful impenitence who, though called, turns away from the wedding feast.

The poet's description of Jerusalem underscores its faithlessness. He calls it "Jherusalem þe ryche" (1159) and describes its citizens as "untrwe" (1161). Although God had always watched over the city and helped it in its need, the citizens abandon their faith, turning to other gods: "And þay forloyne her fayth and folȝed oþer goddes" (1165). The poet also stresses its faithlessness by describing Jerusalem's king, Zedekiah, as a traitor: "Bot of leaute he watz lat to his Lorde hende: / He used abominaciones of idolatrye, / And lette lyȝt bi þe lawe þat he watz lege tylle" (1172–1174). The word "lege" pertains to feudal obligations, and Zedekiah, like Lucifer, is false to his sworn lord and takes God's law lightly. Jerusalem's faithlessness and its king's treason prepare the way for Babylonian capture, as God awakens a foe that will punish an already weakened city. Nebuchadnezzar and "proude men mony" (1177) lay siege to the city, causing a famine. The Babylonians capture Zedekiah when he tries to lead a raid against them; they then conquer the city and bring its citizens to Babylon where they "ar chaunged to chorles" (1258).

The account of Jerusalem's fall is intentionally brief. Following the assessment of Jerusalem's inner weaknesses, the poet swiftly moves on to an account of the Babylonian army, the siege, the consequent famine, the Babylonian victory, the capture of Jerusalem, and the change from gentry to churl. The poet compresses the events of over two years into a compact narrative that underlines the providential nature of human history. Jerusalem's destruction is implicit in its spiritual treachery: Jerusalem having turned from God, God turned from her. After describing the absorption of Jerusalem into Babylon, the poet shifts his attention to the continuing need for purity in a situation that poses severe threats for individual purity. Although Nebuchadnezzar honors those holy things, such as temple vessels, which he has brought from Jerusalem, Balthazar, the subsequent ruler, honors nothing except himself.

The poet underscores the enormity of Balthazar's pride by contrasting him to his father, Nebuchadnezzar.[31] In the poem, two important aspects of Nebuchadnezzar's history reflect his attitude toward God. Though he was responsible for the spoiling of the temple and the capture of its vessels, Nebuchadnezzar protects them from impurity:

> He sesed hem wyth solemnete, þe Soverayn he praysed
> Þat watz aþel over alle, Israel Dryȝtyn;
> Such god, such gomes, such gay vesselles,
> Comen never out of kyth to Caldee reames.
> He trussed hem in his tresorye in a tryed place
> Rekenly wyth reverens, as he ryȝt hade . . .
> (1313–1318)

The poet is careful to specify *how* Nebuchadnezzar treats the vessels—"wyth solemnete" and "wyth reverens." Furthermore, though he acknowledges Nebuchadnezzar's vast temporal power (1321–1323), he also mentions Daniel's role as his spiritual advisor (1325–1328) and Nebuchadnezzar's reverence for God.

In contrast, the description of Balthazar emphasizes only his devotion to himself. The poet introduces Balthazar by suggesting the pride Balthazar takes in his position:

> Bot þenn þe bolde Baltazar, þat watz his barn aldest,
> He watz stalled in his stud, and stabled þe rengne;
> In þe burȝ of Babiloyne þe biggest he trawed,
> Þat nauþer in heven ne [on] erþe hade no pere;
> For he bigan in alle þe glori þat hym þe gome lafte . . .
> (1333–1337)

Balthazar succeeds to the wealth and power of his father, but he acknowledges no authority over him, or debt to any other power. When Balthazar decides to call a feast, the poet attributes his decision to pride: "Thenne þis bolde Baltazar biþenkkes hym ones / To vouche on avayment of his vayneg[l]orie" (1357–1358). The poet then connects the city of Babylon and its magnificent palace with pride: "Prudly on a plat playn, plek alþerfayrest" (1379); "Þat watz a palayce of pryde passande alle oþer, / Boþe of werk and of wunder and walle al aboute" (1389–1390). Balthazar's defilement of the holy vessels is a service to Satan: "Now is sette for to serve Satanas þe blake, / Bifore þe bolde Baltazar wyth bost and wyth pryde" (1449–1450). The words "bolde," "pryde," and "prudly" recur throughout the poet's description of Balthazar and Babylon, contrasting to such words as "reverens" and "solemnete," used to describe Nebuchadnezzar's attitude toward things belonging to God. Balthazar, like his father, has worldly power and wealth, but the son's wealth is merely an appendage to his pride.

The description of Balthazar's invitations to and preparations for his feast is a garish parody of the lord's invitations and preparations in the Parable of the Wedding Feast.[32] The similarities between the two incidents emphasize the essential differences between the two feasts. Whereas God calls men to a banquet of pleasure where clean clothes are signs of purity and service, Balthazar calls men "to reche hym reverens, and his revel herkken, / To loke on his lemanes and ladis hem calle" (1369–1370). Balthazar's invitation is compulsory rather than free, and the reverence Balthazar receives is the product of fear, rather than of love. Moreover, the order of Balthazar's feast is a grotesque imitation of God's order. Balthazar sits in the highest position, assuming the throned seat; around him are the knights, barons, and his concubines, whose "cloþes ful bryȝt" (1400) recall the "wedez bryȝt" of the angels who serve in the celestial court (20). Balthazar's hierarchy only emphasizes the disorderly nature of his court, for at his feast order is merely arrangement. In contrast, the order of both the heavenly court and the wedding feast is a manifestation of spiritual harmony and inner purity.

The feast itself is the occasion for Balthazar's abuse of the temple vessels. Daniel 5:1–4 recounts the feast, saying only that Balthazar called a feast, and the guests drank wine from the golden and silver vessels which had been taken out of the temple, and "praised their gods of gold, and of silver, of brass, of iron, and of wood, and of stone." This incident was thought to describe more than sacrilege, since vessels were frequently used as symbols for souls, and sanctified vessels for the souls of the faithful.[33] Saint Jerome specifically discusses Balthazar's act as a manifestation, not only of heresy, but of the sort of pride that desires heresy in others.[34] Balthazar's heretical act is an act of pride, but it is more serious than simple pride because it tends toward the spiritual downfall of others.

Balthazar's abuse of the temple vessels suggests his pride, sacrilege, and malice. The poet introduces the vessels by recounting their origins: "Salomon sete him s[eve]n ȝere and a syþe more, / Wyth alle þe syence þat hym sende þe soverayn Lorde, / For to compas and kest to haf hem clene wroȝt" (1453–1455). Solomon, who was associated with divine wisdom, had the vessels made; furthermore, Solomon went to the trouble of having them "clene wroȝt." The vessels' purity is an integral part of both their identity and their function. The poet then devotes thirty-seven lines to a description of the vessels, emphasizing their beauty, richness, and variety. Balthazar's decision to use these same vessels at the banquet, where he drinks from God's vessels while toasting false gods, is a perversion of the vessels' original identity and essential function.

For example, the poet draws a sharp contrast between the identity of a temple ornament (a menorah) and the way in which Balthazar uses it:

Hit watz not wonte in þat wone to wast no serges,
Bot in temple of þe trauþe trwly to stonde,
Bifore þe sancta sanctorum [þer] soþefast Dryȝtyn
Expouned his speche spyrytually to special prophetes.
                                                    (1489–1492)

The "candelstik" is meant to stand before the Holy of Holies as a sign of God, truth, and light; Balthazar uses it simply as an ornament, denying and defiling what is more than simply a "candlestick." The poet then notes that God is displeased that "his jueles" should find themselves in such a plight and so fouled. The vessels are fouled because they appear in a carnal setting and, now, like the former citizens of Jerusalem, have been changed from what they were intended to be. But this feast, like Arthur's feast in *Sir Gawain and the Green Knight*, is interrupted by a strange event: handwriting appears on the wall, prompting Balthazar to call upon Daniel.

Daniel's explanation of the handwriting on the wall introduces the virtue of humility, the antidote to pride. He warns Balthazar of the consequences of pride by speaking, first, of Nebuchadnezzar. Nebuchadnezzar also took credit for his wealth and power and became proud, but God chastened Nebuchadnezzar's pride by turning him into a beast (see Dan. 5:20–21). After seven years, Nebuchadnezzar repented. The poet suggests the importance of repentance by rephrasing the Biblical account of this incident. Whereas the Book of Daniel says only that Nebuchadnezzar acknowledged the greater might of God, the poet says, "Þenne he l[o]ved þat Lorde and leved in trawþe" (1703). Nebuchadnezzar does not simply admit his lesser might; he learns to love truly. The words "love" and "trawþe" link Nebuchadnezzar to figures such as Noah and Lot, each of whom acknowledges God by loving him.

The poet's use of Nebuchadnezzar's example alerts us to the fact that Balthazar has been amply warned of the consequences of pride. If Balthazar chooses to see it, there is historical precedent for divine justice in the capture of Jerusalem, the punishment of Nebuchadnezzar, and in the handwriting on the wall. Of the latter, the poet notes that it is a warning: "Bot er harme hem he wolde in haste of his yre, / He wayned hem a warnyng þat wonder hem þoȝt" (1503–1504). The poet follows Daniel 5:25–28 in interpreting "Mane, Techal, Phares" as the number, weight, and measure by which Balthazar's kingdom has been judged. Balthazar ignores the warning of the standards of justice, dismisses the story of his father, rewards Daniel with the spoils of false wisdom— gold and power—and continues feasting.

In his depiction of God's punishment of Balthazar, the poet once again elaborates upon the Biblical account. Daniel 5:30–6:1 says that on the same night as the feast, Balthazar was slain, and Darius succeeded to the kingdom. The poet's account is far more dramatic. After the feast, "Baltazar to his bedd with blysse watz caryed, / Reche þe rest as hym lyst, he ros never þerafter" (1765–1766). He does not rise again from his drunken sleep because Darius and his men scale the city walls when no one is aware of their presence and beat Balthazar to death in his bed. The poet alludes to the providential nature of Balthazar's death by referring once more to his abuse of the temple vessels. Like Lot's wife, Balthazar receives swift justice, a punishment that gains added resonance in the overall context of the poem, in which Daniel's warning is equivalent to an invitation to the wedding feast and Balthazar's rejection of that warning is a sign that he prefers his own impurity.

In the poem, Daniel has both an advisory and a prophetic function. As a former counselor to Nebuchadnezzar, he is the repository of exemplary history in Babylon; as a prophet of Israel, he foretells the future as he knows it from God. He is thus a figure of special wisdom, a man whose knowledge supersedes scientific or worldly knowledge. The poet's emphasis upon Daniel's special knowledge is most apparent in lines 1550–1640, which describe the handwriting on the wall and Balthazar's efforts to find an interpreter (see Dan. 5:5). The poet expands the Biblical account by noting the visual reality of the script which cannot be read by all the "scoleres" of Babylon. Balthazar reacts by promising wealth and power to any who can read and understand the words, and one of his concubines mentions Daniel. She describes Daniel in terms of his former service to Nebuchadnezzar and distinguishes between the false wisdom of scholars and Daniel's true wisdom: "'His sawle is ful of syence, saзes to schawe, / To open uch a hide þyng of aunteres uncowþe'" (1599–1600). This emphasis upon Daniel's visionary function reflects the medieval understanding of Daniel as a seer, a sage, and a righteous man.[35] Daniel, like Noah and Abraham, serves God, remains pure, and is thus granted special knowledge. This final Old Testament story differs from the first and second because there is no account of a safe landing, or of an escape. The pictures of Noah and Lot and their renewed love and service to God have no corollary in the story of Jerusalem and Balthazar. Historically, in the reign of Cyrus, king of Persia, those citizens of Jerusalem who are willing are sent back to rebuild the city under Nehemiah; but the poet makes no reference to this event, or to any sequel to Darius's capture of Babylon. The poet possibly omits any such reference because, in his three exemplary tales, he is also suggesting the choices human life affords. The story of the Flood was seen as embodying the ideas of purity associated with baptism; the charitable intervention of Abraham and Lot's flight from Sodom were thought to suggest certain ideas about New Law charity and penitential reform. In the final incident, the poet describes the absorption of Jerusalem into Babylon, a situation that reflects the conditions of the world, wherein the two cities of God and of man are intermingled. The two cities will be identified and separated at the Second Coming, day of judgment for the unjust, day of mercy for the just.[36] Darius, whom the poet describes as proud (1772), claims Balthazar as his spoil; and Babylon falls to a pride greater than its own. Those who prefer Jerusalem will return to what they had lost.

It is therefore possible that the final incident suggests the final sorting out, the time when there are no more opportunities for baptism or penance. While this is only a suggestion, it is given credence by the figure of Daniel who plays so important a role in Babylon. Daniel, unlike Noah and Abraham, was specifically associated with apocalyptic prophecy, for the Book of Daniel describes the events of the Last Days. Thus, while exploring the lures of lust, avarice, and pride, which may entice a man to reject God, the poet may also be adumbrating the span of human life and of human time. To this end, the first great event in human history after the Fall is the Flood, an event linked to purification through baptism. After the Flood, the earth became soiled again, just as everyman soils his baptismal garments. The remedy for this condition is penance, operating through the sacramental Church. Finally, to everyman and to the world comes death, a day of judgment which will catch the earth unaware and which can catch a man while he sleeps. If a man has not taken advantage of the opportunity for reform, he becomes fixed for eternity, like Balthazar, in the uncleansed impurities of his life.

Conclusion

By means of the Parable of the Wedding Feast, the poet offers us two perspectives upon the history his poem recounts. He summarizes the lessons of the parable by quoting Matthew 22:14: "Thus comparisunez Kryst þe kyndom of heven / To þis frelych feste þat fele arn to called" (161–162). The Old Testament history that follows the parable illustrates the statement that many are called; but it also illuminates the latter half of the verse, "But few are chosen." The poem, in fact, illustrates the process of selection by describing the standard for selection. If purity is the means by which a man may "see God," or attend the wedding feast, each man must choose whether he wishes to attend the feast. The poet, however, does not define purity, but makes it possible for his audience to arrive at a definition by studying the poem. As the introductory parable suggests, the poet adopts Christ's method of teaching. In the parable, the poet suggests the joys of heaven by establishing an analogy between heaven and a contemporary banquet. The orderly and bounteous nature of an earthly banquet should awaken a desire for an even more splendid banquet. Furthermore, clothing and behavior that would appear unsuitable and insulting for an earthly lord appear even more insulting to the king of heaven. Thus, the picture of the banquet and the poet's emphasis upon external signs of respect prepare us to understand the nature of purity and impurity by observing the external actions of the pure and impure figures in the Old Testament stories. To this end, *Purity* is filled with complementary pictures. Sara's laughter over the angels' prophecy is less unsettling when juxtaposed with the outright scorn and disobedience of Lot's wife. Lot's peril is highlighted when we compare the portraits of Lot and Abraham. The hierarchy, beauty, and harmony of the heavenly court and of the wedding feast provide a standard for all other social bodies: Sodom's fairness and Babylon's magnificence pale before the fairness and magnificence of heaven. The poet balances events and scenes in *Purity* in a way that recalls his manipulation of Camelot and Hautdesert in *Sir Gawain and the Green Knight*. The three stories in *Purity* form a kind of elaborately framed triptych, in which the meaning of any single picture depends on its individual pictorial content, its relation to the other parts of the work, and the design of its frame.

The artistic unity of *Purity* offers a foil to the disunity that results from sin. Near the end of *Purity*, the poet describes the effects of impurity in a way that hints at the predominant characteristic of sin in general: "unclannes tocleves in corage dere / Of þat wynnelych Lorde þat wonyes in heven" (1806–1807). The word "tocleves" means tear asunder and thus connotes multiplicity, lack of unity—implicitly, chaos. While the poet applies "tocleves" to the effect man's impurity has on God, the word may also apply to the poet's examples of impurity. Whereas the pure in *Purity* are very much alike, the impure are as apparently diverse as the long list of sins the poet enumerates in lines 177–188. There, he lists the ways in which men may forfeit heaven, and the ways are as numerous as the opportunities the world affords: lying, covetousness, harlotry, thievery, ribaldry, dishonesty, treason, and tyranny.

Although the poet describes the apparent variety of sin, ultimately the poet suggests the limitations of vice. He does this in several ways. First, the poet organizes what appears to be a limitless topic around the triad of lust, avarice, and pride, the classic sins of the sons of Adam, and the sins by which man brought death into the world. The fact that so huge a subject as impurity can be ordered so neatly suggests the repetitive nature of sin. Second, although the figures of impurity seem to retain a good deal of individuality, ultimately their devotion to self suggests the constrictive nature of willful disobedience. For example, Lot's wife is willful, shrewish, determined to assert herself, while Balthazar is loud and arrogant. The cries of Adam's descendants may evoke a more empathetic response from a reader than the ordered thanksgiving of Noah and his family; but these figures, though they are perhaps more recognizable than the almost bland figures of purity, are finally as limited as the medieval types they embody.

In its use of types, Purity is similar to the mystery plays. Balthazar is all too familiar to anyone who has observed such characters as Pharaoh and Herod, types of pride that recur throughout the cycle of time chronicled by the mystery plays. Balthazar, like other figures of pride, is characterized by hyperbolic speech, a single-minded devotion to self, and the desire to dominate others. Lot's wife, like Noah's wife, especially the Wakefield Uxor Noe, is disobedient and shrewish. In Purity, the poet establishes the ultimate limitations of vice by linking these characters to Lucifer, whom he describes as a traitor and a rebel. Furthermore, the reward each of these figures receives for his "individualism" is as static and as barren as man is when he removes himself from God, whom the poet acclaims, "þe gropande God, þe grounde of alle dedez" (591).

The poet also suggests the limitations of impurity by the decreasing empathy with which he describes the punishment of the wicked. The cries of the antediluvian world are human cries and thus evoke sympathy. But in the second tale he focuses upon Lot, rather than on the fears of the Sodomites. Finally, in the third tale, he omits any description of the horrors of the Persian capture of Babylon. The poet, in reversing the ordering of the excuses as they appear in the parable, and in moving from lust, to avarice, to pride, thus indicates the increasing danger of each type of vice.[37]

The story of the Flood, like the sin of lust, is relatively simple. The population of Sodom is avaricious, but it is also carnal. Babylon's pride embraces the pleasures of the world and of the flesh. Babylon is a more dangerous environment for the pure than either the antediluvian world or Sodom because Babylon is devoted to the malicious soiling of pure vessels, a situation that is more serious than either the simple lust of Noah's neighbors or the curiosity of the Sodomites. The poet thus suggests that vice, in becoming more complex, dehumanizes its object. It is only in Babylon that gentry are changed to churls and clean vessels changed to drinking cups. Babylon threatens the very nature of its captives, who face a final choice between justice and mercy.

For the medieval world, God's mercy worked through the sacraments of the Church, so it is suggestive that *Purity* begins by admonishing priests to remain pure. The poet emphasizes the responsibility a priest has, for he "handles Christ's body" (11), and serves God for others. The poet goes on to warn the clergy against impurity. Significantly, Noah, Abraham, and Daniel are described in a way that suggests their functions as servers, or as mediators between God and man. The sequence of the three figures appears even more important when we recall that two out of the three were linked with the three states of the Church—Noah with the prelatical state and Daniel with the contemplative. Job was commonly used as a figure for the active, or married, state. As Saint Gregory says, in Noah we find an example of a spiritual leader or guide, in Daniel an ascetic and a seer, and in Job a figure for the "bonorum conjugam." These three states are those avenues of perfection the Church offers, and the three figures from Old Testament history prefigure the states as they are fulfilled under the dispensation of the New Law.[38] The poet uses Abraham rather than Job, but underlines his condition as, not only a married man, but a married man who has his wife well under control. The portrait of Abraham conveys married harmony and fruitfulness. The poet warns against the temptations of human life and describes the punishments for impurity; but he also offers us a remedy for human life in the sacraments of the Church as they are channeled through its clean priests, who act as spiritual guides, mediators, and seers. The simplicity of the pure perhaps reflects the definition of purity as unmixed or unalloyed. Hence, there is little to distinguish between Noah, Abraham, and Daniel. Each of them serves and acquires his identity from his function as a steward. Noah is described simply as a man who serves God and obeys his laws. Abraham absorbs his meaning from his relation to the great tree, from his priestly function at the feast he prepares, and from his role as patriarch. Daniel's identity is inseparable from his function as prophet and seer. The poet reinforces these implicit links between purity and service in the final lines of the poem:

Ande clannes is his comfort, and coyntyse he lovyes,
And þose þat seme arn and swete schyn se his face.
Þat we gon gay in oure gere þat grace he uus sende,
Þat we may serve in his syȝt þer solace never blynnez.

(1809–1812)

Poetically, *Purity* ends on a note of repose, shifting the emphasis from negative to positive in a way that reflects the poet's method of teaching. His hortatory purpose has been to warn, and his exempla have chronicled punishment; but here he speaks of "comfort," "seme," "swete," and "solace," concluding with words of delight similar to those that described the wedding feast and all moments of safety in the poem. His final reference to clothing is also positive, shifting from the negative man in foul clothes to "we gon gay in oure gere," a construction that communicates the delight the poet finds in purity. Finally, he reinterprets the sixth Beatitude from "he schal loke on oure Lorde wyth a bone chere" (28) to "þat we may serve in his syȝt þer solace never blynnez": the object is no longer to "loke" but to "serve in his syȝt." The reward, then, for purity is joyous, loving service, a reward that is intimated in the orderly and joyous behavior of each of the pure characters in the poem.

However, without the doctrine of penance, purity is humanly impossible; and, without penance, the poem and the history it recounts remain a record of justice. The sacrament of penance, which distinguishes the pure from the impure, is a sacrament of individual recognition and of choice. The poem's figures of purity demonstrate the effects of purity, in behavior that testifies to the harmony purity effects between the human and the divine wills. That harmony arises from conscious choice, and it is for this reason that the poet emphasizes the element of choice in historical selection. Each of the impure characters chooses before he is punished, just as the invited guests and the man in foul clothes choose something other than the feast. The passage connecting the second and third Old Testament narratives reiterates man's opportunity for choice through grace: in Christ, God offers man a means of perfection through penance. The human diseases of sin have a remedy, a physician, in Christ. Through penance, a man may redirect his love, and the poet's continual emphasis upon purity, love, and service points to the real message of the poem. That message is a positive one because it urges the audience toward a recognition of true delight—a marriage banquet, safety, harmony, sweet smells, roses, songs—"to be couþe in his corte, þou coveytes þenne."

Four

Pearl

Whereas, in *Purity*, the poet concentrates upon the outward manifestations of purity in behavior, in *Pearl*, he focuses upon the inward man, describing the process of spiritual expansion that allows a man to shift his desire from an earthly to a heavenly love and thus to long for the opportunity to identify himself as a loving steward. The poet vivifies this process through a narrator, whose grief over a lost "pearl," a child or a maiden, has come to dominate his life, rendering him incapable of any action except mourning his loss. In a state of grief and torpor, the narrator falls asleep in the same garden in which he lost his pearl and experiences a vision. In his dream, he encounters his lost pearl, now a bride of Christ, who leads him away from his preoccupation with his own loss by teaching him about grace, the court of heaven where she now lives, and spiritual marriage. These revelations fill the dreamer with a desire to see the holy city. Upon seeing the celestial Jerusalem and the procession of the Lamb, the dreamer attempts to cross a river the maiden has warned him not to cross. With that attempt, he awakens, still without regaining his lost pearl. That he has gained something of greater value, however, is borne out by the closing stanzas of the poem in which he testifies to a renewed love for Christ, his hopes for the afterlife, and the nourishment he derives from the sacrament of Communion. The poem, a first-person account of grief and consolation, leads the audience away from the constrictions of earthly love to an awareness of spiritual love, a love transcending mortality.

In his efforts to explore the nature of human grief and to dramatize the Christian remedy for grief, the poet draws upon various literary and Biblical traditions. First, *Pearl* owes formal and thematic debts to the consolation; for the narrator, like protagonists before and after him, comes to an understanding of his loss through an instructional dialogue with a figure who, like Lady Philosophy in *The Consolation of Philosophy*, provides him with a perspective upon the loss of a transient good.[1] Second, *Pearl* is a dream vision; so a study of *Pearl* in relation to other dream visions reveals its debts to literary dream poetry and to Biblical visions, most notably Saint John's vision of heaven in the Book of Apocalypse.[2] However, distinctions were made in the Middle Ages between various types of dream visions, distinctions based upon the problems the protagonist explores in his dream. In *Pearl*, the narrator's problem is love: he has lost his beloved. The poet underlines this problem by evoking the lush pastoral imagery and by using the ardent language of the Song of Songs, the classic example of the Biblical epithalamium. Thus, *Pearl* can be called a consolation, a dream vision, or, more specifically, a love vision.[3]

But the source of the narrator's problem is not merely love; the source of his problem is death. In this sense, *Pearl* is also an elegy, which, like others in the language, mourns the death of a special person but ultimately records the mourner's own affirmation of the cycles of the natural world and recognition of a reality removed from that world.[4] The opening stanzas of *Pearl*, which describe the narrator's situation in a grass-covered area and his lamentations for something that has dropped from him into the ground and that now rots, would have alerted the audience to the nature of the poem's setting and to the narrator's immediate problem. The fact that this "pearl" turns out to be a maiden who died before the age of sin would have reinforced the immediacy of these opening stanzas; for, as Philippe Ariès reports, in the late Middle Ages, the very young were buried in cemeteries rather than in churches.[5] Thus, the narrator's description of his setting, like his account of his problem, suggests death, burial, and decay.

When it is viewed as an elegy, whether an occasional piece like the *Boke of the Duchesse*, or possibly a more personal record like the *Vita Nuova*, the other sources and strategies of *Pearl* begin to emerge. In an effort to capture the impact of death, the poet must appeal to a general experience of grief and, in order to direct his audience beyond grief to hope, must touch the audience in a way that allows it to generalize about death while still empathizing with the narrator's predicament. The archetypal instance of death to which the *Pearl*-poet could appeal was the death of Christ, a death that the audience relived each Good Friday and that was sacramentally reenacted in the celebration of the Mass. The desolation of Christ's mourners is captured in the four Gospel accounts of Easter morning when the Marys and Mary Magdalene come to the garden to tend the body of Christ. Three of these accounts, of course, had a good deal of literary influence in the *quem quaeretis* trope, used to vivify the message of resurrection for Easter worshipers. The fourth, Saint John's, which had an enormous impact on medieval spirituality, is perhaps the most moving. Mary Magdalene's encounter with Christ, known to art historians as the *noli me tangere* episode, is central to the poet's purpose in *Pearl* and is, in many ways, a source of the poem's spiritual power.

The scene itself has much in common with *Pearl*:

1. Both works explore death and provide a solution in Christian resurrection.
2. Both take place in a garden/graveyard, or in a pastoral setting.
3. Both mourners are doubly frustrated by a physical loss: the narrator of *Pearl* has let a pearl slip into the grass; Mary cannot find Christ's body.
4. Both mourners seek a means of alleviating grief through remembrance.
5. Both mourners at first fail to recognize the person who addresses them.
6. Both the poem and the Biblical passage contain a dia-

logue between the mourner and the dead but risen love. In both cases, the dialogue is consolatory.

7. Both mourners wish to confirm the fact of resurrection by sensual perception. Mary wishes to touch Christ; the narrator of *Pearl* wishes to see the heavenly Jerusalem, then to cross the river.

8. Both mourners have strictures placed upon their actions. Mary must not touch Christ until the Ascension. The narrator must not cross the river until he is pure.

9. Both mourners receive counsel that directs them back to the world. Christ tells Mary to go and tell the other disciples, in short, to bear witness. The maiden directs the dreamer back to the sacramental life of the communal Church and to the duties of daily Christian life.

Not only does the Biblical scene have a good deal in common with the setting, dialogue, characters, and message of *Pearl*, but the way in which the scene was understood in the Middle Ages illuminates the poet's use of the narrator as a witness who testifies to a new doctrine of love. The poet's characterization of the narrator grows out of the series of concerns associated, in exegetical and in devotional writing, with the figure of the Magdalene, who, as lover, mourner, penitent, and visionary, was central to many areas of medieval Christian life. Furthermore, the lessons Mary was thought to have learned from Christ on Easter morning are the lessons the narrator of *Pearl* learns from the maiden. Most notably, Mary's dialogue with Christ was thought to have suggested a new way of seeing the world around her, of seeing it as a sign of another, more real, world. The relationship I am suggesting between the *noli me tangere* episode and *Pearl* does not obviate the relevance of other literary traditions to *Pearl*. The Magdalene, or the figure known as the Magdalene in the Middle Ages, figures in discussions of visionary ecstasy, of the Song of Songs, and of consolatory dialogue. From the various traditions that informed the medieval understanding of Mary Magdalene and her pastoral encounter with

Christ, the poet creates a poem that, on all its levels, proclaims the message of transformation that Mary heard from her risen master.

Given the parallels between the *noli me tangere* episode and *Pearl*, a consideration of Mary Magdalene within the context of medieval themes and forms is illuminating, for the theme of spiritual growth thought to be implicit in her encounter with Christ is revealed through the narrator's own spiritual growth in *Pearl*. Thus, the first section of this chapter focuses upon the figure of the Magdalene. The second section focuses upon the figure of the narrator in *Pearl* and the poet's dramatization of the narrator's growing apprehension of a transcendent realm. As the third section illustrates, our recognition of the narrator's growth offers a key to understanding the complex imagery of *Pearl*. In his use of the imagery of growth and of visionary apprehension, the poet suggests the expansion of spirit that the narrator shares with his New Testament analogue, Mary Magdalene. Through his evocation of Mary Magdalene, his manipulation of the narrator, and his charged use of imagery, the poet thus describes a timeless pattern of spiritual reversal, a pattern inherent in the elegiac form of *Pearl*.

The Magdalene: Mourner and Lover

The poet draws upon the *noli me tangere* episode in order to universalize the narrator's recognition that the limits of the mutable world need not be the limits of man. His use of this episode can, perhaps, be best understood in relation to Dante, who clearly recognized the potential of such Biblical prototypes. As Charles S. Singleton has demonstrated, Dante used certain significant Biblical events, such as the death of Christ in the *Vita Nuova* and the Exodus in *The Divine Comedy*, as figures, or patterns, that universalize his own private experience of conversion.[6] In his discussion of the *Vita Nuova*, Singleton uses the term "analogy" to describe the relationship Dante establishes between the death of Beatrice and the

Crucifixion. He insists that Dante establishes such a resemblance between the two events, not because he intends us to read Christ for Beatrice, but because for Dante, Beatrice is Christlike. Beatrice, or Dante's love for her, thus becomes his means of approaching the new life. The author of *Pearl* employs the *noli me tangere* episode in a similar manner: the links between that incident and the narrator's experience should alert us to the universal relevance of this account of private conversion. As moderns, we can have the same problems with *Pearl* that increasingly secular ages have had with Dante, since the poet uses the relationship between the Biblical figure and the situation the poem describes as a means of drawing us toward the mourner and hence to the spiritual resolution with which the poem concludes. He expects his audience to recognize the universal in the specific, for the maiden's death is more "real" because of Christ's death, not vice versa, as a modern writer might put it. For the poet, each death is like the one; and each mourner, like Mary, should move beyond the grave to a renewed understanding of the problem of love and loss. By glimpsing Mary Magdalene behind the dreamer and Christ behind the maiden, we may more fully participate in the dreamer's education in spiritual love.

Saint John's account of Easter morning dramatically captures an experience of grief, recognition, and renewed hope in Mary's encounter with her risen lord:

But Mary stood at the sepulchre without, weeping. Now as she was weeping, she stooped down, and looked into the sepulchre, and she saw two angels in white, sitting, one at the head, and one at the feet, where the body of Jesus had been laid. They say to her: Woman, why weepest thou? She saith to them: Because they have taken away my Lord; and I know not where they have laid him. When she had thus said, she turned herself back, and saw Jesus standing; and she knew not that it was Jesus. Jesus saith to her: Woman, why weepest thou? whom seekest thou? She, thinking that it was the gardener, saith to him: Sir, if thou hast taken him hence, tell me where thou hast laid him, and I will take him away. Jesus saith to her: Mary. She turning, saith to him: Rabboni (which is to say, Master). Jesus saith to her: Do not touch me, for I am not yet ascended to my Father. But go to my brethren, and say to them: I ascend to my Father and to your Father, to my God and your God. Mary Magdalen cometh, and telleth the disciples: I have seen the Lord, and these things he said to me.

(John 20:11–18)

The scene is focused by Mary and her dramatic reversal from grief to joy. Until Christ speaks her name, the emphasis is upon her tears. John makes it clear that she is distraught because the body of Jesus is gone. In her grief, she does not recognize a living Jesus when she encounters him. Only when the man she mistakes for the gardener calls her name does she recognize and, it seems, reach out for him. However, Jesus imposes a limit upon her actions: she may not touch him until his ascension. Presumably, once he ascends, Mary may "touch" him in another way.

The relationship between John 20:11–18 and *Pearl* appears more clearly when we consider the medieval interpretations of the Biblical scene and the medieval use of the figure of the Magdalene. John's account was thought to teach the value of spiritual love and understanding rather than of corporal love and understanding. In other words, Mary's encounter with Christ directed her beyond mutable concerns, such as providing for dead bodies and touching her risen master, to the concerns of spiritual love. Furthermore, Mary figured in discussions of vision, and the language used to describe her love for Christ was, like the *Pearl*-dreamer's, the language of fervid passion, or the language of the Song of Songs. In fact, the figure of the Magdalene, or the "medieval figure" of the Magdalene, is the focus for many of the themes and concerns that also converge in *Pearl*.

The figure of Mary Magdalene was a composite one for the Middle Ages, a combination of the woman taken in adultery, the woman who washed Christ's feet with her tears, the sister of Martha and Lazarus, and the woman in the Easter garden.[7] As such, she was relevant to many of the concerns of medieval spirituality, as Henri Marrou notes in the preface to Victor Saxer's *Le Culte de Marie Madeleine en Occident.* Mary was a type of repentant sinner; a model for moral renewal, or for conversion; and a type for the contemplative life, important to hermits and others who followed the interior path to God.[8] Saxer himself, while underlining the relationship between the Magdalene and the relics at Vézelay, asserts that her popularity as a saint was also inspired by her links with the meditative life.[9]

It is possible to trace the growing importance of the saint in England by looking at the maps Saxer appends to his first volume. In the eleventh century, there were nine English foundations devoted to her cult, thirteen in the first half of the twelfth century, and twenty-two in the second half. The years between 1200 and 1278 saw a decline in foundations with only eight, while from 1279 to 1399, there were twenty-three, with a noticeable decline in the fifteenth and sixteenth centuries in England. He notes that many of these were hospitals or lazar houses and that under Edward III there was a renewal of royal patronage in foundations associated with her cult.[10] Saxer links the influence of the Crusades, England's Angevin rulers, and the role Vézelay played in medieval spiritual and political concerns; he also reckons the influence of the intense Christocentric spirituality of Saint Bernard and the *Life* composed at Clairvaux by the pseudo-Rabanus. Near the end of the twelfth century, the feast of Mary Magdalene was elevated from a simple to a double rite, especially in Benedictine abbeys.[11]

The widespread interest in the Magdalene suggests the many areas of Christian life to which she appealed, but, in relation to the poet's use of the narrator in *Pearl*, there are two important aspects of the Magdalene's legend to consider. First, as a mourner, the Magdalene is the focus for a dialogue of consolation with her lost beloved, Christ. Second, as a lover, she is the focus for discussions that chart the progression from earthly to spiritual love, for she was frequently linked with the bride of the Song of Songs.

Perhaps one of the most interesting documents capturing the impact of the *noli me tangere* episode is the pseudo-Origen *De Maria Magdalena*. It is a Latin text, probably of the twelfth century, which has been attributed to Origen, Saint Bernard, and Saint Anselm. Whoever its anonymous author was, it is a product of the devotional concerns associated with these writers and enjoyed a wide circulation that in some measure reflects the appeal of Mary Magdalene.[12] John McCall reports that there are more than a hundred thirty manuscripts of the Latin text, twenty-eight of which are in England alone.[13] He finds that in the fourteenth and fifteenth centuries, the *planctus* appears in devotional miscellanies that "focus on certain themes, such as repentance, sorrow at Christ's death, the contemplative life, and the mystical experience, or in genre collections of complaints and laments."[14] In fact, Rosemary Woolf labels it a meditation rather than a homily and stresses its medieval popularity.[15]

The most exciting aspect of the *De Maria Magdalena* for a literary critic is its handling of the Biblical episode. Its author realized the inherent drama of Saint John's account of Easter morning, much as earlier writers had used the *quem quaeretis* trope for affective liturgical purposes. The *De Maria Magdalena* reads as though it was intended to be read dramatically. Although a narrator frequently comments upon Mary's speeches, the piece also contains the voices of Mary, the angels, and Christ. When we recall that much of medieval literature was probably read by one person using various voices and that medieval sermons were also known for their dramatic appeal, the dramatic possibilities of a religious piece like the *De Maria* become more clear.[16] The *De Maria* is intended to engage its audience; as Saxer notes, the piece is less concerned with the divinity of Christ than with those elements that unite him with us.[17] Whereas it may be difficult to identify with the king of heaven, it is relatively easy to identify with a grief-stricken woman who meets and talks with a loving master whom she thought dead. The dramatic

structure of the *De Maria* underlines its hortatory intent.
Like the debates of the Four Daughters of God and other
medieval debates, the *De Maria* teaches through conflict.[18]
Mary reasons with all the sorrowful blindness of man him-
self; and through her sorrow, confusion, and ultimate joy, the
author projects identifiable human emotion upon a historic
and emblematic scene. By empathizing with Mary, the au-
dience may participate in the incredible joy of the Resur-
rection.

Despite its emotional appeal, the lessons of the *De Maria*
are intellectual. The narrator, whose voice guides our re-
sponse to Mary, suggests the effects of grief upon the senses:
"Feeling, she did not feel, seeing, she did not see, hearing,
she did not hear."[19] The narrator then links Mary's sorrow
with a fruitless search or quest: "She sought him and did
not find him; and on that account, she stood by the tomb,
totally mournful, totally miserable." Mary's paralyzing grief
is the result of not finding the body of Christ in its tomb,
and her physical incapacity arises from a corporal cause. That
the author of the *De Maria* intends more than emotional
empathy is verified by the narrator, who shifts our attention
away from Mary's grief to the nature of her grief. He ques-
tions the quality of her faith: "O Mary, what has been your
hope, your counsel, or your understanding that you stand
alone at the tomb as the disciples depart?" A few lines later,
the narrator reminds her of Christ's promise to rise on the
third day. The narrator thus makes it clear that Mary has a
theoretical knowledge of resurrection, a knowledge that
should rest on faith, rather than on experience.

The first section of the *De Maria* engages both our emo-
tions and our intellects. Mary Magdalene herself provides
the emotional focus of the piece. The author conveys her
grief and bewilderment by her choppy pattern of speech:
"'Alas! Woe is me! What do I do? Where do I go?'" He also
suggests the immediacy of her grief through the terms she
applies to Christ; Chirst is her "dilectus," her "gaudium,"
her "amor," her "dulcedo": "'To what place did my beloved
depart? To what place did my joy depart? Where is my love

hiding? Where is my sweet one?'" By evoking the traditional love between Mary and Christ, the author heightens our sympathy for Mary, who has lost her dearest love.[20] Intellectually, however, the author of the *De Maria* forces us to understand the nature of grief, the inherent blindness and lack of awareness that can accompany emotional abandonment. Her language suggests her inability to remember Christ's promise of resurrection and her failure to put into practice the lessons he taught her before his death.

Mary's incapacity is more marked in her inability to recognize Christ when he actually speaks to her; she mistakes him for the gardener. The narrator implies that Mary thinks of literal gardeners, rather than of metaphoric gardens and gardeners: "O Mary, if you search, why do you not recognize Jesus? Behold, Jesus comes to you, and he whom you seek searches for you, and you suppose him a gardener! . . . It is indeed Jesus, and he is the gardener, who himself plants the good seed in the garden of your soul and in the hearts of the faithful. . . . You therefore seek the dead and do not know the living." Mary is blind because she searches for the wrong thing; in other words, she thinks literally rather than metaphorically. The narrator's words here point to her need for an education in wisdom, manifested in her need for a more flexible use of language. The literal world no longer circumscribes human existence because Christ has defied its limits. Mary looked in a garden for a physical object, a body; she might have looked in her heart and found there what she sought in the garden.

The author of the *De Maria* does not dramatize the final eucatastrophe of the scene, but ends by discussing Mary's love for Christ. Although her love is, at first, limited, it nonetheless is the beginning of her new understanding and her spiritual renewal: "Therefore, merciful and just judge, love, which she had for you, and sorrow, which she had for you, may excuse her in your regard if she erred greatly; do not attend to the error of the woman, but to the love of the disciple, who, not through error, but through sorrow and love, wept and said to you: Lord if you removed him, tell me where you laid him and I will take him away." Though Mary perhaps loved blindly, she did love; and because of her love, she is able to move beyond the sensory world and sensory love to spiritual love.[21]

The author of the *De Maria* captures the "sense" of exegetical commentary on the sequence in John 20. Christ's words, *noli me tangere,* and his request that Mary not touch him until the Ascension occasioned numerous discussions of this scene as denying the value of faith which depends upon the senses.[22] Bruno Astensis stated most succinctly what was a conventional way of understanding Christ's dictum: "Tangere enim, intelligere est" (Therefore, to touch is to understand). Christ commands Mary to believe, or to understand, only when all corporal proof has been removed.[23] That Mary obeyed was thought to be verified by the final verse of John's account, "Mary Magdalen cometh, and telleth the disciples: I have seen the Lord, and these things he said to me." Rather than passive and grief-stricken, she becomes active, the bearer of tidings of hope.

The *noli me tangere* episode and the many commentaries on it provide a focus for Mary's role as mourner. Her appearance in the Easter garden, however, drew much of its emotional credibility from her role as a lover of Christ. Though the relationship between Mary and Christ was never described as physical, the language used to evoke their relationship was frequently the passionate language of ardent love. Furthermore, Mary's reputation as a woman of the world turned religious made it natural for writers to use her as the focus for discussions of the higher ecstasies of prayer, a connection strengthened by her associations with the contemplative life.

Mary's associations with the contemplative life are so widely known that they need little commentary in this study. Briefly, the text of Luke 10:38–39, which is used for the Feast of the Assumption, one of the suggested "dates" of the *Pearl*-dreamer's complaint and vision,[24] establishes Mary as a representative of the contemplative life.[25] Martha and Mary, like Leah and Rachael, are the figures of the active and contemplative ways, and Christ's statement in Luke 10:42, that "Mary hath chosen the best part," established the superiority of the contemplative life. But, lest there be too much enthusiasm among the general population for a way that demands a great deal of spiritual discipline, medieval writers frequently advised religious enthusiasts to discipline themselves by accepting the duties and frustrations of the active life before taking on themselves the spiritual discipline of the way of contemplation.[26] In terms of the relationship between active and contemplative Christianity, Mary's legend provided a perfect model, for her encounter with Christ is followed by her duty of announcing the Resurrection. Only after a long career as a missionary, whose duty is similarly that of announcing her private revelation to others, does she retire from the world to a life of prayer and vision.

Because of her importance as a visionary, Mary Magdalene became a model for those concerned with the life of prayer. The late medieval interest in the saint coincided with the growing absorption with affective piety, and she became a figure whose love, grief, duty, and ecstasy were used as spiritual touchstones. Using her in this way, Saint Anselm, one of the inspirations behind affective piety and the poetry of meditation, prays that Mary's fervid love may quicken his own spirit.[27] Mary, once the woman taken in adultery, the passionate lover of the world, became the saint whose love prepared her for revelation, first in the garden, later in the ecstasies of prayer. Her ability to love passionately was considered the seed from which revelation sprang. The fact that she, in John's account of Easter morning, mistakes Christ for the gardener gave medieval writers the opportunity to discuss the growth of love by playing upon the pastoral language of John's account.[28] The garden became a figure for Mary's heart, or for the human heart, in which Christ, the gardener, plants the seed of charity. This seed, which was connected to the mustard seed (see Matt. 13:31; Luke 13:19), was the impetus behind Mary's search for Christ. Because she loved, she searched; and revelation was her love's reward.

As a visionary, Mary was a compelling figure; but her rep-

utation as a lover made her an even more important figure
for the spiritual life of the Middle Ages. First, her early rep-
utation as a fallen woman and her passionate conversion at
the feet of Jesus contain the elements of dramatic spiritual
reversal, something the *Mary Magdalene* in the Digby Mys-
teries demonstrates. In its use of this theme of conversion,
the Digby *Magdalene* reflects medieval convention. For ex-
ample, Saint Gregory, likewise focusing upon Mary's capac-
ity for love, suggests that the fire of divine love purified the
fires of carnal love in Mary, the stronger fire burning out the
weaker.[29] This emphasis upon passionate love can also be
seen in the *De Maria Magdalena*, most notably in Mary's
speeches. There, her language is represented as that of the
distracted lover, searching for her lost beloved. In so doing,
the author of the *De Maria*, like writers before and after him,
drew upon the language of the Song of Songs, or of the Bib-
lical epithalamium.

The medieval understanding of the epithalamium is im-
portant to *Pearl* both explicitly and implicitly. First, the poet
certainly drew upon many of the characteristic scenes, im-
ages, and rhetorical devices of the Song of Songs.[30] Second,
Mary Magdalene, as the lover of Christ, was linked with the
bride of the marriage celebrated in the Canticle. Third, the
types of issues that were considered in discussions of Biblical
love poetry are issues that also figure prominently in discus-
sions of the Magdalene and that are given a more literary
form in *Pearl*.

E. Faye Wilson, in her study of the medieval conception of
the epithalamium, has pointed out that both the Song of
Songs and Psalm 44 were felt to be epithalamia and were
subjected to formal and thematic scrutiny.[31] Formally, the
Biblical epithalamium was thought to celebrate a marriage
between two persons of unequal rank. The bridegroom of
Psalm 44 is a king, the bride a plebeian; the bridegroom of
the Song of Songs is princely, the bride, a Shulamite. The
pastoral setting of both Biblical poems suggested the use of
pastoral or agricultural metaphors. The dramatic nature of
the Song of Songs, with its parts for bride, bridegroom, at-

tendants, and others, linked the epithalamium with the debate, or with a use of dialogue, as Wilson notes. The marriage itself was thought to be the climax of a longer process of frustration, or of searching. The fact that the bride of the Song of Songs searches for the bridegroom and the fact that some of the book at least seems to imply visionary searching suggested an association between the love-search or love-hunt and the dream vision.[32] The hunt, or the vision, would then culminate in marriage or in the fulfillment of the desire that inspired the search. The marriage itself created a harmony between disparate elements, binding male and female, king and pauper, together in the unity of love.

Thematically, what are literally poems about love, desire, and marriage were thought to outline a progression of spiritual love, desire, and marriage. Man's soul, as the bride, searched for the beloved bridegroom, Christ. Hence, the epithalamium naturally embraced such themes as penance, grace, holy love, and spiritual understanding, themes likewise associated with Mary Magdalene and, in particular, with the dialogue between Mary and Christ on Easter morning. The clearly amorous language of the Song of Songs was thought to convey the delights of spiritual love, to describe what is noncorporal, using the language of physical delight. The pastoral metaphors and landscape of the Biblical epithalamium likewise underwent a sea-change and were used to discuss the garden of the human heart or of the Church and the vegetative growth of spiritual desire. The bride's search for her beloved culminated in penance, symbolized by the clean marriage garment she receives. Her penance made possible a marriage between persons of unequal rank, the human soul and God. The epithalamic form thus sketched a progression from frustration to new knowledge, frequently manifested in a radical expansion of love.

Mary Magdalene, who begins her career as a lover, was in many ways the natural New Testament complement to the bride of the Canticle, likewise a lover and a searcher. Mary's quest for the body of Christ evoked the bride's search for her beloved, or Christ.[33] The many exegetical discussions comparing Mary to the bride of the Canticle find vernacular expression in scenes like the *noli me tangere* play of the Digby Mysteries:

> I haue sought, & besely inquerid
> Hym whom my harte all-way has desired,
> And so desiries still.
> Quem diligit anima mea, quesiui;
> Quesiui illum, et non inueni!
> When shall I haue my will?
> . . . .
> Filie Ierusalem, Wher-os ye goo,
> Nunciate dilecto meo,
> Quia amore langueo:
> Of Ierusalem, ye uirgyns clere,
> Schew my best loue that I was here!
> Tell hym, os he may prove,
> That I am dedly seke /
> And all is for his love.[34]

Her language here, like the language of Mary in the *De Maria Magdalena*, is that of the distracted bride of the Canticle. Like the bride, Mary suffers from love sickness; and the author of the play strongly suggests the relationship between the two searchers by echoing the Latin of the Biblical epithalamium, by his emphasis upon searching (see Cant. 3:1–3, 5:6–8), and by having Mary call on the daughters of Jerusalem (see Cant. 3:11, 5:8). Both female figures search within a pastoral frame; both suffer from love-sickness, and both move beyond love's frustrations by arriving at a new understanding of love.

Perhaps the most explicit discussion of Mary's relevance to the Canticle is the series of sermons by Saint Bernard. In these sermons, Saint Bernard outlines a theory of dynamic love, or a progression from corporal to spiritual love that is like what we tend to call the ladder of love. In Sermon XXVIII of this series, he focuses upon the dialogue between Mary and Christ on Easter morning as a means of linking true, or spiritual, love with mature faith and knowledge. Like other discussions of the *noli me tangere* episode, Saint Bernard interprets Christ's injunction not to touch him as a statement about faith. Faith, or love, should have its basis, not in sensory perception (touch), but in spiritual perception; and Christ's statement that Mary should touch him after the Ascension, for Saint Bernard, becomes a command to live by the spiritual senses: "'. . . by prayer, not by vision; by faith, not by the sense. . . . Touch with the hand of faith, with the finger of desire, with the caress of devotion, touch with the eye of the mind.'"[35] Saint Bernard's use of the language of physical love in relation to spiritual love suggests the relationship between corporal and spiritual faith and love. Whereas Mary's original love for Christ was redemptive, her love was nonetheless dependent upon sense and thus vulnerable to loss, or death. By moving from corporal to spiritual love, she moves beyond the realm of mutability and experiences a higher type of love which draws its strength from a nonmutable source.[36] That this lesson is also the lesson the *Pearl*-dreamer learns is less coincidence than design. The dreamer, like Mary, begins with corporal loss and moves beyond a preoccupation with the mutable to a desire for nonmutable things and loves.

The movement beyond sense to spirit is likewise a lesson embodied in other medieval literary forms. Both the consolation and the dream vision conventionally sketch a progression from frustration or despair to revelation or fulfillment, and there are many fine studies linking *Pearl* to these literary forms. Both the consolation and the dream vision are records of inner experience and are, to use A. C. Spearing's apt phrase, "spiritual adventures." While *Pearl* is both a consolation and a dream vision and uses elements of the epithalamium, it is finally an elegy and hence records the movement from grief and death to hope and life. The source of its elegiac power and the analogue for its record of spiritual movement are Mary's lament over Christ's death and her renewal of spirit. In her grief, vision, consolation, new love, and fulfillment, she is the figure who stands behind the

Pearl-dreamer, who learns from the maiden, as Mary learns from Christ, of spiritual marriage, dynamic love, and the duties of faith.

Pearl and the Theme of Dynamic Spiritual Growth

The themes and lessons of *Pearl* are transmitted through its narrator, so it is important to understand what he learns, how he learns, and where he begins his spiritual growth. As Charles Moorman has noted, "It is first of all, a fiction presented from a clearly defined and wholly consistent point of view; we accompany the 'I' of the poem through his vision, and it is through his eyes that we see the magical landscapes and the girl."[37] Moorman provides an important clue to the poem's message because, in order to understand the poem, we must understand the voice that tells the poem, the voice that recounts its own spiritual experience. The experience, beginning in the garden where the narrator lost his pearl and ending with the spiritual sustenance of the Mass, changes the narrator by offering him a new perspective on the physical world.

In order to vivify the lessons the narrator learns, the poet focuses upon the reality of human grief and the apparently meaningless waste of death. The narrator's spiritual problem, the loss of the maiden, has a universal application, since all men experience the frustrations of death and grief. The poet intimates the universal or exemplary relevance of the poem by omitting any biographical data about either the narrator or the maiden. By providing only a few stark facts— the maiden was young, the narrator loved her—he releases the situation from the limitations of time and place. By also describing this maiden as a pearl, a gem connected with purity, Christlikeness, and the kingdom of heaven, he shifts our attention from the maiden's earthly identity to her importance to the narrator and to her role in his education.[38] *Pearl*, from its opening stanzas, testifies to the poet's sense of economy: the poem is about a man struggling with grief; he has an experience that changes him. Clearly it is with these few facts that the poet wishes us to begin our own efforts to understand the lessons the poem offers its readers. The narrator's experience falls into three general stages. The first stage of his spiritual education is grief and the desolation that he experiences in the garden in which he comes to mourn. Like his spiritual analogue, Mary Magdalene, the narrator returns to a garden of death in order to focus upon the past, to alleviate his grief by a physical act of remembrance and mourning. This stage culminates in his recognition of the *Pearl*-maiden, a scene evoking the effusive "Rabboni" of the Magdalene when she recognizes her risen Lord. However, recognition is not the end of his spiritual education, for the first stage leads into a longer second stage wherein the *Pearl*-maiden tries to educate him in the realities of the physical and spiritual realms, offering him a new understanding of love. The lessons the maiden teaches him correspond to those lessons thought to be implicit in the exchange between Mary and Christ. The second stage of the narrator's education ends with his effort to cross the river into heaven, an act that both literally and figuratively reflects Mary's implied attempt to touch Christ and her more obedient response to his *noli me tangere*. The third stage of the narrator's experience begins with his awakening. This stage, however, concerns the present, rather than the past, and is a record of his continuing belief in spiritual love. In the final lines of the poem, the narrator testifies to the fact that he has transferred his allegiance from the physical to the spiritual world, from a physical maiden, his pearl, to Christ, the prince who cherishes pearls. Like the Magdalene, the narrator moves away from a concern with *temporalia* and toward a devotion to a love uncircumscribed by the limits of the physical world.

In the first five stanzas of *Pearl*, the poet depicts an extreme state of spiritual torpor, despair, or depression. The narrator asserts that he has lost a pearl, the most precious of his possessions, in a garden. Now he languishes from "lufdaungere." These two statements alert us to the narrator's problem—love and loss—a problem manifested in his preoccupation with his loss, beyond which he cannot move. Thus, he notes in the second stanza that he frequently returns to the "spot" where he lost the pearl. There, he relives the loss itself and the likely effects of death upon what was a perfect pearl: "For soþe þer fleten to me fele, / To þenke hir color so clad in clot" (21–22). By concentrating upon the degenerative effects of death and by his persistent vigil in the landscape of his loss, the narrator has circumscribed his own freedom of physical and spiritual mobility. The garden to which he returns has become a monument to decay, and he seeks to assuage his despair by focusing upon what was physical and mutable.

His loss and the landscape of the garden inspire him to muse upon the process of germination in a way that underlines his spiritual despair. In the third stanza, he considers decomposition, the fact that nature feeds herself with the compost from dead grass and plants: "For vch gresse mot grow of grayneʒ dede; / No whete were elleʒ to woneʒ wonne" (31–32). These lines paraphrase John 12:24–25, "Amen, amen I say unto you, unless the grain of wheat falling into the ground die, itself remaineth alone. But if it die, it bringeth forth much fruit." Although these verses refer to the death and resurrection of Christ and should inspire hope in the narrator, he links the grain of wheat with his pearl, sadly speculating, "So semly a sede moʒt fayly not" (34). His theoretical knowledge of resurrection provides him with no comfort. Like Mary Magdalene in the Easter garden, he cannot apply what he has heard to his own situation.

The fifth stanza suggests his spiritual and physical inability to help himself by describing his actions upon a visit to the garden in August:

Bifore þat spot my honde I spenned
For care ful colde þat to me caʒt;
A deuely dele in my hert denned,
Þaʒ resoun sette myseluen saʒt.

(49–52)

His search for the physical object he has lost is unsuccessful. His "care ful colde" and the "dele" in his heart lead finally to utter collapse:

> My wreched wylle in wo ay wraȝte.
> I felle vpon þat floury flaȝt,
> Suche odour to my herneȝ schot;
> I slode vpon a slepyng-slaȝte
> On þat precios perle wythouten spot.
>
> (56–60)

His love-wound, his vain search, and his remembrance of the pearl outline a state of incapacitating grief, much like the grief associated with the Magdalene. Both mourners mourn the loss of a beloved; both search, but find, not what they expected—a physical object—but rather a risen love.

After the narrator has fallen asleep, the poet presents the dreamer's gradual visionary recognition of the maiden (161–180). It is a highly dramatic scene, capturing his growing awareness of a transcendent realm. The dreamer's comic confusion recalls Mary's, for the poet emphasizes the dreamer's amazed dependence on his senses. At first, he sees merely a child, a maiden who looks familiar: "I knew hry wel, I hade sen hyr ere" (164). In a passage that slows down the tempo of the poem, he recalls the length of time before he recognizes her as his pearl. "On lenghe I loked to hyr þere; / Þe lenger, I knew hyr more and more" (167–168). Because he is human, his sense perception is the means by which he begins to know her, but it is also the faculty that confuses him. Though his senses identify her, he is confused by the strangeness of her setting: "Bot baysment gef myn hert a brunt. / I seȝ hyr in so strange a place, / Suche a burre myȝt make myn herte blunt" (174–176). From this mixture of joy and confusion proceeds fear, and the paradoxical process of recognition continues until the maiden speaks to him in line 235. With the verifying evidence of sound, the dreamer, like the Magdalene, bursts into speech. Mary cries "Rabboni"; whereas the dreamer says, "'O perle . . . in perleȝ pyȝt, / Art þou my perle þat I haf playned'" (241–242).

The dreamer's startled recognition of the maiden is at once the climax of the first stage of his spiritual experience and the prelude to a second stage. Thus far, his experience runs parallel to Mary Magdalene's in the Easter garden. The dreamer begins in a state of loss and languor. He then uses his loss as the impetus for a search: he returns to the garden of death. Like Mary, who looks for a body, the narrator looks for a tangible pearl. In that garden his expectations are reversed; he finds not death but life. The maiden guides the second stage of his spiritual experience, a stage that corresponds to what was considered the meaning of Mary's Easter dialogue with Christ. The maiden, however, as Christ was thought to have implied to Mary, attempts to focus the narrator's attention on the spiritual, rather than the physical world. She tries to teach him to use his spiritual senses.

The nature of the dreamer's coming education is suggested by the initial dialogue between the dreamer and the maiden in section 5 of *Pearl*. Upon recognizing her, the dreamer breaks forth into a thoroughly self-centered complaint. He says that while he has been "pensyf" and "payred" (broken, worn), she has been living without strife in paradise. He then mourns "wyrde," which has stolen his jewel, placed him in grief and "daunger," and left him a joyless jeweler. His obvious errors in reasoning are those that the maiden attempts to rectify:

"Bot, jueler gente, if þou schal lose
Py ioy for a gemme þat þe watȝ lef,
Me þynk þe put in a mad porpose,
And busyeȝ þe aboute a raysoun bref;
For þat þout lesteȝ watȝ bot a rose
Pat flowred and fayled as kynde hyt gef."

(265–270)

The maiden first addresses herself to his implicit assumption of ownership, his feeling that the pearl was his. She tells him the pearl was *lent* to him, not given, that he loved as an owner not as a steward. His sense of loss is increased by his possessiveness, and the maiden intimates that he must reconsider his relationship to the physical world. She then undercuts his own metaphoric presentation of his dilemma. He refers to her as a pearl, to himself as a jeweler. She redefines herself, or her corporal nature, as a rose, something that is part of a natural cycle in which death is inevitable. The "rose" has become a pearl in heaven, and the dreamer must learn to see the physical world in a more healthy way and hence to see it as mutable, not fixed.

The lessons the maiden will teach him are the lessons of love and language. The dreamer must learn to love spiritually and to use language properly. That the dreamer does not understand what she has said is emphasized near the end of section 5. He begs her pardon for his gaffes and then says that, now that he has found the pearl, he will begin to rejoice, dwell in this spot forever, and love God and his laws. The maiden's answer is even more stern, and in it the poet underlines the themes of the second stage of the dreamer's experience:

> "Þou says þou traweʒ me in þis dene,
> Bycawse þou may wyth yʒen me se;
> Anoþer þou says, in þys countré
> Þyself schal won wyth me ryʒt here;
> Þe þrydde, to passe þys water fre—
> Þat may no ioyfol jueler."
>
> (295–300)

First, the dreamer must learn to believe without the luxury of corporal proof. Second, the dreamer does not understand the requirements for living in "þys countré." Third, his assumption that he can cross the river is, at the least, naive; at the worst, presumptuous. The second state of the dreamer's education will therefore concern the nature of faith or knowledge in relation to corporal proof, the nature of paradise and of the spiritual love and marriage there, and the means by which a man may cross the river. Her education of the dreamer is designed to redirect his desire from herself to Christ, from the physical world to the spiritual.

The dreamer's education in language and in love adumbrates a progression from the mutable to the immutable. His use of language throughout most of the poem is literal and limited. He calls "wyrd" a thief (249–250) for depriving him of his pearl; he calls the pearl a seed but does not glimpse the hope implicit in the metaphor; he argues with the maiden about her position as a "queen" and a "bride of Christ" and about the location of Jerusalem. The maiden's attempts to expand his understanding of language provide a parallel to her attempts to expand his conception of love. She offers him the conception of spiritual marriage which begins in sorrow, or penance, but progresses to purity, eternal love, and true satisfaction. In this sense, the second broad stage of the account is a debate between a literal-minded dreamer and an allegorically minded maiden. The maiden frequently uses words in their metaphoric sense, calling herself a rose, a queen of courtesy, a citizen of Jerusalem; the dreamer uses words in a rigid and legalistic way. His movement toward spiritual love is manifested in the dreamer's efforts to replace a literal sense of words with an allegorical one. Once the dreamer begins to live and think allegorically, he will have applied the lessons the maiden teaches, which are likewise the lessons of Easter morning; do not touch me, for I am not yet ascended to my Father.

Although the dreamer's initial conception of love is limited and self-involved, his love for the maiden is, nonetheless, the seed from which his spiritual renewal germinates. In fact, his ardent love for her produces the desperation that brings him to the garden in the first place and is thus the impetus for his search. Here, too, he is like Mary Magdalene, for both mourners become searchers because they love, and it is their love that precedes their desire to know. Charles Williams has noted that Beatrice is Dante's "knowing," suggesting that from Dante's initially limited and overwrought love of Beatrice comes a way of knowing that supersedes any knowledge he might gain through corporal love.[39] The many medieval discussions of Mary Magdalene suggest a similar causal relationship between love and knowledge: Mary's love brings her to the garden where she begins to know; she then learns to know by faith. Similarly, though the dreamer's early perceptions are woefully limited, his ability to love—in particular, his love for the maiden—causes him to question her closely about the splendor of her dress, her life in paradise, and her exact role there.

In attempting to satisfy his curiosity, the maiden prompts a dialogue that ultimately directs his attention beyond the limits of his own grief. She answers his question by saying that she is a bride of Christ and enjoys a state of love and harmony that supersedes any joys she might have had on earth. The literal-minded dreamer replies that she is too young to be either a queen or a bride. The maiden responds with the Parable of the Vineyard in Matthew 20:1–16, emphasizing God's grace. She then underlines the necessity for innocence or purity before a man may reap the benefits of grace, benefits she received for her extreme youth, but which the dreamer may receive only through penance. The dreamer counters the maiden's discussion of grace with an assertion of divine justice. The maiden meets justice with mercy and speaks of the joys of the celestial Jerusalem. The dreamer argues that Jerusalem is in "Judee" (922), and the maiden tells him of the existence of two cities, one earthly, one heavenly. Finally, the dreamer is both interested enough and skeptical enough to request a sight of this city, and the maiden grants his request by showing him Jerusalem, the procession of the Lamb, and the Lamb himself. Though the maiden guides the dialogue, its shape is set by the dreamer's questions, by his persistent efforts to define heaven in earthly terms. Throughout, he is literal-minded, seeming to prefer a world of fixed rules and laws to one of interdependent courtesy and love. The maiden helps to change the way he sees the world and hence heaven by providing him with a glimpse of a higher reality. She implicitly suggests that he should see earth as a "sign" of heaven, rather than see heaven as an extension of earth.

The maiden's attempt to alter the dreamer's sense of perspective is most apparent in their discussion of Jerusalem in section 16 of *Pearl*. The dreamer questions the city in which she says she lives:

> "Þou tellez me of Jerusalem þe ryche ryalle,
> Þer Dauid dere watz dyȝt on trone,
> Bot by þyse holtez hit con not hone,
> Bot in Judee hit is, þat noble note.
> As ȝe ar maskelez vnder mone,
> Your wonez schulde be wythouten mote."
>
> (919–924)

The dreamer's perceptions are still those of this world: he can conceive only of one Jerusalem, and that one not fit for a maiden who is "maskelez." The maiden replies by explaining the relationship between the earthly and the heavenly Jerusalem. The earthly Jerusalem was the setting for the Passion, the old city where man's "olde gulte watz don to slake" (942). The heavenly or new Jerusalem is the true reality and is the celestial city of the Lamb. The maiden here provides the dreamer with an elementary lesson in allegory, or in two-dimensional perception. The earthly city is a "sign" of a heavenly "thing," to use Saint Augustine's terms, and thus what exists on earth derives its meaning and its purpose from its heavenly referent. The dreamer must learn to see earth from the perspective of heaven, not vice versa.

Whereas the maiden's ability to see allegorically characterizes her use of language, the dreamer uses words as if the words themselves were the reality. For example, his elaborate conceit of the pearl, whereby the maiden is a lost pearl and he a bereaved jeweler, fixes him in grief. The maiden undercuts the conceit by defining herself as a rose, something that can and will die, and by asserting that now she is a pearl wearing a pearl. The dreamer describes his grief "as wallande water gotȝ out of welle" (365). The maiden later echoes his metaphor but turns it to another purpose by defining God's graciousness as, "he laueȝ hys gyfteȝ as water of dyche" (607). The dreamer sees himself as circumscribed by sorrow. The maiden (661–664) recommends penitential sorrow. The dreamer links his despair to the "spot" where he lost the pearl; the maiden is without "spotte" and thus liberated from the spatial constrictions of earthly graveyards. The maiden uses language more freely than the dreamer: she recasts metaphors; she makes puns; she encourages him to consider words as signs, as possibilities. She uses words with an awareness of their flexibility, manifesting her spiritual freedom in her linguistic freedom.

Just as the maiden uses the dreamer's own words and metaphors to ameliorate his despair, so she uses his love for her to move him from a literal to an allegorical world. His love for her has a doubly redemptive potential. The impetus for his search—his love—finally inspires him to be like her. As the maiden is "like" Christ, the dreamer's yearning for imitation can be the means by which he moves, through her, to Christ.[40] The poet suggests the redemptive potential of the dreamer's love by stressing his continual yearning. In fact, for most of the poem, the dreamer yearns better than he understands or sees. When he first finds himself in a dream state and sees the stream and the land beyond the stream, he says, "And euer me longed ay more and more" (144). His yearning never abates, and the maiden uses his yearning to draw him closer to Christ. He wishes to be with her, but, in order to be with her, he must be like her. Thus she describes herself:

"Iesus con calle to hym hys mylde,
And sayde hys ryche no wyȝ myȝt wynne
But he com þyder ryȝt as a chylde,
Oþer elleȝ neuermore com þerinne.
Harmleȝ, trwe, and vndefylde,
Wythouten mote oþer mascle of sulpande synne,

Quen such þer cnoken on þe bylde,
Tyt schal hem men þe ȝate vnpynne."

(721–728)

The maiden is pure, "harmleȝ, trwe, and vndefylde, wythouten mote"; the dreamer is neither a child, nor in a state of spiritual purity. The maiden directs the dreamer to penance, the bridge between purity and impurity and the means by which a man avails himself of grace:

"Grace innogh þe mon may haue
Þat synneȝ þenne new, ȝif hym repente,
Bot wyth sorȝ and syt he mot hit craue,
And byde þe payne þerto is bent."

(661–664)

Only through penance, or creative sorrow, can a man "haue" grace and imitate the state of childlike innocence that is figured in the pearl the maiden wears: " 'For hit is wemleȝ, clene, and clere, / And endeleȝ rounde, and blyþe of mode, / And commune to alle þat ryȝtwys were'" (737–739). The pearl she wears is a sign of her inward purity and hence a sign of her marriage to Christ. The maiden's discussion of penance points the dreamer toward a new understanding of love because penance is the preliminary to spiritual marriage. Her marriage is the result of her purity, and she echoes the language of Canticle 4:7 in her description of her espousal to the Lamb, " 'Com hyder to me, my lemman swete, / For mote ne spot is non in þe.'" (763–764) The dreamer, however, must gain purity through penance. The type of love she offers the dreamer is an expansion of the love he already feels for her. By using his desire and grief as the first stages in holy love, he may move toward penance and thus toward Chirst and marriage to the Lamb. He, too, may become a pearl and not a bereft jeweler.

The maiden's discussion of love and spiritual marriage, which builds upon emotions and perceptions the dreamer himself experiences, is remarkably similar to the discussions of holy love found in studies of the Biblical epithalamium. Saint Augustine's discussion of the nature of the Biblical epithalamium outlines a movement from impurity to purity that culminates in marriage.[41] Saint Augustine, describing Psalm 44, notes that it celebrates the marriage between a king and a plebeian, a distinction the maiden herself makes when she says, "Me ches to hys make, alþaȝ vnmete" (759). To describe the nuptial purity of the bride, Saint Augustine uses the metaphor of clean marriage garments; in line 766, the maiden says of her own marriage, "In hys blod he wesch my wede on dese." Saint Augustine describes the search of love, the hunt for the beloved, and the need for noncorporal understanding and love. He also uses the pastoral metaphors of the psalm to describe the growth of love, or spiritual agriculture ("germinat," "erumpat," "crescat"). The maiden, too, expands upon the dreamer's early use of agricultural imagery and tells the Parable of the Vineyard as a way of explaining her position in heaven. The stages in and nature of spiritual marriage according to Saint Augustine's outline—the unequal match, the love-hunt, the need for purity, the need to move beyond sense, the vegetative growth of love—are also those stages the maiden describes. She begins with the dreamer's own frustrated yearning and grief and outlines a type of love that begins with desire and grief (penance) and moves toward purity and spiritual marriage.

Not only is the emphasis upon penance as a preliminary to spiritual fulfillment shared by the *Pearl*-maiden and commentators on the Biblical epithalamium, but it is also found in discussions of Mary Magdalene. In fact, for the Middle Ages, the Magdalene was the saint whose life most embodied the ideals of penance. As the free-spirited lover whose remorse turned her to a love of Christ, she stood as a reminder of the efficacy of penance, as Chaucer's Parson asserts in his praise of true chastity: "Thise manere wommen that observen chastitee . . . been the vessel or the boyste of the blissed Magdelene, that fulfilleth hooly chirche of good odour."[42] From Donatello's statue of the Magdalene, dressed in penitential rags and wracked by grief and fasting, to the more elegant figures carrying vessels of ointment, the figure of the penitent saint is a familiar one in medieval art. Her penitential attitude is intended to remind us of the higher joys she will experience when finally reunited with her beloved in heaven. In *Pearl*, the maiden recommends penance to the dreamer as a means of achieving purity before marriage. The maiden, in describing purity, translates the *sine macula* of the Song of Songs as "wythouten mote," hinting at the progression from penance, to purity, to spiritual ecstasy.

The second stage of the dreamer's experience is educational, but this state ends with frustration rather than with spiritual fulfillment. His love for the maiden inspires him to request a sight of her dwelling place, the celestial Jerusalem. His account of the city, in sections 18–19 of *Pearl*, is a faithful rendering of Saint John's description of the celestial city in the Book of Apocalypse. The climax of the dreamer's description comes in the final stanza of section 19, when, after recounting the wonders of heaven, the procession of the Lamb, and the Lamb himself, he suddenly sees his pearl:

Þen saʒ I þer my lyttel quene
Þat I wende had standen by me in sclade.
Lorde, much of mirþe watʒ þat ho made
Among her fereʒ þat watʒ so quyt!
Þat syʒt me gart to þenk to wade
For luf-longyng in gret delyt.

(1147–1152)

His language here is particularly suggestive because it is the language of sensory delight. The *sight* of the maiden awakens "luf-longyng" and "delyt" in him, and he attempts to wade the river he has been forbidden to cross.

His reaction to seeing the maiden is regressive in the sense that it recalls his earlier earthbound reactions both to the landscape of his dream and to the maiden herself. For example, when he first finds himself in a spiritual landscape, his sensual enjoyment of its beauties temporarily banishes his grief: "The adubbement of þo downeȝ dere / Garten my goste al greffe forȝete" (85–86; see also 121–124). Similarly, upon first seeing the maiden, the sight itself gladdens him: "The more I frayste hyr fayre face, / Her fygure fyn quen I had fonte, / Suche gladande glory con to me glace" (169–171). While there is nothing unusual or wrong in his reactions to the beauty of a pastoral landscape, of the maiden, or of heaven, the fact that his reactions are still inspired by physical faculties suggests his dependence upon sense and sensory perception. His desire to cross the river into heaven has its roots in his sensory reaction to the *sight* of heaven's splendor and, especially, to the *sight* of the maiden in the procession of the Lamb. The "luf-longyng" which his "lyttle quene" arouses in him recalls the "luf-daungere" which described his original state of grief and depression. Finally, for the dreamer, his desire for the maiden is stronger than his desire for the Lamb, one more indication that his love and faith are still dominated by earthly concerns. In the next stanza, the first of section 20, the poet underlines the physical or sensory motivation for the dreamer's actions: "Delyt me drof in yȝe and ere, / My maneȝ mynde to maddyng malte; / Quen I seȝ my frely, I wolde be þere" (1153–1155). The emphasis here is upon physical delight—the visual and auditory delights of his vision drive him to frenzy. Moreover, in line 1155, the poet stresses the source of the dreamer's frenzy—"Quen I seȝ my frely," the maiden herself, who, despite her account of her marriage to Christ, remains for the dreamer "my fair one." The dreamer, therefore, disobeys the injunction "not to cross," tries to "touch," and awakens in loss.

Whereas the first stage of the dreamer's spiritual experience begins in loss and ends in recognition, the second stage begins in a mood of untutored optimism and ends in loss. The fact that his emotional frenzy ends in loss of vision may reflect some of the concerns of the late fourteenth and early fifteenth centuries, a time when the attractions of lay mysticism and of religious enthusiasm were beginning to disrupt organized worship to the growing concern of many religious thinkers.[43] The poem itself bears witness to the dangers of emotionalism, or of purely affective faith, in the dreamer's early despair, in his simple-minded reactions to the maiden's instructions, and in his futile attempt to cross the river alone. As the poem implies, emotion on its own is vulnerable to self-involvement, ultimately to despair; and the believer must learn to live by faith, not by touch. The dreamer's actions likewise echo the scene between Christ and Mary on Easter morning: Mary wants to affirm Christ's resurrection by touching him; he forbids it. The dreamer metaphorically tries to touch and awakens. In the third and continuing phase of his spiritual experience, however, he attempts to live and love by noncorporal faith, to affirm a world beyond sense.

The third stage of the dreamer's spiritual experience, though it receives relatively brief treatment, is a remarkable account of spiritual reorientation. The narrator begins this final stage by recognizing his loss. He awakens in the same garden ("þat erber wlonk," 1171), in the spot where he originally lost his pearl. His first words are those of resignation: "And, skyng, to myself I sayd, / 'Now al be to þat Prynceȝ paye'" (1175–1176). His initial resignation is followed by depression:

> Me payed ful ille to be outfleme
> So sodenly of þat fayre regioun,
> Fro alle þo syȝteȝ so quyke and queme.
> A longeyng heuy me strok in swone . . .
>
> (1177–1180)

Not only has he lost his pearl, but he has lost the "fayre regioun" of his vision, a loss that reawakens longing or frustration in him. However, rather than succumbing to despair, the narrator begins to recall his experience, finally stating:

> "If hit be ueray and soth sermoun
> Þat þou so stykeȝ in garlande gay,

So wel is me in þys doel-doungoun
Þat þou art to þat Prynseȝ paye."

(1185–1188)

The sequence is a record of spiritual struggle, an account of the jarring loss of visionary ecstasy and of the narrator's ability to begin to use his memory of vision for his own spiritual health.

The remaining three stanzas of the poem testify to the narrator's success. In particular, the last four lines of *Pearl* attest to the nature of the narrator's spiritual renewal. In these lines, the narrator first considers the sacrament of Communion and the foundations of faith, then the images of the pearl and of the laborer, which are now for him interrelated:

Þat in the forme of bred and wyn
Þe preste vus scheweȝ vch a daye.
He gef vus to be his homly hyne
Ande precious perleȝ vnto his pay.

(1209–1212)

The first two lines concern the corporal foundations of faith and the necessity for allegorical perception. The words "forme" and "scheweȝ" underline the visible reality of the sacrament; however, "þat" refers to Christ who is present in the elements of the Eucharist. A communicant must depend on the elements' being other than they appear and must, in fact, be able through faith to see Christ in the bread and wine of the Mass. In terms of the narrator's former reliance on visual proof, these lines testify to his growth. Previously, he believed only what he saw; by the end of the poem, he believes what he cannot see.

The narrator not only bears witness to his faith, but, in these last lines, also confirms his status as a worker, or his active charity. Sacramental observance was frequently likened to worthwhile labor, for, by devotion to the sacraments, man keeps himself from idleness, substituting a useful, healthy exercise for torpor and spiritual sloth.[44] Whereas the poem's opening stanzas appear to evoke a graveyard, its closing stanzas suggest an altar. The narrator thereby intimates a physical progression complementary to his spiritual progression; for he moves from death to life, from without the church, in its graveyard, to its interior, the center of its life. In his use of the phrase "homly hyne," the narrator signifies his activity, echoing in his choice of words the Parable of the Vineyard which the maiden tells the dreamer in order to warn him of the dangers of an idle existence. However, the final line of *Pearl* suggests a balance between work and grace, for he looks forward to becoming a harvested pearl and existing for his prince's pleasure. He wishes to see himself no longer as a jeweler, possessive and ultimately disappointed, but as a pearl set in its setting of heaven, reflecting beauty not his own.

Through the voice of the narrator, which recounts the experience of the past and the resolutions of the present, the poet outlines a movement from despair and grief to faith, love, and renewed life that is similar, both in situation and content, to the scene between Mary Magdalene and Christ as it was understood in the Middle Ages. The similarities of situation and theme, however, do not necessarily imply that the poem is an allegory that conceals the New Testament encounter behind the veil of a contemporary account. Rather than suggesting that *Pearl* is an allegory, the similarities point to the poet's use of analogy. Again, it is helpful to turn to Dante and to Singleton. Singleton calls the *Vita Nuova* an "analogy of proportion," insisting that "if this is analogy, it is only such a one as may enter into a work of art. . . . The *Vita Nuova* sees as poems see, not as mathematics sees, or logic."[45] Neither is *Pearl* an allegory although it teaches allegory: the poet creates an analogous situation and only hints at allegory in the final stanzas of the poem when the dreamer himself begins to perceive a two-dimensional world. *Pearl* does not say anything different from what it appears to say. Both explicitly and implicitly, *Pearl* teaches renewal and expansion through love. The poet heightens the impact of this lesson by his manipulation of the narrator and the maiden, figures whose setting, situations, and dialogue evoke the Easter morning dialogue between Mary Magdalene and Christ. Furthermore, in his choice and use of imagery, the poet not only draws upon elements of the *noli me tangere* episode, but suggests, once more, the process of expansion that was thought to be implicit in the *noli me tangere* episode, the Biblical epithalamium, and the dream vision.

The Images of Growth and Expansion

The narrator learns of the radical possibilities of love in what is technically a love vision. Like the Dante of the *Vita Nuova*, like Amant of the *Roman de la Rose*, and like the narrator of the *Boke of the Duchesse*, the narrator of *Pearl* experiences visionary revelation about the nature of love. For each of these protagonists, dreams are a direct result of problems associated with love; it is therefore fitting that their dreams provide them with a means of approaching their problems. The *Pearl*-poet's use of the formal and thematic implications of the love vision is particularly suggestive because he draws upon elements of the Song of Songs for much of his pastoral imagery, and he draws upon the visionary experience—notably Saint John's in the Book of Apocalypse—for the way in which he manipulates images. The landscape for *Pearl* is primarily pastoral and many of the images vegetative, but *Pearl*'s imagistic flexibility also owes a good deal to the progressive character of visionary experience, the upward motion of the soul toward God.

In combining elements of Saint John's Apocalypse with elements of the Canticle, the poet follows medieval convention. The relationship between love and vision is stressed in glosses on the Canticle, which frequently discuss vision in reference to the bride's statement that she searches for her beloved at night while she sleeps (Cant. 3:1, 5:2). As vision was seen as a component of holy love, so discussions of holy love can be found in glosses on the Book of Apocalypse. Saint

John's account of the marriage of Christ and the Church in Apocalypse 21 and his eloquent description of the heavenly Jerusalem (the archetype for the Church) in the following chapter suggested marriage or union as the final event of sacred history. Both texts, then, were thought to link the themes of love and vision, and, more important, both texts describe a progressive experience that culminates in vision.[46]

Thus, exegetical discussions of the Song of Songs, or of the Biblical epithalamium, and of the Book of Apocalypse frequently share certain themes and metaphors with discussions of the *noli me tangere* episode. First, all three texts were thought to describe radical change. The bride's and the Magdalene's growing recognition of the nature of love is a progressive experience similar to Saint John's growing apprehension of the celestial realm. Second, the end of all three experiences was seen as a more spiritual knowledge of God. Third, all three texts are focused by their uses of a pastoral setting. For both the bride of the Canticle and the Magdalene, the garden is the scene of the search. The pastoral settings of both texts inspired many writers to discuss love in vegetative terms and to play upon the figurative meanings of the two pastoral landscapes. Paradise was also conceived of as a garden, a regained Eden, whose tree of life, or the cross, provided the antidote to the fruit of the tree man had first eaten in Eden. Saint John's description of paradise as a garden, of course, inspired the plans of many monastic gardens throughout medieval Europe, themselves figures for the garden the monks hoped to inhabit after death. Thus, when we consider the implications of all three texts, the garden is not only the landscape of man's search for love, but also the landscape of fulfillment.

In *Pearl*, the poet draws upon what are interrelated traditions by manipulating the pastoral landscape, which is the setting for the narrator's search for the maiden. Thus, though *Pearl* is an imagistic tour de force, as many fine studies have demonstrated,[47] the imagery should be viewed in relation to the narrator; for in his apprehension of what he sees, we may chart his growing apprehension of the nature of love. For example, the narrator begins by seeing things as distinct from one another. His "spot" of loss, his pearl, his garden, are distinguished from all other spots, pearls, and gardens because of their importance to him. However, in vision he encounters multiple pearls and heavenly gardens, learning that each thing he sees reflects Christ. He finally learns to recognize Christ in apparently disparate elements.

The maiden has already acquired the ability to see Christ around her, for she describes the citizens of heaven as bound together in Christ:

"Of courtaysye, as saytȝ Saynt Poule,
Al arn we membreȝ of Jesu Kryst:
As heued and arme and legg and naule
Temen to hys body ful trwe and tryste,
Ryȝt so is vch a Krysten sawle
A longande lym to þe Mayster of myste."

(457–462)

The maiden adopts Saint Paul's description of the Church as one body (see 1 Cor. 12) in her efforts to describe the interdependence that characterizes the kingdom of Christ. Although different members may have different functions, all are one in Christ. Each member draws his identity from his relationship to the whole body, or Christ; and thus each member is Christlike, just as in a mathematical equation, when $x = z$ and $y = z$, then $x = y$. Through his vision, which opens up to him the nature of heavenly love and spiritual marriage, the dreamer begins to acquire the maiden's ability to see Christ in the various things around him. The poet indicates the narrator's growing spiritual understanding by describing the narrator's gradual reevaluation of the meaning and uses of the natural world.

The Garden and the Imagery of Spiritual Agriculture.
Since the garden was the conventional landscape of human love, loss, and fulfillment in medieval literature, it could reflect the transformations of the human heart. Biblically, the garden is the setting for man's fall and for his rebirth,

and the significant gardens of Christian myth found their ways into secular literature.[48] The Garden of Eden where man lost himself, the love garden of the Canticle, the garden of Easter morning, and the garden of paradise form a backdrop to and participate in the providential history of human salvation. For medieval poets and exegetes, gardens had a good deal of figurative potential because of their associations with human failure, desire, and renewal. The poet's use of the garden in *Pearl* prompts these associations, and in his use of the pastoral landscape we may find indications of the narrator's state of mind. Initially, the garden in *Pearl* reflects the narrator's grief and despair. As the dreamer grows, the poet introduces other gardens—the splendidly heightened garden of the first stages of the dreamer's vision; the garden of labor, or the vineyard, which the maiden describes; the heavenly garden of paradise; and, finally, the original garden, which has been transformed into the landscape of resurrection.

The garden of *Pearl* undergoes a series of transformations parallel to the dreamer's capacity for vision or sight. Initially, it is a place of ill fortune ("Allas! I leste hyr in on erbere," 9), which commemorates the dreamer's loss and thus his grief: "I dewyne, fordolked of luf-daungere" (11). The reference to "luf-daungere" places the garden within a literary tradition which also includes the garden in the *Roman de la Rose*. The similarities between the two gardens suggest the dreamer's spiritual condition at this stage of the poem. Amant, of the *Roman*, wanders into a garden which, like the garden in *Pearl*, is sweet-smelling and filled with flowers; there he gazes into the pool of Narcissus, conceives a passion for a rose reflected in it, and is struck by Cupid as he gazes. The *Pearl*-dreamer, as the poem begins, has already been struck with "luf-daungere" and has thus transformed his garden into a reflection of his own despair. Like Amant, whose major mistake was gazing into Narcissus's pool,[49] the dreamer testifies to his own fatal self-involvement:

ȝet þoȝt me neuer so swete a sange
As stylle stounde let to me stele.

For soþe þer fleten to me fele,
To þenke hir color so clad in clot.

(19–22)

Death, which defines his spiritual condition, also defines his surroundings. The sweet songs that arise from the dreamer's proximity to the garden turn again on his despair. In line 37, the poet indicates the importance of the garden to this stage of the dreamer's love: "To þat spot þat I in speche expoun" and again, in line 49, "Bifore þat spot my honde I spenned." The narrator's garden is a monument to his own grief; like the garden the Magdalene visits on Easter morning, the garden has become a memorial. The poet underlines the narrator's spiritual torpor by intimating the garden's associations with memory: it is a symbol of past loss and of present grief. The narrator's garden has no "future," unless the future is to continue the limitations of the present. Moreover, the similarities between Amant's condition and his garden and the *Pearl*-narrator's condition and his garden suggest both protagonists' frustration. Like Mary Magdalene before she recognizes Christ, Amant and the narrator of *Pearl* focus upon the mutable and carnal. Thus, the gardens they inhabit are landscapes of torpor and self-involvement.

The author of *Pearl*, however, describes a transformation of the narrator's pastoral landscape that is parallel to the narrator's spiritual renewal. The poet follows the tradition of the Biblical epithalamium by suggesting that visionary revelation may follow desire (see Cant. 3:1, 5:2). The garden is therefore not only the nexus for the narrator's grief and self-involvement, but also the physical location for his visionary experience. The poet suggests a relationship between the pastoral landscape of search and frustration and visionary revelation. To this end, the narrator first notes his search of the spot where he lost the peral, "Bifore þat spot my honde I spenned" (49), and then the creative potential of the garden itself, "Fro spot my spyryt þer sprang in space" (61). For the entire "time" of his vision, or the "time" occupied by the body of the poem, the dreamer remains in "þat spot," which he likens to a grave: "My body on balke þer bod in sweuen" (62). Upon awakening, he is therefore in the same garden that appeared in the first section of *Pearl*. He verifies this in lines 1171–1173: "Þen wakned I in þat erber wlonk; / My hede vpon þat hylle watȝ layde / Þer as my perle to grounde strayd." The garden is, however, enriched by the preceding vision: it is no longer merely a grave or a monument to "luf-daungere" and a departed love. In the final stanza of the poem, the dreamer says, "Ouer þis hyul þis lote I laȝte, / For pyty of my perle enclyin, / And syþen to God I hit bytaȝte / In Krysteȝ dere blessyng and myn" (1205–1208). The garden of the end of the poem is the same physical place that was at the beginning, but at the end it has become a means of remembering not death, but life.

That the maiden is aware of these associations between a pastoral landscape and renewal is hinted at in an early interchange between herself and the dreamer. The narrator sees himself as ill used: his jewel has been torn from him; and, from his earlier remarks about losing his pearl in the grass, it is clear that he associates his garden with loss. The maiden counters his remark by saying that she now inhabits another, eternal garden:

> "Sir, ȝe haf your tale mysetente,
> To say your perle is al awaye,
> Þat is in cofer so comly clente
> As in þis gardyn gracios gaye,
> Hereinne to lenge for euer and play,
> Þer mys nee mornyng com neuer nere."
>
> (257–262)

She compares the garden she now inhabits to a "cofer" that heightens the beauty of the gem it encloses. Both literally and metaphorically, she has been reset. Her new setting is not a monument to the past nor is it circumscribed by mutability; it is a living garden. The difference between the narrator's and the maiden's perceptions of the garden highlights the narrator's lack of understanding: as he perceives human nature and human love, so he perceives the garden which is the landscape for the interchange of love.

The intimate association between the narrator and his landscape is reinforced by medieval discussions of gardens. Frequently gardens were likened to the soul or to human nature insofar as they are at once landscapes of potential fruitfulness and landscapes governed by the laws of mutability.[50] Alanus de Insulis, for example, in discussing the similarities between the garden and human nature, refers to Mary Magdalene and the *noli me tangere* episode. He uses that scene to underline the transformation of the human heart, or garden, which Christ effected through the Resurrection: by becoming human and thus assuming the strictures of human nature, Christ added a new dimension to human life. Metaphorically, by entering into the garden, or human nature, Christ changed the garden from the landscape of death and loss to one of renewal and eternal life.[51]

The poet's use of the garden in *Pearl* suggests his awareness of this progression. The initial connection between the garden and death points to an association between mortality and the garden, reflecting the Magdalene's similar appraisal. Originally, the garden's limits are the limits of the dreamer. The *Pearl*-maiden's sudden appearance begins to expand what was a finite space, as Christ's sudden appearance in the Easter garden is a transformation of space. In line 805 the maiden alludes to the limited scope of earthly space when she says, "'In Jerusalem watz my lemman slayn.'" But her later discussion of marriage denies the limits or reality of death. There, she shifts to the present tense and gives notice of what is real and continuing, "'Forþy vche saule þat hade neuer teche / Is to þat Lombe a worthyly wyf'" (845–846). The reversal from past to present tense, from death to life, suggests a transformation of the dreamer and his garden. In the final lines of the poem the dreamer first refers to the "hyul," which formerly defined his grief, and then alludes to the sacrament of the Eucharist. He has not only shifted to present tense himself, but uses a plural pronoun, implicitly linking himself with the body of Christ: "Þe preste vus scheweʒ vch a daye" (1210).[52]

However, between the garden of death at the opening of the poem and the garden of life at the end lies the vineyard of labor. The Parable of the Vineyard appears in Matthew 20:1–16 and illustrates the rewards of grace in exchange for spiritual diligence.[53] Every laborer, whether he began work at the first hour or at the eleventh, will receive a penny as his wage. Like the rewards of heaven, the wages for labor are equal for all who work. The last verses of the parable summarize its message:

> And receiving it they murmured against the master of
> the house, saying: These last have worked but one hour,
> and thou hast made them equal to us, that have borne
> the burden of the day and the heats. But he answering said
> to one of them: Friend, I do thee no wrong: didst thou
> not agree with me for a penny? Take what is thine, and
> go thy way; I will also give to this last even as to thee.
> Or, is it not lawful for me to do what I will? is thy eye evil,
> because I am good? So shall the last be first, and the first
> last. For many are called, but few chosen.

In *Pearl*, the poet captures both the tone and the message of the Parable of the Vineyard by placing it within a specific context; the maiden tells it to the dreamer in response to his unwillingness to believe she is a queen in paradise:

> "That cortaysé is to fre of dede,
> ʒyf hyt be soth þat þou coneʒ saye.
> Þou lyfed not two ʒer in oure þede;
> Þou cowþeʒ neuer God nauþer plese ne pray,
> Ne neuer nawþer Pater ne Crede;
> And quen mad on þe fyrst day!"
>
> (481–486)

The dreamer's exclamation echoes the workers' dissatisfaction in the Biblical parable that all shall receive the same wage. The narrator seems to think it unfair that a child who could neither please God knowingly, pray, nor recite the Pater Noster or Creed should enjoy so exalted a position in heaven—and should be elevated on the first day. He ends his complaint by lamenting, "'Bot a quene! Hit is to dere a date'" (492). The narrator here falls into the trap of justice: how unfair that she who did not work should receive the same reward that I—or any other worker—will receive for a long, hard life of service.

The theological controversy about the poet's use of this parable has in some ways shifted attention from its context and message to the issue of the poet's orthodoxy. D. W. Robertson, Jr., has pointed out that the poet indeed uses the parable in an orthodox manner; Bruno Astensis also glossed the eleventh hour as that when newly baptized children approach the kingdom. Neither is the poet's statement of the equality of heaven heretical, as Robertson shows by citing Saint Augustine.[54] In fact, by quarreling over heaven's equality, we run the risk of focusing, like the narrator, on the equity of the workmen's wages rather than on the parable's message. The maiden uses the parable to illustrate the necessity for spiritual labor because man must work in order to deserve the "peny," which is like the kingdom of heaven. The dreamer misses the point; for he asks for justice, or wages based on merit, not for the mercy that bestows the "peny" on unworthy man. The dreamer focuses upon the literal components of the parable, ignoring its spiritual implications.

We should, however, view the poet's use of the parable within the frame of the narrator's quarrel with divine justice. The maiden directs the parable at the narrator's idleness, for she underlines the necessity for work. Without work, there is no "peny." However, she also uses the parable to point out God's graciousness. Once more, she opens up to him a world larger than the one he inhabits. He quarrels, "'Hit is to dere a date.'" She replies by replacing a narrow definition with an expanded one, "'Per is no date of hys godnesse'" (493). Whereas the narrator wishes for limits on grace, the maiden argues for grace as limitless as love.

Through the parable, the maiden promises grace in exchange for work, implicitly linking the garden of labor, or the vineyard, to the "garden" of the Church. Like other exegetes, she associates the vineyard with both the Church and the kingdom of heaven.[55] Labor in the former is rewarded by the "peny" wage, a simile for the latter. Thus, while the maiden follows Matthew in saying, "'My regne . . . is lyk on hyȝt / To a lorde þat hade a uyne, I wate'" (501–502), she describes the labor of the vineyard as labor before death:

"Anon þe day, wyth derk endente,
Þe niyȝt of deth dotȝ to enclyne:
Þat wroȝt neuer wrang er þenne þay wente,
Þe gentyle Lorde þenne payeȝ hys hyne."

(629–632)

Faithful Christians, like agricultural laborers, must work with one eye on the clock. Death, like night, precludes labor, and what is to be done must be accomplished while light lasts. Her emphasis upon work has a particular relevance for the dreamer, who has described himself as torpid and idle. The maiden implicitly offers the dreamer another sort of garden—not a garden of loss, despair, and memory, but a garden of toil, activity, community, and, ultimately, of fulfillment.

She may also offer him a warning. The fact that September is the traditional month for the "labor" of the vineyard may underline the urgency behind the maiden's use of the parable.[56] September, signified by the Scales, or Libra, was the month traditionally associated with judgment, with the ending of things, as Chaucer implies in the Prologue to the Parson's Tale.[57] The scales which weigh actual agricultural fruitfulness metaphorically weigh human fruitfulness and stand as signs of spiritual judgment. The poet seems to reflect the association between the gathering of the grapes and judgment by using "date" as a link word in this section of Pearl and by having the maiden preface her account of the parable with a triple stress on the time of year. She connects the time for work in the vineyard with man's recognition of the need for such labor: "'Of tyme of ȝere þe terme watȝ tyȝt,

/ To labor vyne watʒ dere þe date. / Þat date of ʒere wel knawe
þys hyne'" (503–505). Correspondingly, the parable ad-
dresses the urgency of labor ("'Wy stonde ʒe ydel þise dayeʒ
longe?'" 533) in the face of the "date's" passing: "'Þe day
watʒ al apassed date'" (540). By noting that the day of harvest
is known only by God ("'The date of þe daye þe lorde con
knaw,'" 541), the maiden stresses the necessity for spiritual
cultivation. With death, the opportunity for labor ceases be-
cause time ceases for the individual; at the Last Judgment,
time ceases for the world.

The emphasis upon both time and work makes fruitful-
ness the parable's central message. If man may earn the "peny"
only by laboring in the vineyard, and if the "peny" is a meta-
phor for the kingdom of heaven, man should direct himself
to the arts of cultivation. Because the vineyard is *like* either
the Church or heaven, the work done in it is clearly spiritual.
Man engages in spiritual cultivation through worship and
active charity. The motivation for such labor is love, a point
that Saint Augustine makes in his consideration of this par-
able and a point that applies to the dreamer's own situa-
tion.[58] The dreamer, like Mary Magdalene and the bride of
the Canticle, seeks out of a sense of love and loss; the searcher
or lover metaphorically becomes a laborer in order to be-
come a bride. The progression from lover to worker to bride
is one the maiden herself hints at, for she follows her dis-
cussion of agricultural labor with a discussion of her mysti-
cal marriage to Christ. The dreamer, like other lovers, must
become spiritually fruitful before he attains the fulfillments
of spiritual marriage. He comes to the garden to mourn, but
the garden has become a place of labor. Christ, in John 20:17,
directs Mary back to the community of the disciples with
the command to testify to the Resurrection; with its mes-
sage of spiritual labor, the parable functions as a similar
command to the dreamer.

The parable implicitly embodies a message of duty; it also
embodies a message of hope. Therefore the dreamer's literal-
mindedness, evident in his quarrel over the equality of the
workmen's wages, is foolish because he asks for justice rather
than for mercy. He does not understand the parable. The

maiden responds by discussing the abundance of grace in literal terms. Section 11 contains five stanzas. The body of each stanza deals with basic human folly and ends with an affirmation of grace. Each stanza ends with "For þe grace of God is gret innoȝe." Even the best men fail, but mercy is always there to shore up human nature:

"Where wysteȝ þou euer any bourne abate,
Euer so holy in hys prayere,
Þat he ne forfeted by sumkyn gate
Þe mede sumtyme of heueneȝ clere?
And ay þe ofter þe alder þay were,
Þay laften ryȝt and wroȝten woghe.
Mercy and grace most hem þen stere,
For þe grace of God is gret innoȝe."

(617–624)

This explanation of human imperfection and divine grace is simple enough for a child to understand. The maiden's discussion of purity emphasizes the necessity for childlike innocence. The dreamer must regain innocence through penance; he must put off his peevish sophistry and accept grace as simply as a child.

The Parable of the Vineyard and the *Pearl*-maiden's explanation of it illustrate the balance between grace and works. She ends by telling the dreamer that work is a duty but never sufficient, and only grace rewards the laborer after all. Appropriately, after the parable, she explains grace, her purity, and the meaning of Jerusalem. The message of duty and grace embodied in the parable is the dreamer's preparation for his sight of the celestial Jerusalem. In terms of the parable, the dreamer must choose either to work in the garden or to mourn in it; his vision of heaven allows him to balance one garden with another. The garden he knows is an extension of himself, of his preoccupation with death; the garden of heaven is a garden of life, and he may enter it only through the vineyard, the garden of labor, expecting grace in exchange for work.

The poet's use of the garden provides us with a means of

understanding the narrator's gradual apprehension of the nature of heavenly love. The poem opens in a conventional enough way, with a solitary lover, who haunts a garden of "luf-daungere." He perceives the garden as a landscape of loss, turning it into a memorial to death. However, that initial garden expands to include a celestial garden, the new and living setting for his lost pearl. While the narrator lies exhausted in the garden of death, his spirit inhabits a garden he had not considered, a garden of life that is potentially immanent in the garden of death. While wondering at this lovely place of water and colors and greenery, he learns of yet another garden, one that requires toil. He then sees the garden of paradise, set in the midst of the celestial city:

> Aboute þat water arn tres ful schym,
> Þat twelue fryteȝ of lyf con bere ful sone;
> Twelue syþeȝ on ȝer þay beren ful frym,
> And renowleȝ nwe in vche a mone.
>
> (1077–1080)

The garden of paradise, containing trees of life whose fruit is eternally renewed, stands as the archetypal garden of the poem, the garden manifested in all earthly gardens. But, upon awakening, the narrator finds himself back in the original, earthly garden. "His" garden now includes more than memories of death. It includes memories of all the other pastoral landscapes he has encountered and, for him, is now linked to the communal garden of the Church. The garden of the end of *Pearl*, though literally the same space, has become a place of spiritual labor, a way station for heaven's garden of love and marriage. The transformation of pastoral space is fitting, for the poet allows the traditional landscape of love to reflect the growth of love.

The poet's use of the garden also alerts us to the dreamer's altered conception of time. He begins by associating the garden and the imagery of vegetation with mutability. Initially, the narrator cannot move beyond a recognition of mutability to its implications of harvest, ultimately of fruitfulness. He can understand time because he can perceive its effects, but he cannot understand its use. The maiden begins to alter his understanding of time by the very fact that she appears to him, thereby alerting him to time's powerlessness. The time that at first delimits his conception of human love is further placed in a new perspective by the Parable of the Vineyard because time becomes the medium for labor and growth, the preparation for love's fulfillment. Finally, he is granted a sign of the celestial city and the eternally ripening trees of life. The garden he thought evidence of mutability is transformed into an emblem of eternity. Once the narrator learns to see his garden as a manifestation of the heavenly garden, rather than as a reflection of change and mutability, he signifies his ability to escape the effects of time by transcending it.

Vision and the Imagery of Vision. *Pearl* teaches a radical expansion of love, a lesson reflected in the poet's manipulation of the pastoral elements of the poem and a lesson thematically suited to the visionary framework he employs. The poem's subject, the dreamer's problem, is love, and the dreamer's attitude toward love is changed by a vision wherein he first speaks with his dead beloved and learns of heaven's perfect love and then "sees" the reality of this love in the celestial Jerusalem. The change in him is effected by the vision itself which moves his spirit upward, away from earth and earthly "luf-daungere," to the immutable courtesy and life of paradise. As the dreamer moves upward, so do the poem's images—toward their source in heaven.

In linking vision with change, the poet reflects the formal awareness of the dream vision as it was conceived of in the Middle Ages. Classical dream visions like the Dream of Scipio and *The Consolation of Philosophy*, Biblical dream visions like those of Ezechiel and Saint John, and medieval dream visions such as the *Roman de la Rose*, the *Vita Nuova*, and *The Boke of the Duchesse* associate vision with the acquisition of knowledge, knowledge that, ideally, should lead to change or to a new perspective. In linking vision with love, the poet is on equally firm ground, for vision was considered a part of the Biblical epithalamium, and numerous medieval poets explore the problems of love using a visionary frame.

Beginning with the first major commentary on a literary dream vision, Macrobius's *Commentary on the Dream of Scipio*, there evolved standards for judging the nature of vision as a way of determining how meaningful a dream was. A dream might be called a nightmare or a vision, depending upon the circumstances under which a dreamer falls asleep and upon the types of things he sees in his dream. Lethargy, or spiritual sloth, was frequently thought to induce meaningless dreams, or nightmares that could effect no spiritual change. The sleep of the virtuous was thought conducive to revelation because a virtuous man falls asleep already prepared for the acquisition of wisdom.[59] Virtuous sleep is particularly conducive to vision because the body and the carnal faculties, both literally and metaphorically, are at rest; and the soul is free to receive noncarnal impressions. The higher consciousness is potentially receptive and is most alert when separated from the sensual preoccupations of the waking state.[60] The potential for revelation through dreams is likewise suggested by Canticle 5:2, "I sleep and my heart watcheth," a verse that received frequent mention in medieval discussions of sleep and dreams. The love vision, in particular, may culminate in a vision of the celestial Jerusalem, as both Saint Augustine and Saint Gregory suggest in their discussions of spiritual love. Thus, the meaningful dream ideally begins in virtuous sleep, proceeds to a revelation of the workings of divine love, and often culminates in the beatific vision of the celestial Jerusalem.

The medieval understanding of vision, which inevitably influenced the literary dream vision, was firmly based on formal considerations of works such as Saint John's Book of Apocalypse and prophetic Old Testament visions. Whether or not authors patterned literary dream visions upon either a specific Biblical vision or upon an exegetical discussion of vision, the progression—starting from a certain type of sleep and leading on through revelation, frequently dialogue, and beatific vision to subsequent awakening and change—remained a conventional sequence. There were, of course, numerous variations upon such a pattern, but the concern of this study is *Pearl* and the way in which the poet uses the visionary framework to suggest the dreamer's spiritual change.

The poet's use of the visionary frame in *Pearl* implies his awareness of these medieval conventions and suggests that he uses the conventional elements of the dream vision to underline the narrator's experience of what can be called spiritual resurrection. The narrator himself does not begin in a particularly auspicious frame of mind for a meaningful dream. Rather, he begins in a state of frustration, sloth, and sorrowful love, qualities that appear to foreshadow something other than a redemptive dream. However, the ominous beginnings of the narrator's love vision lead to a spiritual change which begins with the onset of sleep and continues through his awakening. His spiritual change is manifested in the dreamer's upward movement, from the limitations of an earthly garden to the infinite space of a celestial garden. In fact, from the moment the narrator falls asleep, it is clear that the poet will be describing the redemptive movement of the mind because the movement of the narrator's spirit is upward and its interest is directed outward.

The poet marks the shift in the dreamer from one kind of sleep to another kind of sleep as a way of preparing us for and heightening the sense of awakening at the end of the poem. Lines 57–60 prepare us for a certain kind of dream vision: "I felle vpon þat floury flaȝt, / Suche odour to my herneȝ schot; / I slode vpon a slepyng-slaȝte / On þat precios perle wythouten spot." The dreamer here testifies to his lethargy and sensual abandonment. His sleep is the result of languor and dolor, and he seems an unlikely candidate for a revelatory dream. However, with line 61, the poet begins to reverse our expectations by suggesting that, while the dreamer's body fell on earth, his spirit ascends, or springs, toward God: "Fro spot my spyryt þer sprang in space; / My body on balke þer bod in sweuen. / My goste is gon in Godeȝ grace / In auenture þer meruaⳉley₃ meuen" (61–64). In describing the sleeping dreamer, the poet seems to reflect the conventional view that sleep could bring revelation because the body with its carnal preoccupations is at rest, or dead to the world, and the spirit, or higher consciousness, is free to apprehend truth. Thus the dreamer exists, for most of the poem, in two places at once: his body is "on balke"—in fact, on the "spot" of his loss, perhaps a grave—and his spirit moves toward life.

The dreamer's situation has a number of applications to our understanding of the poet's meaning. First, that part of him frustrated by physical loss is quite rightly left on the earth, tied to one "spot," enervated by the apprehension of mutability. His spiritual faculties, those faculties that are not constricted by time, move quite easily toward a vision of infinite splendor and timeless love. Second, the moment of awakening when his spirit "rejoins" his body is a moment when his spiritual perceptions assume mastery over his physical loss and direct the whole man toward the sacrament of the Mass—nourishment for both the physical and the spiritual man. Hence, the moment of awakening is a moment of resurrection: the body arises from its memorial "spot" and moves beyond recognition of death to hope and renewed love. Third, the dreamer's situation duplicates the situation of man in general—the human body is implicitly tied to death, to a "spot" of earth, while the human spirit is capable of infinte movement. In terms of Christian theology, the spirit can banish the threat of the grave by availing itself of the possibilities of grace. Finally, lines 61–64 prepare us for a redemptive love vision by echoing Canticle 5:2, a verse that was linked with this process of spiritual cognition. The dreamer's spirit "springs up," finding itself standing in a landscape of heightened clarity and splendor, a landscape he sees with his spiritual eye.[61]

Throughout his dream, the narrator's spirit undergoes a process of cognition or of awakening. First, he realizes that the landscape of his dream is new to him ("I ne wyste in þis worlde quere þat hit wace," 65), but he senses that he has an innate familiarity with it:

Forþy I þoȝt þat Paradyse
Watȝ þer ouer gayn þo bonkeȝ brade.
I hoped þe water were a deuyse
Bytwene myrþeȝ by mereȝ made;
Byȝonde þe broke, by slente oþer slade,
I hoped þat mote merked wore.

(137–142)

While his description does not represent true recognition, it is similar to his feelings of familiarity when he first sees the maiden: "I hade sen hyr ere" (164). It points to the perceptive abilities of his spirit when liberated from his body and hence to the faint human memory of paradise. The dreamer's increased visual clarity underlines his increased receptivity. The movement of spiritual education is implicit in the poet's description of the onset of vision ("My goste is gon in Godeȝ grace," 63) and, later, in his description of the dreamer's reaction to the figure of the maiden ("I hoped þat gostly watȝ þat porpose," 185), in which the word "goste" links the spirit of the dreamer with the purpose of his vision.

The vision is intended to alleviate his despair by offering him a new understanding of love; like the Biblical love vision, *Pearl* charts a progression from frustration and lack to satisfaction and love's plenitude. The movement in *Pearl* from the single dreamer to the celestial Jerusalem and its diverse harmony of love may also owe something to medieval discussions of Biblical love poetry. Many of these discussions culminate in discussions of the celestial Jerusalem, sketching a progression from an individual visionary to the unified multiplicity of the Church. Both Saint Augustine and Saint Gregory end their considerations of spiritual love with a paean to the Church and its heavenly archetype. For both writers, the individual's movement toward God ends in a vision of communal ecstasy, and both use the ardent language of physical ecstasy to describe the visionary apprehension of celestial marriage. The poet's description of the procession of the Lamb in section 19 is likewise an account of visionary ecstasy. For this section, the poet uses "delyt" as a link word, a word that captures both the dreamer's attitude toward what he sees and the nature of celestial love.

The poet also appears to reflect the formal progression of Biblical love poetry in the more general outlines of the dreamer's experience. He begins with a single dreamer and a single maiden and enlarges the scope of the poem to include heaven's many lovers. The garden at the end of the poem is implicitly communal because it is peopled by the dreamer's memories of heaven and because it is linked to the rite of the Mass, a sacramental affirmation of community. The dreamer arrives where he began, but vision has altered his perception of a familiar landscape.

The movement from garden to garden through vision is analogous to the movement from pearl to pearls. In the opening of the poem, the dreamer says of the maiden, "I sette hyr sengeley in synglere" (8). At the end, this statement is transformed to: "He gef vus to be his homly hyne / Ande precious perleȝ vnto his pay" (1211–1212). Between the two references, the first singular, the second plural, lie his vision and his realization that his pearl is one of a company of 144,000 pearls, in a city of pearls. The dreamer progresses from a fixation on a single pearl to the sight of countless pearls, eventually merged into a single love. "A God, a Lorde, a frende ful fyin" (1204), and a desire to be a pearl among pearls. Discussions of the Canticle and of Psalm 44, both marriage poems, thus provide a possible direction for vernacular poetry of love and vision, a progression common to Dante and to the *Pearl*-poet. The *Pearl*-poet emphasizes the movement from one to many. As the vegetative imagery illustrates, the poem begins with one dreamer, one pearl/seed, one garden. The visionary dialogue introduces other figurative seeds and gardens. By the end of the poem, the only single thing is the godhead who unites all multiplicities. Paradoxically, by expanding the original images through vision, the poet finally contracts them into one inclusive, limitless thing.

The poet's manipulation of the elements of the dream vision reveals at once his familiarity with its conventions and his shrewd sense of the potential flexibility of the form. Not only does the poet employ the dream vision as a frame for the narrator's experience, but he allows the upward and expansive nature of the visionary experience to inform each aspect of this section of *Pearl*. Both physically and spiritually, *Pearl* describes upward movement: the dreamer's spiritual movement is reflected in his movement through the landscape of his vision, for, both spatially and spiritually, he moves upward toward God. Moreover, the dreamer, while moving steadily upward, also undergoes an expansion of spirit which may be called a growing apprehension of likeness. Thus, as he moves, he also begins to see differently, or begins to see things in terms of their similarities. Both types of movement complement the poem's visionary frame because, ideally, vision is such a movement up, toward a recognition of unity in love.

From the moment he falls asleep, the dreamer begins to move spatially upward. Lines 61–63, which note that his spirit springs into space and goes with God's grace, alert us to the direction he will take throughout the poem. His spirit then finds itself in a landscape of remarkable beauty and splendor, and here, by a stream he cannot pass, he talks with the maiden. After their dialogue, she directs him further "up": "'Bow vp towarde þys borneȝ heued'" (974). He moves up the stream to a hill, and from this vantage, which he compares to Saint John's hill of revelation, he sees the celestial Jerusalem, consisting of twelve levels with the city towering over all. Upon awakening, he blesses the "hill" upon which his head lay and resolves to become a laborer and a pearl, testifying to his desire to return to the heights that he saw in a dream.

Spiritually, he also moves toward God because he begins to lose the heaviness of heart that has tied him to one spot of memorial earth. His first impression of the visionary landscape—the colors, the splendor, the gleaming gems, the birds—begins to assuage his grief: "The adubbemente of þo downeȝ dere / Garten my goste al greffe forȝete" (85–86). His grief abating, he begins to take pleasure in the beauty of the

spot, finally approaching a stream whose beauty lightens his
spirit even more: "The dubbement dere of doun and daleȝ, /
Of wod and water and wlonk playneȝ, / Bylde in me blys,
abated my baleȝ, / Fordidden my stresse, dystryed my payneȝ"
(121–124). Not only is grief forgotten, but he experiences
happiness, finally coming to the maiden on the other side of
the water. When he sees her, even his bliss is heightened by
the "gladande glory" (171) she awakens in him. His feelings
later, upon seeing the holy city, are even greater, and the poet
suggests the dreamer's heightened joy by his persistent use
of "delyt" in this section (19) of the poem. As the dreamer
moves up, the light grows more dazzling, the landscape more
clear, and his spirit lighter. He begins to experience sensa-
tions of spiritual ecstasy as he moves farther away from the
body sleeping on the "spot" of death and closer to God, the
source of life and delight.

It may therefore be significant that only when the dream-
er's motion is guided by God does it approach God. The
narrator introduces his account of his experience by describ-
ing his grief. That first section tells us a good deal about his
inability to move, either spiritually or spatially, beyond the
evidence of mortality. He continually returns to the place in
which he lost the pearl; he finally sinks to the earth, ex-
hausted by grief and despair. However, on falling asleep, his
spirit moves up, in God's grace. Once he finds himself in the
visionary landscape, he wanders without direction. When he
encounters the stream, he naturally moves downstream:
"Doun after a strem þat dryȝly haleȝ / I bowed in blys, bredful
my brayneȝ" (125–126). When he sets his own direction, he
chooses to move down rather than up, whereas the maiden
directs him upstream rather than downstream. The poet's
references to the direction the dreamer's movement takes at
certain points in the poem underline the upward nature of
vision itself, but also suggest that the spirit moves upward
through grace, not of its own inclination.

The poet also suggests the relationship between upward
motion and grace in his use of this stream, which figures in
every stage of the dreamer's visionary experience. When the

dreamer first encounters the stream, he senses, rather than knows, its significance:

Forþy I þoȝt þat Paradyse
Watȝ þer ouer gayn þo bonkeȝ brade.
I hoped þe water were a deuyse
Bytwene myrþeȝ by mereȝ made;
Byȝonde þe broke, by slente oþer slade,
I hoped þat mote merked wore.

(137–142)

He senses that the stream divides the landscape in which he stands, that it is a "deuyse," separating him from paradise. That the water is indeed a barrier is clear from his two references to trying to cross it (143, 150–153), but the maiden herself tells him what type of barrier it is: "'Þou wylneȝ ouer þys water to weue; / Er moste þou ceuer to oþer counsayle: / Þy corse in clot mot calder keue'" (318–320). The maiden links the stream with the "Jordan," the river man crosses in death. However, it is only when the dreamer moves upstream and sees the holy city that the stream begins to acquire another symbolic dimension. From his hill of revelation, he sees, "byȝonde þe brok" (981), the city and a celestial river: "A reuer of þe trone þer ran outryȝte / Watȝ bryȝter þen boþe þe sunne and mone" (1055–1056). He sees the river of life of Apocalypse 22:1, a river that Pearl's audience would almost certainly connect with baptismal water.[62]

For the dreamer, the stream has two interrelated functions: by following the stream upward to its source, he may see paradise; while he may not cross over as a living man, he may find this stream on earth in the baptismal font and cross it there, freeing himself from the judgment of eternal death. The maiden's discussion of innocence in section 11 foreshadows his own later realization that he may find a manifestation of heaven in earthly sacraments:

"Innoghe þer wax out of þat welle,
Blod and water of brode wounde.

Þe blod vus boȝt fro bale of helle
And delyuered vus of þe deth secounde;
Þe water is baptem, þe soþe to telle,
Þat folȝed þe glayue so grymly grounde,
Þat wascheȝ away þe gylteȝ felle
Þat Adam wyth inne deth vus drounde."

(649–656)

Discussing baptismal innocence, the maiden identifies the source of that water as the side of Christ.[63] Metaphorically, both streams, one issuing from God's throne, the other from Christ's side, are rivers of life and hence are the same river; for with the water of grace, man washes away the guilt that brings death.

The fact that the river flows downward from heaven to earth underlines the hierarchy between heavenly things and earthly signs that the poem continually suggests, but it also suggests that the signs of heaven that earth provides may be used as guides. What is initially a barrier is revealed as a means, a directional guide and a sign of the grace heaven offers to earth. By the end of the poem, the narrator can turn his attention to heaven, his humility, penance, and attentiveness to the Mass indicating his ability to use earthly signs or sacraments as channels of grace, but channels that point back to their sources in paradise.

As the poet's use of this river underlines the nature of the visionary experience, his manipulation of the *Pearl*-dreamer's hill of revelation suggests the dreamer's movement toward God and his newly awakened ability to find heaven's reality in an earthly landscape. Significantly, the dreamer falls asleep and awakens on a "huyle," or mound, the place where he lost his pearl. The term is perhaps a reminder of the poem's elegiac purpose simply because a new grave would inevitably be mounded. However, *Pearl* contains more than one hill, and it is *Pearl*'s hills of life and revelation that perhaps help the dreamer to transform his own mound from a site of loss to one of fulfillment. We note that the dreamer sees the celestial Jerusalem from a hill, and it is from this vantage that he receives visionary proof of heaven's new life and love. The poem's third hill is metaphoric and is introduced by the maiden when she quotes Psalm 23:3–4 (678ff.): "Who shall ascend into the mountain of the Lord: or who shall stand in his holy place? The innocent in hands, and clean of heart, who hath not taken his soul in vain, nor sworn deceitfully to his neighbor."[64] The poet emends "Quis ascendit in montem Domini" (verse 3) to read "Lorde, quo schal klymbe þy hyȝ hylle" (678). This particular hill, or mountain, was generally linked with paradise and hence with the need for innocence, an interpretation that is reflected in the maiden's use of the verses and in the end line for this section of the poem: "Þe innosent is ay saf by ryȝt."[65] The need for innocence is one of the functions of the sacramental Church, manifested in the sacraments of baptism and of penance. The relationship between the need the psalm proclaims and the Church is one which both Saint Bernard and the *Pearl*-maiden stress in their discussions of this psalm.

The "hill" of Psalm 23 provides a link between the dreamer's two hills and foreshadows his subsequent vision of paradise. He ascends the hill in the visionary landscape in order to view paradise, and he ascends it after the maiden has described the innocence that is a prerequisite for heavenly citizenship. When he awakens, the hill of revelation has disappeared with his vision, but an earthly hill remains: "Þen wakned I in þat erber wlonk; / My hede vpon þat hylle watȝ layde" (1171–1172). However, the mound has become more than a static site of grief and loss; it has become the site of revelation, the stepping-off place for heaven:

Ouer þis hyul þis lote I laȝte,
For pyty of my perle enclyin,
And syþen to God I hit bytaȝte
In Krysteȝ dere blessyng and myn,
Þat in þe forme of bred and wyn
Þe preste vus scheweȝ vch a daye.

(1205–1210)

The mound has become a memorial to vision, a sign of love uncircumscribed by death, and hence the preliminary to his commitment to the sacramental life of the Church. The earthly hill or mound, then, recalls him to paradise through the channel of grace the Church provides. Just as the river of life is the "source" for earth's baptismal water, so Mount Sion is the archetype for earth's hills and mounds: the dreamer's ability to use earth's symbols as signs of a greater reality testifies to the new life, the resurrection, he has found through vision. Like vision, which comes to a man from God, earth's signs are themselves manifestations of grace which proceeds from heaven to earth in order that a man can follow these symbols to their source in God.

The poet's use of the dream vision indicates his awareness of the form's possibilities. Ideally, the visionary experience is an increasing apprehension of God. The poet underlines the dreamer's gradual spiritual illumination by noting the direction of the dreamer's movement through the landscape of vision. In fact, the parallel the poet establishes between spatial and spiritual movement is fitting because it is literally the dreamer's spirit that is in the landscape rather than his body, which lies fast asleep on the earth. In addition to indicating spiritual change through movement, a technique likewise apparent in the *Roman de la Rose*, the *Boke of the Duchesse*, and *The House of Fame*, the poet establishes a dream landscape that is hierarchical in the sense that it, too, directs us upward toward a celestial reality. Thus the dreamer moves from comparatively lesser to greater wonderment. At each stage the poet heightens the dreamer's descriptive language, indicating the progressive nature of the experience. However, while the dreamer moves through a hierarchical landscape in increasing illumination, the experience *Pearl* describes is less an awareness of the distinction between the stages of illumination than an awareness of their similarity. Though different in degree, the stages in the journey to God are similar in essentials.[66]

The poet suggests this similarity in the language with which the dreamer describes what he sees. For example, in attempt-

ing to convey the effect of certain things he sees, the dreamer
tends to describe what are different things in the same way.
Thus, he recounts the "glemande glory" of the cliffs that
first catch his eye (70); later, he notes that the rocks in the
bottom of the stream "glente" and "glowed"; he likens the
maiden to "glysnande golde" (165), saying that she awakens
in him "gladande glory." Finally, he says that the walls of
paradise are "as glemande glas" (990). The descriptions are
linked by the stress on g, by the fact that each describes light,
and by the repetition of certain adjectives and nouns. Al-
though it is possible to pass off the dreamer's persistent use
of certain sounds and words as due, in part, to the constric-
tions of the alliterative style and to the relative inadequacy
of language to convey ecstatic experience, it is noteworthy
that in section 18, which describes paradise, the dreamer
simply echoes Saint John's description and describes a city
that contains the source of light, the Lamb. Once he arrives
at this source, the "lombe-lyȝt" (1046) or the "lantyrne"
(1047), it becomes clear why the poet has not made an effort
to use a more varied language of description, for the dream-
er's descriptions of earlier stages of his experience fore-
shadow and prepare us for his apprehension of heaven. His
description of heaven is a faithful paraphrase of the Book of
Apocalypse, an account of pure light and love. The other
"lights" he encounters in the visionary landscape are simi-
lar, both in appearance and in effect, because each reflects
the "lombe-lyȝt," also the source of heaven's light. Thus, the
various things he sees that cast light are alike because each
borrows its light from God.

That the poet is indeed consciously using language to sug-
gest the interrelation of all things in God is borne out by the
dreamer's description of the river he encounters. His de-
scription of the rocks in the streambed introduces shapes
and colors and gems that later appear in his account of the
celestial city. As such, his apprehension of the stream fore-
shadows his apprehension of heaven because the effect of
the stream is a foretaste of the effect of the source of color,
light, and shape:

Swangeande swete þe water con swepe,
Wyth a rownande rourde raykande aryȝt.
In þe founce þer stonden stoneȝ stepe,
As glente þurȝ glas þat glowed and glyȝt,
As stremande sterneȝ, quen stroþe-men slepe,
Staren in welkyn, in wynter nyȝt;
For vche a pobbel in pole þer pyȝt
Watȝ emerad, saffer, oþer gemme gente,
Þat alle þe loȝe lemed of lyȝt,
So dere watȝ hit adubbement.

(111–120)

Not only does this description foreshadow that of heaven,
but it foreshadows the dreamer's own illumination and new
life. The stanza contains two similes, each of which points
toward radical spiritual change. The first says that the rocks
gleam as if through glass. The phrase awakens echoes of the
Pauline metaphor for earthly knowledge, through a glass
darkly. These stones gleam brightly, but as if through glass.
Later, when the dreamer sees them in heaven, they will gleam
without a filter. That analogy does not satisfy him; he adds
another—as stars on a winter night when "earth-men" sleep.
This might also serve as a description of the dreamer, who
sleeps in "care ful colde" and "deuely dele" (50, 51) in the
midst of color and light. This second analogy also awakens
echoes—of shepherds sleeping on a hillside, awakened by
the angels' joyous announcement of hope for a dark, cold
world that God has entered human nature. Just as the shep-
herds' despairing darkness is altered by light, so the maiden
will alter the dreamer's darkness. Both of the dreamer's anal-
ogies hint at the progressive character of the visionary move-
ment toward knowledge and illumination. He then notes
that jewels are set ("pyȝt") in the stones, a turn of phrase
that he repeats when he describes the *Pearl*-maiden as "pyȝt"
in pearls. However, his description of the Lamb as "þat gay
juelle" (1124) suggests that the maiden's ultimate value as a
gem lies in her resemblance to Christ, or in the bond of
marriage that unites her to her lord. His language intimates

the relationship between gem and setting that exists in paradise: in heaven, the two are truly bound to one another, and the setting reflects the glory of the gem it holds. On earth, however, a gem may slip from its mortal setting and from its jeweler and be lost in the grass.

The language in which the dreamer's description of the streambed is cast is but one instance of the poet's manipulation of language to indicate the link between the dreamer's experience and the nature of visionary experience in general. Language serves to describe an event in the present while foreshadowing events in the future. In this way, the two tropes that the dreamer employs to describe the rocks in the streambed indicate the splendor of what he sees, but they also suggest the possibilities of even greater knowledge, or light, at some future point. This particular technique, of using language that is both immediate and progressive, complements the poem's visionary frame; for, as vision is a gradual movement toward illumination, so does the poem's language urge us on to the source of beauty and light. The language of the poem reflects its form and reinforces its theme. The maiden teaches the dreamer about a new sort of love wherein each member of heaven is like Christ and bound to Christ and every other member through interdependent love and courtesy. The dreamer's descriptions of what he sees capture, perhaps unknowingly at first, the similitude of each element within the heavenly domain. Through vision he moves toward an awareness of likeness or similarity that the maiden's language has implied throughout their dialogue. Her tendency to pun, to expand upon an image that the dreamer has used in a constricted manner, her explanation of heavenly love, and her likeness to Christ all suggest a world of possibilities and linguistic freedom that he can affirm upon awakening.

Conclusion

Through the narrator, the poet explores what are universal problems of love and death, problems, for the Middle Ages, ultimately related to faith. In order to dramatize these problems for his audience, the poet draws upon a New Testament model for the experience *Pearl* describes. The narrator's love, his despair, his confusion, and his spiritual transformation evoke Mary Magdalene's love for Christ, despair over his death, dialogue of counsel with him, and subsequent reversal from despair to hope and belief. Mary marks her own transformation by bearing a message of eternal life and love to the disciples. The narrator of *Pearl* testifies to his spiritual renewal by describing a past experience. His use of the present tense in the last lines of his account alerts us to the continuing reality of his encounter with the celestial realm. The poet thus uses the narrator as a voice that, like the voice of Saint Augustine in *The Confessions*, recalls past loss and frustration while affirming present fulfillment and certainty. The narrator of *Pearl* speaks as a witness to resurrection.

The poet's use of the New Testament analogue not only illuminates the nature of the narrator's spiritual journey, but gives the narrator's experience an added emotional power and range. As Singleton has noted in reference to the *Vita Nuova*, there is only one drama enacted many times, the drama of reversal, of salvation. Through his handling of the narrator, the *Pearl*-poet dramatizes the impact of this movement from death to life, a movement first enacted by Mary Magdalene in the garden she thought a graveyard. That the *Pearl*-poet should exploit the *noli me tangere* episode and use it and its lessons in a fourteenth-century elegy is not surprising.[67] Experience was exemplary for medieval poets and therefore participated in the timeless. *Pearl* is an elegy in the same way that the *Vita Nuova* and the *Boke of the Duchesse* are elegies: all three poems reach beyond one death to comfort all deaths. All three poems are able to use the particular as a means of addressing the general because of the central truth of the resurrection of Christ. Whether *Pearl* is an elegy for a child (the poet's or a patron's), or for a woman whose virtue inspired the metaphor, it is a poem that seeks to console all mourners in describing the consolation of a single mourner.

The transformation *Pearl* describes is cast in the frame of a love vision, many of whose metaphors were drawn from the epithalamium and the Biblical dream vision. Both the epithalamium and the dream vision were frequently linked with the figure of the Magdalene and, in particular, with the literal and figurative understanding of her encounter with Christ in John 20. The association between that scene and the Biblical epithalamium is much easier to ascertain, for Mary was often cast as the bride of the Canticle, and the lessons, pastoral setting, and use of dialogue in both works could be used interchangeably. The links between the incident in John 20 and the visionary mode are less direct but equally compelling. First, Mary was the focus of many medieval discussions of visionary ecstasy, discussions that, at some point, touch on the love vision intimated by the Canticle. Second, the record in John 20 not only is an account of Christ's resurrection, but was seen as depicting Mary's spiritual revival or resurrection, as the version in the *Meditations on the Life of Christ* suggests.[68] For a medieval poet, dream poetry was a way of protraying spiritual resurrection, for a dreamer might fall asleep in sorrow and awaken with a sense of new life as do the *Pearl*-dreamer, the narrator of the *Boke of the Duchesse*, and Dante at various points in the *Vita Nuova*. Thematically, *Pearl* teaches a new understanding of love; it demonstrates resurrection, and the images of the epithalamium and of vision naturally complement its broader thematic concerns.

Since *Pearl* is built around an extended analogy between John's account of the Resurrection and the dreamer's account of his own experience in a garden of death and memory, it is fitting that most of the poem's central images are similes. The kingdom of heaven is like a man who had a vineyard; it is also like a pearl. The pearl is likened to Christ and to the kingdom of heaven: the maiden, the procession of virgins, and the dreamer himself, in their proximity to the pearl, become like Christ, like the kingdom of heaven. Similarly, the Church is like the vineyard and like the kingdom of heaven. For this reason, when the maiden discusses the procession of the Lamb, she says of its members, "'As lyk to hymself of lote and hwe'" (896). Her use here of the word "lyk," or of the phrase "lyk to," meaning resembling, is significant; for both the word and the phrase were those used to describe similitudes or similes, terms the poet would have used for the more modern term "analogy." In fact, the maiden's method of exposition, the dreamer's gradual apprehension, the poem's imagery, and our recognition of the nature of the poem's lessons are all related to the poet's manipulation of the simile. We, like the narrator, come to see that what is *like* Christ, may lead us to Christ.

Both thematically and imagistically, *Pearl* moves the audience to likeness through love. The success of the dreamer's spiritual adventure depends upon his recognition of similarity. Speaking of spiritual metamorphosis and perfect knowledge, Saint John says, "Dearly beloved, we are now the sons of God; and it hath not yet appeared what we shall be. We know, that, when he shall appear, we shall be like to him: because we shall see him as he is" (1 John 3:2).[69] As this verse suggests, true recognition depends on similarity. The part may stand for and contain the whole because the part is like the whole. Similarly, the poem's images are like one another because each of them expands to include Christ. The poet's use of similes seems to reflect Saint Augustine's definition of God, that he is the way and the end of the way: love is both the way and the end of the way in *Pearl*.

Like the images of the natural cycle and those of vision, the maiden reflects Christ and thus leads the dreamer to Christ. His desire to be like her moves him to an expanded awareness of love which ends by resting in the infinite. This is one reason why the maiden, or pearl, is the most elusive aspect of the poem. She is both thing and sign. The poet insists both on her reality and on her symbolic power. In her own right, she exists in celestial marriage and has achieved her true reality, or to paraphrase Saint John, has become what she should be. But for the dreamer, she is, or should be, a sign. The dreamer first sees the pearl as a "thing," his "thing," not realizing that for him she is a symbol which he must decipher and hence use. He comes to see her reflection of Christ and, instead of desiring her, desires reflective power of his own. His wish to be a pearl at the end of the poem testifies to his transformation. Like the audience, he must move through the appearance of a symbol to what it is like, before his love takes on the infinite and fluid quality of celestial courtesy. As the narrator moves beyond simple mutability, the experiential world begins to reflect the movement between heaven and earth. At the same time, the poet expands his original images, adding simile to simile, until we, like the narrator, come to see them as the same thing. Like the citizens of paradise, the images of *Pearl* are splendidly alike.

The elegiac themes and techniques of *Pearl* reflect the concerns of the fourteenth century. As Rosemary Woolf has demonstrated, the emotional appeal of late medieval dramas and lyrics was intended as the first step of what should be a devotional or meditative response. In this sense, *Pearl* is a document of its time. As Christ's word "Mary" fell on the distracted, grief-stricken Magdalene, so the maiden's voice falls on a blinking, confused dreamer. As empathetic viewers of these encounters, we participate in the miraculous. But the new life must be understood and desired before it becomes a fact—hence the visionary dialogue which teaches the dreamer as it speaks a familiar, but perhaps forgotten, message to the audience. The poem's use of analogy, its emotional appeal, its harmonious imagery speak in the precise and economical language of the fourteenth century. Unlike later elegies, *Pearl* is not concerned with political or ecclesiastical corruption, with lasting monuments, or with the life of poetry. It is concerned with faith and the movement beyond the senses, in love, in faith, and in perception. The poem and its impact rest on reversal or resurrection. In their despair and need for actual proof, neither the figure of Mary Magdalene nor the narrator is unusual. *Pearl*'s first-person narrative underlines the message of resurrection by saying, with Mary, "I have seen it." *Pearl* bears witness to a transformation of memory. This is a part of the poem's message to its world. The narrator's world, like Mary's, and like ours, takes on color and perspective with the new knowledge of rebirth. The process of rebirth begins with love, however limited or foolish: love is catalyst, way, and end of the movement which, for the Middle Ages, rested finally in God.

Conclusion: "He Cryed So Cler"

I began this study by stating that I share the view of most medievalists that the four poems of the *Pearl* manuscript are the creations of a single poet, whose work will bear the closest scrutiny. The poems, in fact, offer many of the characteristic strengths and pleasures T. S. Eliot found in Dante: economy of language, clear visual imagery, and unity of poetic, structural, philosophical, and theological concerns. Not only are the poems unified individually, but they seem to share a common series of interests, themes, assumptions, and techniques which suggests that their being bound together in a single manuscript was not accidental. Though without external evidence it is, of course, impossible to answer definitively the question of common authorship, a study of the poems naturally alerts us to links among them. Taken both individually and as a group, they suggest an artist whose control of style, tone, and theme and whose command of traditional forms and techniques resulted in poems that proclaim a single message.

The manuscript itself hints at an arrangement designed with an eye to thematic coherence. The manuscript begins with *Pearl*, a startling record of inner experience, an experience that alerts us to the need for purity before we can hope to become a cherished pearl, a bride of Christ. In *Purity*, the second poem, the poet also underlines the need for purity by considering the implications of human choice as they can be perceived in the more public record of Biblical history. Both poems emphasize the need for penance: for, without penitential cleansing, we are fit neither for spiritual marriage, nor for the wedding feast. Furthermore, both poems play upon the theme of perception and thus emphasize the faculty of sight, an emphasis that probably owes a good deal to Christ's statement in Matthew that the pure shall "see God." The theme of perception in both poems is ultimately related to the poet's two attempts to portray the kingdom of heaven: in *Pearl* as an interrelated hierarchy of lovers within Saint John's celestial city; in *Purity* as a hierarchical and bounteous wedding banquet. These two poems, exploring both inner experience and the ways in which inner purity is manifested in human behavior, thus seem to complement one another imagistically and thematically. The last two poems in the manuscript, *Patience* and *Sir Gawain*, likewise seem to be paired. Both poems are accounts of protagonists who function as representatives of certain ideals and as figures for everyman. While the poet treats both figures with a certain amount of comedy, pointing up the vagaries of man as he ignores or misunderstands the nature of the demands placed upon him, ultimately the poet uses Jonah and Sir Gawain to stress the need for penance. Both poems are therefore pointed demonstrations of human failure and inadequacy, preparing us for the final section of the manuscript, the depiction of Sir Gawain's renewal. Here, the poet demonstrates the process by which man may turn from an old world to a new; in short, he shows us what we must do before we may hope for status as a pearl, the subject of the first poem in the manuscript.

There are, however, other equally significant connections among the poems in the manuscript. In both *Purity* and *Sir Gawain*, the poet emphasizes the sin of "untrawþe," a word associated in both poems with Adam. Furthermore, both poems consider human inadequacy by drawing upon the triad of sins traditionally associated with the fall of Adam and the temptation of Christ. In addition, *Sir Gawain*, *Purity*, and *Patience* not only link man to Adam, but place man against a backdrop of mythic history, English or Biblical. Thus, all three poems suggest that we see their protagonists as exemplary and history as a record of past action that has an organic and continuing relationship to the present; for, as the poems imply in their use of history, present time may become past time for another age, a memory of former glories, mistakes, and choices. In *Patience* and *Pearl* the poet uses a first-person narrator to heighten the dramatic impact of the poems and to draw us into each account of human experience. Moreover, in Jonah and the narrator of *Pearl*, he creates protagonists who are remarkably similar in their egocentricity, a self-involvement that dominates their actions, their patterns of speech, and their perceptions. *Sir Gawain* and *Pearl* demonstrate, in different ways, the process of radical spiritual change that is, I believe, the underlying theme of the manuscript. Finally, many of the same terms frequently applied to *Pearl* might be used to describe the *Pearl* manuscript; for, like a double diptych, the group seems to fall into two pairs, but each poem also relates to and reflects the concerns, allusions, language, and technique of the other three. We are left with four poems whose affinities appear integral and fundamental, and not merely ornamental.

Most obviously, the poems display similar rhetorical strategies. To borrow a phrase from Coleridge, each poem has its tail in its mouth;[1] for the last lines of each poem echo its opening lines, reminding us of the series of considerations with which it begins. However, the verbal similarity between a poem's beginning and its end does not impose a merely artificial sense of unity; rather, the technique serves to remind us of the distance we have traveled from those introductory considerations and impressions. The problems the poet introduces in the opening lines—of the difficulty of attaining patience, of the beauties of purity and the ugliness

of impurity, of insurmountable grief, and of historical flux—
are explored and resolved by the narratives they introduce.
Thus, whereas the opening stanzas of *Sir Gawain* provide no
remedy for man's problems in time, Sir Gawain's experience
suggests an antidote for man's failures, desires, and fears by
indicating a way of transcending those limitations by tran-
scending time. Similarly, each of the poems, though appear-
ing to describe a circle, in fact describes a series of progres-
sions—a spiral?—that only appears to return to where it
began. Dante perhaps provides the best analogy: though the
pilgrim moves in a circle—going from earth to Hell to pur-
gatory to paradise and back to earth—he does not return to
that dark wood except in memory, for his understanding of
earth and of the self has been dramatically altered by the
journey he has taken. Thus, while we return with the *Pearl*-
dreamer to an earthly garden, our vision has been refocused
by his account of heavenly gardens and undying love.

These external similarities, however, are the outward
manifestations of even more striking internal similarities. If
it were necessary to isolate a single technical characteristic
the poems have in common, that choice, I believe, would fall
upon the structural unity of each poem. The poems may be
compared to late Gothic pictures or cathedrals, for each has
a plan that, once discovered, illuminates each of its ele-
ments. To recast a notion of twentieth-century esthetics,
each poem is a tribute to the union of form and function,
eloquence and wisdom. For example, the opening stanzas of
Pearl, which evoke the scene of Mary's search for the body
of Christ, provide the poet with a dominant theme, a range
of imagery, a possible form, and a potential resolution. The
dream vision, the dialogue, the nature of the dialogue, the
action, and the choice and manipulation of images all emerge
from those introductory stanzas in which the narrator mourns
a pearl that has slipped from his grasp. Likewise, the text
with which *Patience* begins, the Parable of the Wedding Feast
in *Purity*, and the introductory stanzas of *Sir Gawain*, a
chronicle of the fall of civilizations, all serve as organizing
principles, or schemes, for each poem.

The poet, of course, shares his interest in organization with his age, for the poems of the *Pearl* manuscript, like other examples of late Gothic style, are informed by the idea of order. Our recognition of such a fundamental belief in order prevents us from taking seemingly insignificant details as mere decoration: we cannot ignore what the Christ child may have in his hands in a painting, the Wife of Bath's spurs, a shield decorated with a pentangle linked to Solomon, a maiden likened to the pearl of great price, or a protagonist who, throughout medieval Europe, was depicted as a type of Christ. Each of these details is finally relevant to the plan that governs the logic of poems or pictures. It is, however, a tribute to the *Gawain*-poet that we must discover the plan for each poem, for he was artist enough to conceal its scaffolding, to create works whose architectonics rarely, if ever, intrude upon our appreciation of them as poems.

Not only do these poems have similar rhetorical strategies, but each bears witness to the poet's sensitivity to language. Working within the obvious restrictions of the alliterative style and frequently employing complicated patterns of rhyme and meter, the poet nonetheless achieves a lively, varied, and fresh effect. For example, the poet, as Gordon notes in the introduction to his edition of *Pearl*, "subjected himself to a double discipline, that of alliterative verse itself, and that of an elaborate rhyme-scheme combined with stanza-linking by echo and refrain."[2] Despite strictures that could easily result—as they do in many medieval alliterative poems—in mechanical language, wordiness, and forced rhymes, *Pearl* evinces a poet who knew how to use language and meter effectively. The end lines to the sections, like the bob-and-wheel refrains of *Sir Gawain*, serve a purpose: the poet uses such techniques to underscore a theme or to offer a new perspective on preceding action. Frequently, these lines alert us to important issues that perhaps went unnoticed upon a first reading of a stanza.

Although a single poem, such as *Pearl*, bespeaks the poet's linguistic dexterity, only if we see that poem in relation to the others do we begin to gauge the full measure of the poet's sensitivity to language. Linguistically, each poem enriches and is enriched by the other three. For example, the phrase "at ese," connoting sensual gratification and physical comfort, is used to describe Sir Gawain's comfort in sleeping late beneath Hautdesert's rich bed coverings and the delights of the guests at the wedding feast in *Purity*; the word "won" (dwelling) describes both the *Pearl*-maiden's home in paradise and Jonah's beneath the woodbine. While there is nothing inappropriate in finding pleasure at the Lord's table or in seeing heaven as a dwelling place, it is less salutory to take too much comfort in either blankets or woodbines. It will not do to ascribe such repetitions to the so-called limitations of Middle English, the richness and flexibility of which both Chaucer and the *Gawain*-poet fully exploit. Sadly, this aspect of the *Gawain*-poet's talent tends to disappear in translation: it is impossible, for example, to convey the felicities of a phrase like "lombe-lyȝt" used to describe Christ in *Pearl*. Like Chaucer, the *Gawain*-poet appears to use words with an awareness of their implied meanings and connotations. Just as Chaucer in *The Canterbury Tales* uses a word such as "pitee" or "quyte" in all sorts of situations, playing with and changing a word's meaning, so the author of these poems seems to expect us to recognize recurring words and phrases and to consider their various meanings. Once we recognize that the Knight uses a word one way and the Reeve another, we should then recognize that the narrator of *Pearl* and the maiden seem to use words differently, whereas Hautdesert and Camelot speak the same debased tongue.

The poet's handling of the rhythms of speech is as effective as his understanding of semantics; here, too, he is rarely explicit, but allows language to suggest meaning. His dramatization of Jonah in *Patience* is, in this sense, a masterpiece of economy. Rather than simply describing Jonah's actions and retelling the Book of Jonah, the poet allows Jonah to speak for himself. Jonah's own use of language—his inflated rhetoric and his continual use of *I*, *my*, and *me*—tells us more about the nature and effects of faulty reasoning than we would learn from a narrator who told us that Jonah's fear and egotism blind him to logic. From listening to Jonah, we can deduce his errors and his lack of charity, which suggests that the poet was certain enough of his abilities to allow us to appreciate the poem and to learn from it without feeling the necessity of glossing each incident. Similarly, the poet draws upon Jonah's conventional typological function but does not belabor the association; instead, those associations inform our understanding of Jonah's actions and make it possible for the poet to evoke both the weaknesses of Adam and the perfections of Christ in his description of the unruly prophet.

The poet's use of images, like his use of language, illustrates his exploitation of medieval tradition. For example, in *Pearl*, he need not describe the narrator's garden in detail, for it is a garden that appears over and over again in medieval literature; the few stanzas he devotes to describing the garden suggest its relationship to other landscapes of love, frustration, and visionary experience. Yet the poet's use of this series of associations is his own. With a few strokes, he sketches the scene, letting the narrator describe the pastoral landscape from his own point of view, thereby alerting us to the type of garden it is, to its relevance to the narrator, and to the narrator's particular problem. That initial garden is the first in a succession of pastoral landscapes the narrator encounters, and, throughout the poem, the poet avoids the trap of making the implicit explicit but allows one garden to succeed another. Our understanding of the poet's use of these pastoral landscapes is cumulative, and in many ways approximates the experience the narrator describes in the poem; for each successive garden enriches our understanding of the original landscape of love and loss until we, too, come to see the narrator's final view of the natural realm as fitting and right. When we find ourselves back, with him, in a graveyard, the monument to death manifests far more than mutability; it stands as an avenue to earthly gardens of labor and as a sign of heavenly gardens of harvest and pleasure. *Sir Gawain* testifies to the same awareness of the uses of imagery: in the subtle comparisons he draws between the accouterments of

Arthur's and Bercilak's courts and in his deft substitution of the girdle for the shield, the poet adumbrates many of the themes of the poem. In realizing the visual impact of certain images, the poet displays a sense of his art; for he throws a picture upon a screen, apparently sure that he can suggest what lesser poets would stop to explain.

Thematically, too, the poems share a common focus: from various perspectives, the poems address the problem of spiritual inadequacy. Sir Gawain's failure in "trawþe," the *Pearl*-dreamer's failures in understanding, Jonah's failure in charity, all reflect the characteristic flaws of the descendants of Adam, whom the poet describes in *Purity* as "a freke þat fayled in trawþe" (236). "Freke" means "man," a word that epitomizes the poet's central theme. Thus, the poet scrutinizes human nature. He offers us Sir Gawain, a man who exists within the framework of English myth and of the ideals of medieval chivalry. He offers us, in *Pearl*, a narrator whose grief and incomprehension are juxtaposed with the fullness and clarity of the celestial realm. He offers us Jonah, who is fearful, egocentric, and uncharitable, seen from the two perspectives of typological and historic time. Finally, in *Purity*, he places man's general desires and failings against the backdrop of providential history, pointing up the choices each man must make in time. In *Purity*, he externalizes our sense of the choices human life affords by drawing upon the strikingly visual image of the wedding garment. Though the other three poems describe more ambiguous situations and are far less explicit, the choice each protagonist faces is the same, whether or not the choice is admitted.

The poet, however, conveys how important it is to acknowledge that choice exists. We find in these poems a sense of urgency, an urgency differently expressed, but similarly intent, by Harry Baily in response to the Parson's deliberation about beginning his tale: "But hasteth yow, the sonne wole adoun." Each poem suggests the necessity of recognizing the choice between God and the self by scrutinizing man within the strictures of time. Nineveh's "time" depends upon Jonah's willingness to preach, thus granting Nineveh an opportunity to repent its sins and giving God the chance to substitute mercy for justice. A similar sense of urgency is apparent in *Purity,* which presents us with three civilizations, each of which refuses the opportunity for penance in time and dooms itself to destruction.

In *Pearl* and *Sir Gawain,* the poet's emphasis upon and handling of time is more subtle but equally purposeful. The narrator in *Pearl,* who languishes from time's effects, dreams in the realm of mutability of an immutable realm. It is the maiden's job to warn the dreamer of time's limits: once the sun is down, there is no opportunity to work in the vineyard and hence no chance to earn a "peny," which is like the kingdom of heaven. In *Sir Gawain,* the poet evokes the theme of fallen cities, placing Sir Gawain and Arthur's court against a background of waste. However, the poet also suggests a remedy for transience in these two poems by providing us with a glimpse of worlds uncircumscribed by time. In *Pearl,* the picture of the celestial realm serves this purpose, offering the dreamer more than a cycle of death and decay. In *Sir Gawain,* the poet juxtaposes his picture of fallen cities and of Camelot's youth and heedlessness with a cycle of sanctified time through his references to the liturgical calendar. His references to certain dates in that calendar point up the stability of the Church year and the belief that time may be ordered according to truths that are themselves impervious to change.

It is his emphasis on man's ability to choose, which is his ability to change, that lightens the poet's seemingly dark depiction of man's limitations and failures; like Chaucer, the *Gawain*-poet preaches penance to his age. Donald Howard has described the Parson's Tale as "a book on sin sandwiched into a book on penitence."[3] Though I would not describe the Parson's Tale as a "book on sin," Howard's term for *The Canterbury Tales* might well apply to the *Pearl* manuscript. What the Parson explicitly urges, the other *Canterbury Tales* and the poems of the *Pearl* manuscript implicitly urge—that we redirect our desires and wills, choosing life and plenitude, rather than the lack (the Parson uses the word "defaute") of sin. That knowledge is crucial to that process of redirection is borne out by both Chaucer and the *Gawain*-poet. Just as Chaucer, through his Parson, allows us to understand the nature of sin by describing its outward manifestation in overly elaborate clothing or in such habits as backbiting, so the *Gawain*-poet allows us to understand sin and failure by depicting or dramatizing them. Hence, we observe Sir Gawain in Hautdesert and so understand something of the complexities of avarice, just as it is to be hoped that we become more aware of the subtle traps the world lays for each one of us. We listen to the narrator of *Pearl* and hear what solipsism sounds like. Chaucer's Parson, however, does not end his tale with sin, but closes by praising the living "fruyt" of that tree of penance; likewise, the *Gawain*-poet describes more than failure. In each poem, he offers us something finer, more delightful, than self and sin, offering us, implicitly, a picture of man redeemed and, thus, truly himself.

Save in *Purity*, the poet's concern with penance is expressed dramatically, rather than didactically. *Purity*'s more overt didacticism is perhaps why it is the least successful of the poems for a modern reader. The poet's more usual approach is that of the dramatist. Even in *Purity*, the poet's rendering of Old Testament history is intended to show us rather than to tell us, and his interpolation of the Parable of the Wedding Feast conveys the delights of heaven by describing the satisfactions of an earthly banquet. Had he altered its tone and refashioned the passages that connect its various narratives, *Purity* would not startle a reader used to the finely drawn comparisons and suggestions of the other three poems.

The poet uses the dramatic appeal of his work to a serious purpose, vivifying in different ways the critical moments of human life. The comic drama of Sir Gawain evading his hostess leads into the serious, but no more dramatic, decision to accept the girdle and not to mention the gift to his host. The *Pearl*-dreamer's awakening is also a dramatization of the mental reversal that makes it possible for the narrator to shift perspectives upon the physical world. Given the vision he has just experienced, he is presented with a choice:

he may pick up his lament where he left off, or he may incorporate his dialogue with the maiden into his views of the world around him. What we see, as we participate in the final stanzas of *Pearl*, is a man who chooses, not without a struggle, to accept the truth of his dream and to live the rest of his life accordingly. Jonah's instability and egotism are a dramatic heightening of human wilfullness and misunderstanding and underline the insufficiencies of man without God.

The poet uses these dramatic moments to draw the audience into the poems. His artistry is directed at empathy: the confusion, anger, fear, and anguish he describes are human and therefore ours. The poems demand that we recognize ourselves and that we recognize human failure for what it is. To ignore the failure is to ignore the remedy. As these poems demonstrate, only the damned refuse knowledge. Balthazar is a prime example: refusing to listen to Daniel, he chooses an ignoble death. As *Sir Gawain* implies, it is better to return to Camelot wearing the badge of self-recognition than to wear the badge without seeking to understand its implications and fall prey to the chaos of time's judgments.

These poems not only reveal an awareness of the various techniques of narrative poetry and an effective use of images and language; they reveal a mind capable of drawing upon and reshaping traditional medieval views. The poems themselves display a knowledge of traditional literary forms—the homily, the dream vision, and the romance—as well as a knowledge of medieval religious thought. However, there are many bad homiletic poems, wooden dream visions, mechanical romances, and numbing poetic accounts of Biblical events in the long history of medieval literature. These four poems suggest a mind flexible enough to use the traditions available to a medieval poet—to combine Biblical stories, to rephrase the formula of the Arthurian romance, to allow exegetical interpretations to inform his use of Biblical passages in ways that are fresh and compelling. The description in *Sir Gawain* of the seasonal cycle is an apt example of the poet's recasting of a traditional literary form. The poet shapes his account of the natural year in such a way that the tone of the passage suggests its meaning for the poem. By paying attention to his use of adjectives describing the winds of each season, to the verbs characterizing the "labors" of each season, to the variations in pace, and to the context of the piece, we can then recognize the urgency of Gawain's and Camelot's position within a world dominated by a natural cycle that hastens to harvest and death. Similarly, in *Pearl*, his handling of the Parable of the Vineyard reinforces the traditional allegorical interpretations of the parable, linking labor in the vineyard to active Christian charity, because he plays upon our awareness of the brevity of any gardener's "day." In short, the poet employs figurative language, Biblical allusions, and traditional forms, but is not employed by them.

To return to where I began, the commonly held assumption that the poems are the work of a single hand is reinforced by a study of the poems in relation to each other. If we take the broader connotations of a term like rhetoric, the four poems share striking rhetorical similarities, just as they share a common focus upon man, inadequate to the task at hand, but splendidly adequate should he graft the new Adam onto the old. In fact, a picture of a certain sort of craftsman emerges from a study of the four poems—an artist who was fully aware of the resources the late fourteenth century offered a poet and who took full advantage of the ideals, traditions, and possibilities of his own English culture. Formally and technically, none of the poems could be written today; on the other hand, few medieval poets were capable of the sorts of things we find in these poems. Too often we find poets dominated by form and poems whose mechanical parts are all too evident.

In contrast, the experience of reading *Pearl* can be simple or complex. Read with an eye to its tone, imagery, and point of view, *Pearl* makes a clear and compelling statement. However, in order to probe the poem's peculiar power, to participate in the haunting situation the poem describes, and to appreciate the source for the extraordinary sense of renewal and release in the closing lines, it is important to glimpse the New Testament drama behind the fourteenth-century scene. The poet's use of analogy in *Pearl* is dramatic and mythic, for he draws upon an episode of enormous significance for his audience. The narrator's grief captures our grief for all things lost on earth precisely because the poet exploits the drama of the *noli me tangere* episode, thereby evoking a universal experience of loss. An understanding of that Biblical episode within the context of medieval thought illuminates the logic that undergirds the poem and places *Pearl* within the framework of a specific series of techniques and concerns. But at no point does the poet sacrifice the poem to its "figure," or poetry to analogy.

The *Gawain*-poet's talents are, however, at the service of his "sentence"; for the poems are ultimately directed at an audience used to thinking of literature as a vehicle for meaning and hence of poetry as something that can be probed and understood by a process of rational thought. Although—and I turn again to Eliot's comments on Dante—we need not share either the poet's concerns or his beliefs in order to appreciate the learning, craft, and imagination with which he treats fundamental issues of medieval life, we must recognize those concerns if we are fully to understand the poems. Since the poet was a Christian Englishman of the late fourteenth century, we need to see him within the context of his country, his religious beliefs, and his age. The poems are the products of a particular mind and point of view; they are directed to an age concerned with national stability and individual reform, and accustomed to hearing those concerns expressed through poetry. As a Christian poet writing for a Christian and, most likely, a sophisticated audience, the poet confronts human problems and offers Christian remedies in narrative poetry designed to interest, prompt speculation, and convey the urgency of the times, for men and for England.

Appendix

Notes

Index

Appendix:
De Maria
Magdalena

Incipit omelia Beati Anselmi super Johannem de planctu Magdalene.

In illo tempore Maria stabat ad monumentum foris, plorans. Et reliqua.

Audivimus, fratres, Mariam ad monumentum foris stantem, audivimus Mariam foris plorantem: Videamus, si possumus, cur staret, videamus et cur ploraret. Prosit nobis illius [illam] stare, prosit nobis illius [illam] plorare. Amor faciebat eam stare, dolor cogebat eam plorare.

Stabat et circumspiciebat si forte videret quem diligebat; plorabat vero, quia sublatum estimabat quem querebat. Dolor renovatus erat, quia quem prius doluerat deffunctum, nunc dolebat ablatum; et iste dolor major erat, quia nullam consolationem habebat. Primi fuit causa doloris, quia vivum perdiderat; sed de hoc dolore aliquantulam consolationem habebat, quia mortuum se retinere credebat. Nunc autem de isto se consolari non poterat, quia vel corpus deffuncti non inveniebat; metuebatque ne amor magistri sui in pectore suo frigesceret, quo viso recalesceret.

Venerat autem Maria ad monumentum, defferens secum

aromata et unguenta que preparaverat, ut, sicut antea pedes viventis unguento precioso unxerat, sic etiam nunc corpus deffuncti totum et unguento ungeret et aromatibus condiret; et, sicut prius ad pedes Domini Jhesu lacrimas fuderat, ita nunc ad monumentum lacrimas funderet. Fleverat prius et lacrimis suis pedes ejus rigaverat pro morte anime sue, veniebat nunc cum lacrimis monumentum rigare pro morte magistri sui. Cum autem non inveniret corpus in monumento, labor unguenti periit, sed dolor lugendi crevit. Defuit obsequio qui non defuit dolori; defuit quem condiret, sed non defuit quem ploraret; eoque magis plorabat, quo ille magis deerat.

Plorabat itaque vehementer Maria, quoniam additus erat dolor super dolorem; duosque dolores ex unios [unico] viro gestabat in corde, quos mitigare volebat lacrimis, sed non valebat. Et ita posita in dolore, mente et corpore defficiebat, et quid ageret nescienbat [nesciebat]. Quid enim ista mulier poterat, nisi plorare, que intollerabilem habebat dolorem? Et nullum inveniebat consolatorem. Petrus quidem et Johannes venerant cum ea ad monumentum: sola plorans, et quasi desperando desperans! Petrus et Johannes timuerunt et ideo non steterunt: Maria non timebat, quia nichil suspicabatur sibi superesse pro quo timere deberet. Perdiderat enim magistrum suum, quem ita singulariter diligebat, ut preter eum nil posset diligere et nil posset sperare. Perdiderat vitam anime sue; et jam melius arbitrabatur fore sibi mori quam vivere, quia forsitan moriens inveniret quem vivens invenire non poterat, sine quo tamen vivere non valebat; fortis namque est ut mors dilectio ejus. Quid namque aliud faceret? Mors in Maria facta erat exanimis, facta erat insensibilis; sentiens, non sentiebat; videns, non videbat; audiens, non audiebat: sed neque ibi erat, quia tota ibi erat, ubi magister suus erat, de quo tamen ubi esset nesciebat. Querebat enim eum et non inveniebat; et ideo stabat ad monumentum et plorabat, tota lacrimabilis, tota miserabilis.

O Maria, quid spei, quid consilii, aut quid cordis erat tibi, ut sola stares ad monumentum, discipulis abeuntibus? Tu ante illos prevenisti et cum ipsis rediisti et post illos remansisti: cur hoc fecisti? Sapiebas plus illis, aut diligebas plus quam illi, quia non metuebas ubi illi.

Certe nil sapiebat Maria, nisi diligere et pro dilecto dolere. Oblita erat timorem, oblita era semetipsam, oblita erat denique omnia, preter illum quem diligebat super omnia. Et quid mirabile est, si sic erat oblita etiam ut ipsum non agnosceretur [agnosceret], in momento enim illum non quereret, sed verba illius in mente retineret, sed de vivente gauderet, nec de sublato ploraret, sed de resurgente exultaret? Dixerat Jhesus quia sic moreretur, quod tercia die resurgeret. Sed pro [proh] dolor! Et nimius dolor cor illius repleverat, et memoriam horum verborum deleverat: sensus nullus in ea remanserat, omne consilium ab ea perierat, spes omnis deffecerat, solummodo flere supererat; flebat ergo, quia flere poterat.

Et dum fleret, inclinavit se et prospexit in monumentum, et vidit duos angelos in albis sedentes, unum ad caput et alium [unum] ad pedes, qui dicunt ei: Mulier, quid ploras?

O Maria, multam consolationem invenisti, et forsitan tibi melius contingit quam sperasti: nam tu querebas unum et duos invenisti. Querebas hominem, et angelos invenisti, et viventesque [viventes] vidisti. Querebas mortuum, et viventes reperisti eos, qui videntur curam de te habere et qui volunt dolorem tuum lenire. Ille vero quem queris dolorem tuum videtur negligere, lacrimas tuas non videtur modo respicere: vocas enim illum et non audit, oras et non exaudit, queris illum et non invenis, pulsas et tibi non apperit, sequeris illum et fugit. Heu! quid est hoc? Heu! quam magna mutacio! Heu! quomodo mutata est res in contrarium! Iste est Jhesus qui recessit a te? Et quomodo? Forte nescio an diligat te. Olim te diligebat; olim a Phariseo deffendebat, et a sorore tua dulciter excusabat. Olim laudabat te, quando pedes suos unguento ungebas, lacrimis rigabas et capillis tergebas. Dolorem tuum mulcebat, peccata tua dimittebat, olim querebat te cum non adesses, mandabat per sororem tuam ut ad se venires: Magister, inquit, adest et vocat te.

O quam cito surrexit Maria ut audivit! Quam cito venit! solito more cecidit ad pedes tuos, o bone Jhesu! Tu quoque cum vidisti eam tristatam, contristatus es; et cum vidisti lacrimantem, lacrimatus es! O quam pie consolando eam dixisti: Ubi posuisti eum? Denique pro dilectione ejus que multum dilexit te, fratrem suum Lazarum suscitasti, et planctum hujus dilecte tue in gaudium convertisti! Et, o dulcissime magister, quid post hec peccavit in te hec discipula tua, aut in quo postea offendit dulcedinem cordis hec amatrix tua, quia sic recedis ab ea? Nos post hec de ea nullum peccatum audivimus, nisi quia valde mane ad monumentum venit ante omnes ferens unguenta quibus ungeret corpus tuum, et cum non invenisset te, cucurrit et nunciavit discipulis tuis. Illi venerunt, viderunt et abicrunt. Hec autem stat et plorat. Si hoc peccatum est, negare non possumus quin ipsa hoc faciat; si autem peccatum non est, nec cesset amor et desiderium quod de te habet. Quare sic recedis ab ea et abscondis te? Tu diligis omnes diligentes te, qui inveniris ab omnibus querentibus te. Tu dicis: Ego diligentes me diligo, et qui mane vigilaverit ad me inveniet me. Ergo mulier ista que valde mane vigilat ad te, cur non invenit te? Quare non consolaris lacrimas quas fudit pro fratre suo? Si tu solito more diligas eam, cur desiderium ejus tam diu protrahis? O verax magister et testis fidelis, recordare testimonii quod olim de Maria reddidisti. Marthe, sorori sue, dixisti enim: Maria optimam partem elegit, quia elegit te; sed quo modo verum est: Que non aufferetur ab ea, si tu es ablatus ab ea? Sed quod ab ea non est ablata pars quam elegit, quare plorat et quid conqueritur? Certe Maria nichil querit, nisi quod elegit, et propter hoc plorare non desinit, quia quod elegit nunc perdidit. Ergo, o custos hominum, aut tu partem, quam elegit, custodi in ea, aut ego nescio quo modo verum sit: Que non aufferetur ab ea, nisi etiam hoc intelligatur qui [quod], licet tu sis ablatus de ore ejus, occulus ejus [tuus] non est ablatus de corde ejus.

Sed, o Maria, quid jam amplius moraris? Quid turbaris? Quid ploras? Ecce habes angelos: sufficiat tibi angelorum visio, quia forsitan ille quem queris, quem ploras, sentit aliquid in te, propter quod non vult videri a te. Pone jam finem dolori tuo. Sit modus lacrimis tuis. Recordare quod dixit tibi

et aliis mulieribus: Nolite, ait, flere super me. Ergo quid est
hoc quod facis? Ipse flere prohibuit, et tu tantum flere non
desinis! Timeo ne plorando ipsum offendas, eoque sic inces-
santer ploras [plores]. Nam si ipse amaret lacrimas tuas, non
posset fortassis, ut olim, continere lacrimas suas. Nunc ergo
audi consilium meum. Susurat [susurrat] tibi angelorum
consolacio; mane cum illis, interroga illos, si forte sciant
quod factum est de illo quem queris et quem ploras. Certe
ego credo quod ipsi ad hoc venerunt, ut testimonium perhi-
beant, et credo quod ipse quem ploras misit ipsos pro se et
pro te, ut annuncient resurreccionem suam et consolarentur
[consolentur] deploracionem tuam.

Dicunt ei: Mulier, quid ploras? Quid est tanta causa do-
loris? Non abscondas a nobis lacrimas tuas. Aperi nobis an-
imum tuum, et nos indicabimus tibi desiderium tuum.

Maria nimio dolore confecta, tota in excessu mentis po-
sita, nullam reperit consolacionem et ad nullum attendit
consolatorem. Sed infra se cogitavit, dicens: Proth dolor!
Qualis visitacio est ista? Quero si sunt in omnes consola-
tores generat modo et non consolentur me. Ego enim quero
Creatorem meum, et gravis est michi ad videndum omnis
creatura. Nolo angelos videre, nolo cum angelis manere, quia
possunt dolorem meum augere, non possunt penitus delere.
Si ceperint michi multa narrare, et si ego voluero eis ad om-
nia respondere, timeo ut amorem meum magis impediant
quam expediant. Denique, ego quero non angelos, sed eum
qui fecit et me et angelos. Non quero angelos, sed mei et
angelorum Dominum. Tulerunt Dominum meum; ipsum
solum quero; ipse me solus potest consolari; sed nescio ubi
posuerunt eum. Circumspicio si videam illum, et non video.
Vellem invenire locum ubi positus est, et non invenio. Heu!
me miseram! Quid agam? Quo ibo? Quo abiit dilectus meus?
Quesivi illum in monumento, et non inveni; vocavi, et non
respondit michi. Heu me! Ubi queram illum? Ubi eum in-
veniam? Surgam certe et circuibo omnia loca que potero.
Non dabo sompnum occulis meis, non dabo requiem pedi-
bus meis, donec inveniam illum quem diligit anima mea.
Effundite lacrimas, occuli mei, plorate et nolite defficere;

ambulate, pedes mei, currite et nolite quiescere. Heu, heu! Quo abiit gaudium meum? Ubi latet amor meus? Ubi est dulcedo mea? Cur dereliquisti me, salus mea? O dolores! O angustie intollerabiles! Angustie enim sunt michi undique, et quid eligam ignoro. Si a monumento recessero, infelix, nescio quo vadam, nescio ubi requiram. Discedere a monumento mors michi est; stare ad monumentum irremediabilis dolor est. Melius est michi sepulcrum Domini mei custodire, quam ab eo longius ire. Si enim longius abiero, forte cum rediero, ipsum sublatum inveniam aut deffunctum. Stabo igitur et hic moriar, ut statim juxta sepulcrum Domini mei sepeliar. O quam beatum erit corpus meum, si fuerit sepultum juxta magistrum meum! O quam felix anima mea que, egrediens de fragili vase corporis mei, mox potest ingredi sepulcrum Domini mei! Corpus meum semper fuit anime mee labor et dolor: sepulcrum Domini mei erit illi requies et honor! Hoc ergo sepulcrum in vita mei [mea] erit consolacio mea; in morte mea erit requies mea. Vivens juxta illud manebo, moriens illi adherebo. Nec viva, nec mortua ab illo separabor. Heu, me infelicem! Quare ergo tunc non prospexi? Quare ergo tunc non steti? Quare monumentum et corpus ejus tunc perseveranter non custodivi? Nunc certe non plorarem sublatum quem ante vi prohibuissem, aut sublatores subsequta fuissem. Sed proth dolor! Ego volui observare legem, et dimisi Dominum legis. Ego legi obedivi, et eum cui lex obedit non custodivi, quamvis cum ipso manere non fuisset legem transgredi, sed adimplere: Pascha enim ab isto deffuncto non contaminatur, sed renovatur. Mortuus iste non polluit mundos, sed mundat immundos; sanat omnes tangentes, sed illuminat omnes accedentes ad se. Sed quid recuso dolorem meum? Abii, redii, monumentum apertum inveni: ipsum autem quem querebam non inveni. Stabo itaque et expectabo, si forte alicubi appareat. Sed quo modo stabo sola? Abierunt discipuli et me solam plorantem relinquerunt [reliquerunt]. Nusquam apparet qui mecum doleat, nusquam apparet qui mecum Dominum meum requirat. Apparuerunt angeli, sed nescio pro qua causa apparuerunt. Si consolari me vellent, causam pro qua ploro non ignorarent.

Si enim non ignorarent cur ploro, cur dicunt michi: Quid
ploras? An interrogant, ut plorare prohibeant? Queso, non
hoc michi suadent [suadeant], alioquin me interficiant. Quid
plura? Ego illis non obediam, et dum vivo [vivam] plorare
non desinam, donec Dominum meum inveniam. Sed quid
faciam, nisi ipsum inveniam? Quo me convertam? Ad quem
ibo? A quo consilium petam? Quem percunctabor? Quis mi-
chi miserebitur? Quis consolabitur? Quis indicabit michi
quem diligit anima mea, ubi positus sit, ubi cubat [cubet],
ubi quiescat? Queso, nunciate illi quia amore langueo et
dolore defficio; nec est dolor sicut dolor meus. Revertere,
dilecte vir, revertere, dilecte volorum meorum! O amabilis!
O desiderabilis! Redde michi leticiam salutaris presencie,
ostende michi faciem tuam. Sonet vox tua in auribus meis.
Vox enim tua dulcis et facies tua decora! O spes mea! Ne
confundas me ab expectacione mea! Demonstra faciem tuam
michi et sufficit anime.

Cum Maria sic doleret et sic fleret, et cum hec dixisset,
conversa est retrorsum et vidit Jhesum stantem et nesciebat
quia Jhesus est, et dicit ei Jhesus: Mulier, quid ploras? Quid
queris?

Ipsa paulo ante occulos suos, cum magno dolore tum cor-
dis sui, viderat speciem suam [tuam] suspendi in ligno, et tu
nunc dicis: Quid ploras? Ipsa in die tercia ante unxerat manus
tuas, quibus sepe benedicta fuerat, et [viderat] pedes tuos,
quos deosculata fuerat et quos lacrimis irrigaverat, clavis af-
figi, et tu nunc dicis: Quid ploras? Nunc insuper corpus tuum
sublatum estimat, ad quod ungendum, ut se quoquo modo
consolaretur, veniebat, et tu dicis: Quid ploras? Quem queris?
Dulcis magister, ad quid, queso, provocas spiritum hujus
mulieris? Ad quid provocas animum ejus? Tu scis quia te
solum querit, te solum diligit, pro te omnia contempnit, et
tu dicis: Quid queris? Tota pendet in te, et tota manet in te,
et tota desperat de se, ita querat [querit] te, ut nichil querat,
nichil cogitat [cogitet] preter te. Ideo forsitan non cognoscit
te, quia non est in se, sed pro te est extra se. Cur ergo dicis
ei: Cur ploras? Quem queris? An putas quia ipsa dicat: Te
ploro, te quero, nisi tu prius inspiraveris et dixeris in corde

suo: Ego sum quem queris et quem ploras? An putas quia ipsa cognoscat te, quamdiu volueris celare te? Ut ipsa existimans quia ortolanus [hortulanus] esset, dixit ad eum: Domine, si tu sustulisti eum, dicito michi ubi posuisti eum, et ego eum tollam. O dolor innumerabilis! O amor mirabilis! Mulier ista, quasi densa dolorum nube obtecta, non videbat solem qui mane surgens radiabat per fenestras ejus, qui per aures corporis jam intrabat in domum cordis sui! Sed quoniam languebat amore, isto amore sic occuli cordis caliginabant, ut non videret quoniam videbat: [non] videbat enim Jhesum, quia nesciebat quia Jhesus est. O Maria, si queris, cur [non] agnoscis Jhesum? Ecce Jhesus venit ad te, et quid queris querit a te, et tu ortholanum [hortulanum] eum existimas! Verum quidem est quod existimas. Sed tamen tu in hoc erras dum eum, si ortholanum [hortulanum] eum existimas, non Jhesum non agnoscas. Est enim Jhesus, et est ortolanus [hortulanus], quia ipse seminat omne semen bonum in orto [horto] anime sue [tue] et in cordibus fidelium suorum. Ipse omne semen bonum plantat et rigat in animabus sanctorum, et ipse est Jhesus qui tecum loquitur. Sed forsitan cumdem non agnoscis, quia tecum loquitur. Mortuum enim queris et viventem non cognoscis. Nunc in veritate comperi hanc esse causam pro qua a te recedebat et pro qua tibi non apparebat. Cur enim tibi appareret, quoniam non querebas eum? Certe querebas quod non erat, et non querebas quod erat. Tu querebas Jhesum et non querebas Jhesum, ideoque videndo Jhesum, nesciebas Jhesum.

O dulcis et pie magister, omnino excusare non audeo hanc discipulam tuam, non possum libere deffendere hunc errorem suum. Sed tamen errabat, quia talem te requirebat qualem te viderat, et qualem te positum in monumento relinquerat [reliquerat]. Videbat quippe deffunctum corpus tuum de cruce et deponi et in monumento reponi; tantusque dolor eam invaserat de morte tua, ut non posset sperare de vita tua, ut nichil posset cogitare de resurrectione tua. Denique Joseph posuit in monumento corpus tuum: Maria pariter sepelivit ibi spiritum suum et ita indissolubiliter sepelivit ibi spiritum suum, et ita indissolubiliter vixit et quodam modo univit cum tuo, ut facilius posset separari animam se vivificantem a vivente corpore suo, quam spiritum te diligentem a deffuncto corpore tuo. Spiritus enim Marie Magdalene erat in corpore tuo [magis] quam in corpore suo, cumque ipsa requirebat corpus tuum, requirebat et pariter spiritum tuum [suum], et ubi perdidit corpus tuum, perdidit cum eo spiritum suum. Quid ergo mirum si te nesciebat, que non habebat spiritum quo scire te debeat? Redde ergo ei spiritum sanctum quem habet in se corpus tuum, moxque recuperabit cor suum et relinquet errorem suum. Sed quo modo errabat, que sic pro te dolebat et sic te amabat? Certe si errabat, indubitanter dico quod ipsa errare se dubitabat, et hic error non procedebat ab errore, sed ab amore et dolore. Igitur, misericors et juste judex, amor, quem habet in te et dolor quem habet pro te, excuset eam apud te. Si forte errat de te, ne attendas ad mulieris errorem, sed ad discipule amorem que, non pro errore, sed pro dolore et amore, plorat et dicit tibi: Domine, si tu sustulisti eum, dicito michi ubi posuisti eum et ego cum tollam. O quam scienter nescit! O quam docte errat! Angelis dixit: Tulerunt et posuerunt eum. Et non dixit: Tulistis et posuistis; quia angeli neque de monumento detulerunt eum [te] neque in aliquo loco te posuerunt. Tibi vero dixit: Si tu sustulisti eum et posuisti, quia revera te ipsum de monumento [sustulisti], et ipsum cognoscis ut non sit necesse querere ab aliis ubi est Jhesus. Sed tu magis indicabis eum, "annuncians aliis [discipulis] quia vidi Dominum et hec dixit michi;" cui est honor et gloria cum Patre et Spiritu Sancto vivit et regnat in secula seculorum. Amen.

Explicit omelia beati Anselmi super Johannem de planctu Magdalene.

—from *La chaire française au XIIe siècle*,
ed. L. Bourgain (Paris, 1879)

Notes

Introduction

1 This study does not include *St. Erkenwald*. Henry Savage first developed the theory that this was the work of the *Gawain*-poet. See *St. Erkenwald*, ed. H. L. Savage (New Haven, 1926). However, Larry Benson in "The Authorship of *St. Erkenwald*," *Journal of English and Germanic Philology*, 64 (1965), 393–405, argues convincingly against Savage's theory. For a discussion of the common authorship of the poems in the manuscript, see A. C. Spearing, *The Gawain-Poet: A Critical Study* (Cambridge, 1970), pp. 32–40; *Saint Erkenwald*, ed. Clifford Peterson (Philadelphia, 1977).
2 Charles Moorman, *The Pearl-Poet* (New York, 1968), p. 113. See also Morton W. Bloomfield, "*Sir Gawain and the Green Knight*: An Appraisal," in *Critical Studies of "Sir Gawain and the Green Knight*," ed. D. R. Howard and C. Zacher (Notre Dame, 1968), p. 34.
3 For studies of the canon, see Moorman, *The Pearl-Poet*; Spearing, *The Gawain-Poet*. For editions of the works that illuminate the relationship between all four poems and between the poems and their sources and backgrounds, see *The Poems of the "Pearl" Manuscript*, ed. Malcolm Andrew and Ronald Waldron (Berkeley, 1979); *The Complete Works of the Gawain-Poet*, trans. J. C. Gardner (Chicago, 1965); *The Works of the Gawain-Poet*, ed. Charles Moorman (Jackson, 1977); *The "Pearl"-Poet*, trans. M. Williams (New York, 1967).
4 Charles Williams, *Arthurian Torso*, ed. C. S. Lewis (Grand Rapids, 1974), pp. 199–200.

5 For studies of the medieval sermon, see T. M. Charland, *Artes Praedicandi* (Ottawa, 1936); G. R. Owst, *Literature and Pulpit in Medieval England* (Cambridge, 1933; rev. ed., Oxford, 1966). For a study of the ways in which medieval art and literature were informed by exegetical techniques, see D. W. Robertson, Jr., *A Preface to Chaucer* (Princeton, 1962). See also David C. Fowler, *The Bible in Early English Literature* (Seattle, 1976).

6 Yves-Marie Duval, *Le livre de Jonas dans la littérature chrétienne*, 2 vols. (Paris, 1973).

7 For discussions of the late fourteenth century, see Morton W. Bloomfield, *Piers Plowman as a Fourteenth Century Apocalypse* (New Brunswick, 1962); D. W. Robertson, Jr., *Chaucer's London* (New York, 1968).

8 Robertson, *A Preface to Chaucer*, pp. 223, 284–285; J. A. Burrow, *Richardian Poetry* (London, 1971), pp. 93–94.

9 Larry D. Benson, *Art and Tradition in Sir Gawain and the Green Knight* (New Brunswick, N.J., 1965), pp. 117–126.

10 Rosemary Woolf, *The English Mystery Plays* (Berkeley, 1972), p. 28. J. A. Burrow discusses the effect *Sir Gawain* might have had as a spoken poem. See J. A. Burrow, *A Reading of Sir Gawain and the Green Knight* (London, 1965), pp. 1–3. Cf. Anne Middleton, "The Idea of Public Poetry in the Reign of Richard II," *Speculum*, 53 (1978), 94–114.

11 HE DO THE POLICE IN DIFFERENT VOICES was Eliot's original title for the opening section of *The Waste Land*. See T. S. Eliot, *The Waste Land; A Facsimile and Transcript of the Original Drafts*, ed. Valerie Eliot (New York, 1971), p. 5. The phrase is from *Our Mutual Friend* by Charles Dickens; see Eliot, p. 125, n. 1. In his recent study of the effects of World War I on modern life, Paul Fussell discusses the literary cast of the war, the fact that the soldiers not only read but recited poetry in the trenches. See Paul Fussell, *The Great War and Modern Memory* (New York, 1976), pp. 155–190. Our generation is perhaps the only one without a tradition of oral delivery.

12 Burrow, *Richardian Poetry*, pp. 43–46, 82.

13 Dorothy Everett discusses the poet's interest in conduct and thus the moral cast of his thought in "The Alliterative Revival," in *Twentieth-Century Interpretations of "Sir Gawain and the Green Knight*," ed. Denton Fox (Englewood Cliffs, N.J., 1968), pp. 13–22.

14 Burrow (*A Reading of Sir Gawain and the Green Knight*, pp.

140, 183–184) discusses Gawain as a figure for everyman; he also notes the fourteenth century's emphasis upon penance, an emphasis that, quite naturally, resulted in a good deal of literary soul-searching. See also E. J. Arnould, *Le manuel des péchés* (Paris, 1940).

15 Benson, *Art and Tradition in Sir Gawain and the Green Knight*, pp. 35–37. See pp. 26–37 for a discussion of *Caradoc* and *Sir Gawain*. For other discussions that suggest the flawed heroism the *Gawain*-poet depicts, see Donald Howard, *The Three Temptations* (Princeton, 1966); "Structure and Symmetry in *Sir Gawain*," in *Twentieth-Century Interpretations*, p. 50; Gervase Mathew, "Ideals of Knighthood in Late-Fourteenth-Century England," in *Twentieth-Century Interpretations*, pp. 68–72; Burrow, *A Reading of Sir Gawain and the Green Knight*, pp. 146, 159. Both A. C. Spearing and Charles Moorman point up the almost vague nature of the dilemmas the protagonists of these poems must face and hence the ambiguous portraits of heroism.

16 I would like to thank D. W. Robertson, Jr., for this insight.

17 Derek Pearsall, *Old English and Middle English Poetry* (London, 1977), p. 156; Benson, *Art and Tradition in Sir Gawain and the Green Knight*, pp. 123, 124.

One: Patience

1 For two recent studies of the figure of Jonah, see R. H. Bowers, *The Legend of Jonah* (The Hague, 1971); Duval, *Le livre de Jonas dans la littérature chrétienne*. Duval's study is a particularly fulsome account of early medieval uses of Jonah, analyzing both Eastern and Western treatments of and references to the prophet. For a discussion of medieval uses of Jonah in relation to *Patience*, see William Vantuono, "The Structure and Sources of *Patience*," *Medieval Studies*, 34 (1972), 401–421.

2 For example, see *The Liturgical Poetry of Adam of St. Victor*, from the text of Gautier, ed. and trans. Digby S. Wrangham (London, 1881), number XIV, "Pascha," p. 84; St. Ambrose, *Expositionis in Lucam*, lib. VII, PL 15, col. 1812; St. Augustine, *De Civitate Dei*, XVIII; *De Symbolo*, PL 40, col. 66; "De Jona propheta," in *Epistolarum Classis II*, PL 33, col. 382; Haymo, *In Jonam Prophetam*, PL 117; Isidore, *Allegoriae Quaedam Scripturae Sacrae*, PL 83, col. 115; St. Jerome, *Commentarium in*

Ionam Prophetam, Corpus Christianorum Series Latina, vol. 76 (Turnholt, 1966); Paschasius Radbertus, *Expositio in Matthaeum, PL* 120, cols. 475–477, 553; Rupert of Deutz, *In Jonam Prophetam, PL* 168; St. Zeno, *De Jona Propheta, PL* 11, cols. 444–450. In "History and Action in *Patience*" (*PMLA,* 86 [1971], 959–965), Jay Schleusener discusses the importance of typology to the poem. See also Malcolm Andrews, "Jonah and Christ in *Patience,*" *Modern Philology,* 70 (1973), 230–233. For a discussion of artistic renderings of Jonah as a type, see Louis Reau, "Le symbolisme typologique" in *Inconographie de l'art chrétien,* 3 vols. (Paris, 1955–59), 1:207.

3 Robertson, *A Preface to Chaucer,* pp. 189–190, 300.

4 Rupert of Deutz, *In Jonam Prophetam,* cols. 404–405. See St. Augustine, "Ps. 93," in *Ennarationes in Psalmos,* Corpus Christianorum Series Latina, vol. 39 (Turnholt, 1966), p. 1321.

5 St. Gregory, *Moralia, PL* 75, col. 746; Petrus Berchorius, *Super Jonam,* in *Reductorium Morale super Tota Biblia,* XXX, in *Opera Omnia* (Colona, 1730); Thomas à Kempis, *Sermons to the Novices Regular,* trans. Dom Vincent Scully (London, 1907), pp. 32, 36. The discussions of patience in *The Imitation of Christ* are remarkably similar to some of the poet's observations; these similarities led me to the sermons. However, a survey of other pietists has revealed nothing further about a thematic link between the figure of Jonah and the virtue of patience within this tradition. Curiously, Jean Gerson in a sermon preached on All Saints' Day, 1402, uses the eighth Beatitude as his text, going on to discuss Jonah's experience in the whale as an example of spiritual refinement. Gerson says that Jonah's tribulations bore fruit in obedience and in the salvation of Nineveh. See Jean Gerson, *Oeuvres complètes,* ed. M. Glorieux (Belgium, 1963), p. 112.

6 All quotations from *Patience* refer to J. J. Anderson's edition of the poem (New York, 1969) and will be cited by line number in the text. For a discussion of the poem's divisions, see Anderson's introduction, pp. 9–10.

7 Cf. Jonah, 1:7; St. Jerome associates the casting of lots with the turbulence of the storm. See *Comment. in Ionam,* p. 387.

8 See Henry Bradley, *A Middle English Dictionary* (Oxford, 1891).

9 In his edition of *Patience,* p. 59, Anderson notes that "OE *sluma,* from which the first element of the compound is derived, has connotations of dullness and sluggishness."

10 For example, the York Adam laments his expulsion from Eden

by saying, "Agaynst his wille þus haue they wrought, / To greeffe grete god gaffe they right noght" (*Adam and Even Driven from Eden*, in *York Plays*, ed. L. T. Smith [New York, 1963], lines 13–14).

11 In particular, see St. Jerome, *Comment. in Ionam*, pp. 377, 392; St. Augustine, *De Symbolo*, col. 66; Isidore, *Allegoriae Quaedam Scripturae Sacrae*, col. 115; Paschasius Radbertus, *Expositio in Matthaeum*, col. 553.

12 The Index of Christian Art includes over forty examples of Jonah cast overboard for Psalm 68. For discussions linking Psalm 129 with penance, see St. Augustine, "Ps. 129," in *Ennarationes in Psalmos*, p. 1889; Cassiodorus, *Expositio Psalmorum*, Corpus Christianorum Series Latina, vol. 98 (Turnholt, 1968), pp. 846–855; St. Gregory, *In Septem Psalmos Poenitentiales*, PL 79, col. 632; Peter Lombard, *Commentarium in Psalmos*, PL 191, col. 1167; St. Zeno, *De Jona Propheta*, col. 447.

13 The poet, both here and in *Purity*, uses clothing as a figure for a spiritual condition; see Anderson, n. 342. See also, D. W. Robertson, Jr., and B. F. Huppé, *Piers Plowman and Scriptural Tradition* (Princeton, 1951), chap. 6.

14 St. Jerome, *Comment. in Ionam*, p. 413; Rupert, *In Jonam Prophetam*, col. 436; St. Augustine, "De Jona Propheta," col. 384.

15 Thomas Brinton, *Sermons*, ed. Sister Mary Aquinas Devlin (London, 1954), Sermon 16, p. 65; Sermon 36, p. 155. In Sermon 101 (p. 465), delivered at Cobham on July 22, 1382, Brinton uses the Ninevites as a figure for true penance, exhorting England to follow Nineveh's example and turn again to God. See also St. Augustine, *De Catechizandis Rvdibvs*, Corpus Christianorum Series Latina, vol. 46 (Turnholt, 1969), XVIII, 32, p. 156.

16 Anderson and others have noted the poet's use of "bour" to describe both shelters.

17 See St. Augustine, "De Jona Propheta," col. 384; St. Jerome, *Comment. in Ionam*, p. 416.

18 See, for example, Marie de France, "The Woodbine," in *The Literature of Medieval England*, ed. D. W. Robertson, Jr. (New York, 1970), pp. 308–309; n. 10, p. 310; Chaucer, *Troilus and Criseyde*, III, 1231; Shakespeare, *A Midsummer Night's Dream*, II, i, 251.

19 Ordelle Hill, "The Audience of *Patience*," *Modern Philology*, 66 (1968–69), 103–109. See also St. Augustine, Sermo CCCXXXIII—"In Natali Martyrum," PL 38, cols. 1463–1464; St. Bernard, "In Festo Omnium Sanctorum," Sermo 1, PL 183, cols. 453–462; St.

Gregory, Homilia XXXV—"In Basilica Sancti Mennae Martyris, Die Natalis Ejus," in *XL Homil. in Evangelis, PL* 76, cols. 1261–1263. See also Jean Gerson, note 5, above.

20 St. Augustine, *De Sermone Domini in Monte,* Corpus Christianorum Series Latina, vol. 25 (Turnholt, 1967), pp. 4, 9, 12–13. For a discussion of Augustine's commentary in relation to *Patience,* see Jay Schleusener, "*Patience,* Lines 35–40," *Modern Philology,* 67 (1969), 64–66. See also St. Bernard, Sermo XXIV, In quo Tractatur de Humilitate et Patientia," in *Sermones in Cantica, PL* 183, col. 961; Alanus de Insulis, "De Patientia," *PL* 210, cols. 140ff. For a discussion of the traditional connection between the steps of wisdom, the Beatitudes, and the Pater Noster, see Rosemond Tuve, *Allegorical Imagery* (Princeton, 1966), pp. 92–102. J. T. Irwin and T. D. Kelly in "The Way and the End of the Way Are One: *Patience* as a Parable of the Contemplative Life," *American Benedictine Review,* 25 (1974), 33–55, also discuss the importance of the Beatitudes to the meaning of *Patience.*

21 For medieval discussions of the virtue of patience, see: St. Augustine, "De Patientia," *PL* 40; St. Benedict, *Codex Regularum,* appendix, "Exhort. ad Monachos et Virgines," *PL* 103 (there are numerous exhortations to aspiring to patience throughout the *Rule*); St. Bernard, "De Obedientia, Patientia, et Sapientia," in *Sermones de Diversis, PL* 183; St. Zeno, "De Patientia," *PL* 11.

22 Chaucer, The Parson's Tale in *Works,* ed. F. N. Robinson (Cambridge, Mass., 1961), X (I), 659–660, p. 249.

23 Origen, "De Prophetia Alia Balaam," in *In Numeros Homilia, PL* 12, col. 692.

24 See St. Augustine, "De Patientia," *PL* 40.

25 See D. W. Robertson, Jr., "The Question of Typology and the Wakefield *Mactacio Abel,*" in *Essays in Medieval Culture* (Princeton, 1980), pp. 218–232. For a discussion of applied typology, see A. C. Charity, *Events and Their Afterlife* (Cambridge, 1966), pp. 148–164. See also Earl Miner, ed., *Literary Uses of Typology, From the Late Middle Ages to the Present* (Princeton, 1977); Tuve, *Allegorical Imagery,* p. 47.

26 See my article, "Psalm 93 and *Patience,*" *Modern Philology,* 74 (1976), 67–71.

27 For critical discussions of Jonah's human, and therefore comic, traits see Charles Moorman, "The Role of the Narrator in *Patience,*" *Modern Philology,* 61 (1963–64), 90–95; *The Pearl-Poet*

(New York, 1968), pp. 64–77; A. C. Spearing, "*Patience* and the *Gawain*-Poet," *Anglia,* 84 (1966), 305–320; *The Gawain-Poet* (Cambridge, 1970), pp. 74–95; David Williams, "The Point of *Patience,*" *Modern Philology,* 68 (1970–71), 127–136.

28 We may find a similar approach in Rupert of Deutz's Commentary on Jonah. Rupert finds the virtues of obedience or humility and of patience in suffering illustrated in the Book of Jonah. Linking Jonah's experience in the whale with the lesson of obedience, he deduces the lesson of patience from the entire narrative (cols. 408, 425).

Two: Sir Gawain and the Green Knight

1 Throughout this study I have used *Sir Gawain and the Green Knight,* ed. J. R. R. Tolkien and E. V. Gordon, revised by Norman Davis (Oxford, 1967). All quotations from the poem refer to this edition and are cited by line number in the text.

2 For the only other consideration of the various levels of time in *Sir Gawain,* see John Kenny Crane, "The Four Levels of Time in *Sir Gawain and the Green Knight,*" *Annuale Medievale,* 10 (1969), 65–80.

3 For an account of the literary uses of the legend of Troy, see Arthur M. Young, *Troy and Her Legend* (Pittsburgh, 1948). For suggestions about the importance of Troy to medieval Englishmen, see Robertson, *Chaucer's London,* pp. 2–4.

4 William Caxton, *Eneydos,* eds. W. T. Culley and F. J. Furnivall, Early English Text Society, E.S. 57 (London, 1890), p. 10. This passage appears in Caxton's translation of the Prologue of the French translation of the *Aeneid.*

5 For a discussion of the ways in which the Middle Ages drew upon Rome for its standards of military discipline, see M. H. Keen, *The Laws of War in the Late Middle Ages* (London, 1965). For discussions of Vegetius in relation to medieval military standards, see Christine de Pisan, *The Book of Fayttes of Armes and of Chyualrye,* trans. William Caxton, ed. A. T. P. Byles, Early English Text Society, 189 (London, 1932), pp. xxxvi–xxxviii; *Knyghthode and Bataile, A XVth Century Verse Paraphrase of Flavius Vegetius Renatus' Treatise 'De Re Militari,'* ed. R. Dyboski and Z. M. Arend, Early English Text Society, 201 (London, 1935), pp. xxiv–xxvi; M. Jähns, *Geschichte der Kriegswissen-*

schaften, in *Geschichte der Kunstswissenschaften* (Royal Academy of Munich, 1889), 1:186–187, 350.

6 Thomas Brinton, Sermon 38, in *Sermons,* p. 167.

7 Lydgate, *Fall of Princes,* ed. Henry Bergen, Early English Text Society, E.S. 121–124 (London, 1924), vol. 121, I, line 6068, p. 171.

8 Ibid., lines 6110–6111, p. 171.

9 See, for example, Ranulph Higden, *Polychronicon together with the English Translations of John Trevisa and of an Unknown Writer of the Fifteenth Century,* Rolls Series (London, 1865), V, v, pp. 335, 337.

10 N. Denholm-Young, "The Tournament in the Thirteenth Century," in *Collected Papers of N. Denholm-Young* (Cardiff, 1969), pp. 108, 107.

11 Higden, *Polychronicon,* VIII, vii, p. 63.

12 Mary E. Giffin, "Cadwalader, Arthur, and Brutus in the Wigmore Manuscript," *Speculum,* 16 (1941), 109–120.

13 May McKisack, *The Fourteenth Century, 1307–1399* (Oxford, 1959), p. 97; Joan Evans, *English Art, 1307–1461* (Oxford, 1949), p. 56.

14 Joan Evans, *English Art,* p. 57. Evans's note to the ewer reads "Inventory of 1370; Polgrove, III, 264."

15 See, for example, Lydgate, *Fall of Princes,* vol. 123, VIII, lines 3130–3164, pp. 910–911. For a consideration of the figure of Arthur, as a possible lesson in fortune, see Robert W. Hanning, *The Vision of History in Early Britain* (New York, 1966), chap. 5; Russel A. Peck, "Willfulness and Wonders: Boethian Tragedy in the Alliterative *Morte Arthure,*" in *The Alliterative Tradition in the Fourteenth Century,* ed. B. S. Levy and P. E. Szarmach (Kent, Ohio, 1981), pp. 153–182.

16 Hanning discusses this sort of historical perspective in *The Vision of History* in relation to Gildas.

17 See also Bernard Silvestris, *The Cosmographia,* trans. Winthrop Wetherbee (New York, 1973), p. 116.

18 In the dream Nebuchadnezzar had of a statue composed of different elements, the Middle Ages found a Biblical figure for the Ovidian idea of decay. See Daniel 2:31–45. For a contemporary observation about decay in relation to Nebuchadnezzar's dream, see John Gower, *Confessio Amantis* in *The Complete Works of John Gower,* ed. G. C. Macaulay (Oxford, 1901), Prologue, lines 585–662.

19 John of Salisbury, *The Statesman's Book, being the fourth, fifth, and sixth books, and selections from the seventh and eighth books, of the Policraticus,* trans. John Dickinson (New York, 1927), VI, 16, p. 226.

20 See Froissart, *Oeuvres,* ed. Kervyn de Lettenhove (Brussels, 1870), I, 1, pp. 419, 440. Chaucer's "Lak of Stedfastnesse" is perhaps his most succinct statement of decay.

21 Higden, *Polychronicon,* I, p. 3. Corollary to the idea that knowledge might be redemptive is the Chartrian recognition of the intellectual labors as part of the divine scheme of salvation. See Emile Mâle, *The Gothic Image,* trans. Dora Nussey (New York, 1958), pp. 75–82.

22 See Lawrence Stone, *The Family, Sex, and Marriage in England, 1500–1800* (New York, 1977), pp. 4–6, 85–119. Stone points out that in the Middle Ages young people were expected to act like adults and childish behavior was not praised.

23 See also Burrow, *A Reading of Sir Gawain and the Green Knight,* pp. 33–36; Theodore Silverstein, "The Art of *Sir Gawain and the Green Knight,*" *University of Toronto Quarterly,* 33 (1964), 258–278.

24 Bernard Silvestris, *The Cosmographia,* p. 126.

25 Gower, *Confessio Amantis,* Prologue, lines 655–662. For a survey of late medieval ways of considering history, see Bloomfield, *Piers Plowman as a Fourteenth-Century Apocalypse,* pp. 98–103. See also Burrow, *A Reading of Sir Gawain and the Green Knight,* p. 34.

26 See Sherman Hawkins's discussion of time in "Mutabilitie and the Cycle of the Months," in *Form and Convention in the Poetry of Edmund Spenser,* Selected Papers from the English Institute, ed. William Nelson (New York, 1967), pp. 76–102.

27 The Feast of the Holy Innocents (December 28) is not mentioned in the poem, but see Tolkien and Gordon, *Sir Gawain and the Green Knight,* n. 1022.

28 See *Missale ad Usum Insignis et Praeclarae Ecclesiae Sarum,* ed. F. H. Dickinson (Hants, England, 1969), cols. 953–956.

29 *The Golden Legend; or, Lives of the Saints of England,* trans. William Caxton, ed. F. S. Ellis (London, 1935), vol. 6, pp. 97, 102. For "the debt of interchanging neighborhood," the Latin reads "debitum mutuae vicissitudinis." See Jacobus de Voragine, *Legenda Aurea,* ed. Th. Graesse (Leipzig, 1850), p. 720. Caxton's translations are accurate for those passages I have cited.

30 *The Golden Legend,* trans. Caxton, vol. 6, p. 102.

31 Ibid., pp. 102–103. For "covenant," the Latin reads "pactum." According to Lewis and Short (*A Latin Dictionary* [Oxford, 1879]), "pactum" was used to refer to a Biblical covenant, such as "pactum Domini." See Deut. 29:25; 3 Kings 11:11; 2 Par. 6:14. For "chivalry," the Latin reads "militiam."

32 *Missale . . . Ecclesiae Sarum,* col. 957.

33 The penitential tone of the day is underlined by the use of the Dies Irae sequence for the feast. F. J. E. Raby (*A History of Christian-Latin Poetry* [Oxford, 1953], pp. 443, 449) notes that the sequence was used liturgically for this feast during the lifetime of Bartholomew of Pisa (d. 1401). The Sarum Missal does not contain the Dies Irae, but the responses and prayers for the day reflect a similar awareness of judgment and, consequently, an emphasis upon penance.

34 Hugh of St. Victor, Sermo V—"In Adventu Domini," in *Sermones Centum, PL* 177, col. 911. See also Berchorius, "Adventus," in *Dictionarium Morale,* p. 84.

35 For an allegorical reading of these preliminary battles, see Schnyder, *Sir Gawain and the Green Knight,* chap. 4. The *Glossa Ordinaria* (*PL* 114, col. 179) says of the wilderness, "Ubi vicit diabolus. . . ." The fourteenth-century Holkam picture Bible, on one page, juxtaposes three pictures—of John the Baptist preaching, of his recognition and baptism of Christ, and of the temptation of Christ. The series underlines the relationship between Advent, the wilderness, and temptation (London: Mus., British Add. 47682 fol. 19ro.).

36 See Hugh of St. Victor, Sermo XXIV—"In Nativitate Domini," in *Sermones Centum,* col. 948; Sermo XLVIII—"In Nativitate," col. 1031. In Sermon 48, Hugh of St. Victor employs the metaphor of the spiritual warrior, or knight. See also Raymond Oliver, *Poems without Names* (Berkeley, 1970), pp. 56–57; Berchorius, *Super Apocalypsim* in *Opera,* cap. XXIII, p. 248.

37 Owst, *Literature and Pulpit in Medieval England* (Cambridge, 1933; rev. ed., Oxford, 1966), pp. 81–82. The Devil's Castle also contains Sloth as a chamberlain, "who draws the curtains and makes men lie for long in wantonness, and makes priests to celebrate after midday, fearing more to give offence to their lords than to God."

38 *The Golden Legend* verifies these dates and offers a compilation of popular legends and sermons associated with each one. See

also C. R. Cheney, *Handbook of Dates for Students of English History*, Offices of the Royal Historical Society (London, 1961); *Missale . . . Ecclesiae Sarum.*

39 In Scotland and in some parts of northern England, December 31 was called Hogmanay, a day on which children received oatmeal cakes or on which gifts were given.

40 Berchorius, *Super Apocalypsim*, cap. XXIII, p. 248.

41 See Peter Lombard, *Sententiae* (Florence, 1916), IV, I, cap. vii, pp. 748–749. In IV, III, cap. viii, p. 761, Peter Lombard discusses the original significance of circumcision in relation to its New Law significance. See also Bruno Astensis, *Sententiae*, PL 165, IV, v, col. 987.

42 Hugh of St. Victor, Sermo XLIX—"In Circumcisione Domini," in *Sermones Centum*, col. 1039.

43 St. Bernard, "In Circumcisione Domini," Sermo III, PL 183, col. 139. See also Bernard S. Levy, "Gawain's Spiritual Journey: *Imitatio Christi* in *Sir Gawain and the Green Knight*," *Annuale Medievale*, 6 (1965), 65–106.

44 St. Bernard, "In Circumcisione Domini," col. 142. In *Il Convivio*, IV, viii, Dante says that *discrezione* is the most beautiful branch that springs from the root of reason.

45 One of the meanings the *OED* assigns to "axe" is that instrument used by the headsman on condemned traitors; in addition, it is a weapon. The ax acquires further significance as an instrument of justice because Saint John the Baptist used it as a metaphor for Jerusalem's destruction. This association is evoked by John of Salisbury in the *Policraticus*, for he frequently refers to the ax of the Day of Judgment and the punishment it will render upon impenitent societies. See, for example, *Policraticus*, IV, 12. See also St. Gregory, Hom. XX, in *XL Homiliarum in Evangelia*, PL 76, col. 1164; Rabanus Maurus, *Commentaria in Matthaeum*, PL 107, col. 771; Filippo Picinelli, *Mundus Symbolicus* (Colona, 1687), XVII, xxvi, p. 215.

46 See Tolkien and Gordon, *Sir Gawain and the Green Knight*, n. 298.

47 For a discussion of this scene, see Burrow, *A Reading of Sir Gawain and the Green Knight*, pp. 127–133.

48 "Man's Disobedience and Fall from Eden," in *York Plays*, ed. L. T. Smith (New York, 1885; rpt. 1963), lines 175–176, p. 28. Trevisa (in Higden, *Polychronicon*, II, p. 215) uses much the same wording to describe the human condition: ". . . profit of berþe is

sorwe and care in lyuynge. . . ." Cf. Burrow, *A Reading of Sir Gawain and the Green Knight*, p. 140.

49 For a discussion of one such hero, see my article, "The Medieval Hector: A Double Tradition," *Mediaevalia*, 5 (1979), 165–182.

50 See Marcel Simon, *Hercule et le christianisme* (Paris, 1955), p. 129. See also Robertson, *A Preface to Chaucer*, p. 224.

51 The three standard medieval commentaries on the *Aeneid* are those of Servius, Fulgentius, and Bernard Silvestris: Servius, *In Virgilii Carmina Commentariorum* (Harvard Edition, 1946); Fulgentius, *The Mythographer*, trans. L. G. Whitbread (Columbus, 1971); *Commentum Bernardi Silvestris super Sex Libros Eneidos Virgilii*, ed. G. Reidel (Gryphiswaldae, 1924). See also D. Comparetti, *Vergil in the Middle Ages*, trans. E. F. B. Benecke (London, 1895).

52 For a discussion of the idea of pilgrimage, see Christian Zacher, *Curiosity and Pilgrimage* (Baltimore, 1976), pp. 42–45.

53 *The "Gest Hystoriale" of the Destruction of Troy*, ed. G. A. Panton and D. Donaldson, 2 vols. (London, 1869 and 1874), XXIX, lines 11957, 11973. See also Tolkien and Gordon, eds., *Sir Gawain and the Green Knight*, p. 70; Higden, *Polychronicon*, II, p. 415.

54 Hanning, *The Vision of History in Early Britain*, p. 157. For the legend of Brutus, see Geoffrey of Monmouth, *History of the Kings of Britain*, chaps. 2–28. Laʒamon's *Brut* also reveals its Vergilian antecedents in the prophecy that directs Brutus to England. In this case, it is Diana, and not Venus, who appears to Brutus in a dream and outlines his goal.

55 Arthur G. Brodeur, *Arthur, Dux Bellorum*, University of California Publications in English (Berkeley, 1939), pp. 263, 264, 282. See also C. G. Loomis, "King Arthur and the Saints," *Speculum*, 8 (1933), 478–482; J. S. P. Tatlock, *The Legendary History of Britain* (Berkeley, 1950), pp. 178–229.

56 Benson, *Art and Tradition in Sir Gawain and the Green Knight*, pp. 3–55.

57 See Jessie L. Weston, *The Legend of Sir Gawain* (London, 1897), pp. 2, 8, 14, 51.

58 Petrus Berchorius, *Reductorium Morale*, lib. XIV, p. 565, in *Opera*. Sir Frederic Madden first mentioned this tale in *Sir Gawayne: A Collection of Ancient Romance-Poems* (London, 1839), p. xxxii.

59 See Jane Chance Nietzche, *The Genius Figure in Antiquity and*

the Middle Ages (New York, 1975), p. 54. See also Bernard Silvestris, *De Mundi Universitate*, bk. II. The classic study of the mythic overtones of this pattern is Joseph Campbell's *Hero with a Thousand Faces* (Princeton, 1949).

60 For discussions of chivalry see: *Knyghthode and Bataile, A XVth Century Verse Paraphrase of Flavius Vegetius Renatus' 'De Re Militari,'* lines 276–277; *Livre d'Enanchet*, ed. Werner Friberg (Leipzig, 1938), p. 18; Geffroi de Charney, *Le livre de chevalerie*, reprinted in Froissart, *Oeuvres*, I, 2, p. 513; *The Book of the Ordre of Chyualry, trans. and printed by William Caxton from a French version of Ramon Lull's "Le Libre del orde de cauayleria," together with Adam Loutfut's Scottish Transcript*, ed. A. T. P. Byles, Early English Text Society, 168 (London, 1926), p. 31; *Moralium Dogma Philosophorum*, ed. J. Holmberg (Uppsala, 1929); *Le livre des manières*, ed. Kremer (Marburg, 1887); Bonizo, *Liber de Vita Christiana*, ed. Ernst Derels (Berlin, 1930); Jean Priorat, *Li Abrejance de L'Ordre de Chevalerie*, ed. U. L. L. Robert (Paris, 1897); *The Book of Fayttes of Armes and of Chyualrye; The Epistle of Othea*, translated from the French text of Christine de Pisan by Stephen Scrope, ed. C. F. Buhler (Oxford, 1970). For modern discussions of the ideals of chivalry, see Keen, *The Laws of War in the late Middle Ages*, p. 20; Mathew, "Ideals of Knighthood in Late-Fourteenth-Century England," in *Studies in Medieval History Presented to F. M. Powicke*, ed. R. W. Hunt, W. A. Pantin, R. W. Southern (Oxford, 1948), pp. 354–362; G. V. Smithers, "What *Sir Gawain and the Green Knight* Is About," *Medium Ævum*, 32 (1963), 171–189.

61 For comments upon Satan's powers of deception and thus the strengths a knight, metaphoric or actual, must have, see: St. Jerome, *Commentaria in Epistola ad Ephesios, PL* 26, col. 577; Peter Lombard, *In Epistola ad Ephesios, PL* 192, cols. 218–219; Alanus de Insulis, "Ad Milites," in *Summa de Arte Praedicatoria, PL* 210, cols. 185–187; Trevisa, in Higden, *Polychronicon*, lib. II, p. 427.

62 See Evans, *English Art*, p. 58. See also *The Book of the Ordre of Chyualry*, p. 81.

63 For an analysis of Gawain's shield, see R. H. Green, "Gawain's Shield and the Quest for Perfection," *ELH*, 29 (1962), 129–135; R. W. Ackerman, "Gawain's Shield: Penitential Doctrine in *Sir Gawain and the Green Knight*," *Anglia*, 76 (1958), 254–265; Roger Lass, "Man's Heaven: The Symbolism of Gawain's Shield,"

Mediaeval Studies, 28 (1966), 354–360. See also A. Kent Hieatt, "Sir Gawain: Pentangle, Luflace, Numerical Structure," in *Silent Poetry*, ed. Alastair Fowler (New York, 1970), pp. 116–140.

64 For a discussion of the medieval treatment of Solomon, see Fowler, *The Bible in Early English Literature*. For a medieval account of Solomon, see the sections in the *Cursor Mundi* chronicling Solomon's reign. That the legends surrounding Solomon retained their vitality is borne out by Du Bartas's long sixteenth-century poem, *Divine Weekes and Workes*, and Sylvester's seventeenth-century English translation. *Le livre des manières* begins by referring to Solomon and his writing of Ecclesiastes; Dante in *Il Convivio* and John of Salisbury in the *Policraticus* also frequently allude to Solomon and his salient advice to young men. Curiously, in *De Inventione Linguorum* (*PL* 112, col. 1584), Rabanus Maurus discusses Solomon in relation to a sign. He discusses certain monograms which form pictures for the imagination, providing Solomon with the following monogram:

Salo-   mon.

Re   x

paci-   ficus

This monogram is a little too complicated to be considered an analogue for the pentangle on Gawain's shield; as D. W. Robertson, Jr., remarked to me, it would be nice to find one like this:

Although I cannot claim such good fortune, it is possible to conjecture that something like it may have existed.

65 The *Gawain*-poet's emphasis upon the visual and moral harmony of Gawain's shield is reminiscent of Harmony herself in book IX of the *De Nuptiis*. Harmony enters, carrying in her right hand a shield embroidered with striking figures. Harmony's shield does not depict a pentangle, but circular chords, which encompass one another; from their intertwinement pours a concord of

all the tones. See Martianus Capella, *De Nuptiis Philologiae et Mercurii*, ed. Adolfus Dick with F. Preax (Stuttgart, 1969). See also W. H. Stahl and R. Johnson, with E. L. Burge, *Martianus Capella and the Seven Liberal Arts* (New York, 1971); Fanny Le Moin, *Martianus Capella: A Literary Re-evaluation* (Munich, 1972).

66 For medieval comments upon the figurative understanding of hunting, especially Satan's talent for hunting, see *An Exposition of 'Qui Habitate' and 'Bonum Est' in English*, presumably by Walter Hilton, ed. Björn Wollner (Lund, 1954), p. 7: "Hunters are fendes þat are dedly enemyes to þe rihtwis mon & pursuwen him to sleen, nat bodily but gostly." Cf. St. Augustine, "In Psalmum XC," in *Enarrationes in Psalmos*, Corpus Christianorum Series Latina, vol. 39 (Turnholt, 1956), pp. 1254ff.; St. Bernard, Sermo III, "In Psalmum XC," *PL* 183, col. 190. Psalm 90 was thought to prefigure the temptation of Christ and was seen as outlining the dangers the world posed to the armed Christian warrior. For a discussion of hunting in relation to Aeneas, see the *Policraticus*, I, 4; VI, 22. The fact that Bercilak the hunter is also the Green Knight makes him even more suspect in light of the associations assigned to the color green. See D. W. Robertson, Jr., "Why the Devil Wears Green," *Modern Language Notes*, 69 (1954), 470–472. See also *The Book of Fayttes of Armes and of Chyualrye*, p. 290; *On the Properties of Things*, John Trevisa's translation of Bartholomaeus Anglicus, *De Proprietatibus Rerum*, 2 vols. (Oxford, 1975), II, xix, 19, p. 1291. What I mean to suggest, however, is not that Bercilak is the devil, but that, like the devil, Bercilak tests, or hunts out, the weaknesses of his opponents.

67 For comments about Simon Magus, see Peter Lombard, *Sententiae*, II, vii, cap. vi, pp. 336–337. See also St. Augustine, Sermo II "In Psalmum XC," in *Enarrationes in Psalmos*, pp. 1272–1273. There are numerous references to Simon Magus in *The Golden Legend*.

68 Howard, *The Three Temptations*, pp. 44–56. For discussions of the connections between Bercilak's hunts and Gawain's temptations, see Robertson, *The Literature of Medieval England*, p. 407; H. L. Savage, *The Gawain-Poet* (Chapel Hill, 1956), pp. 31–48; Hans Schnyder, *Sir Gawain and the Green Knight* (Bern, 1961), pp. 55–66. For a discussion of the partial relevance of the triad of lust, pride, and avarice to Gawain's experience with his hostess, see Howard, *The Three Temptations* (Princeton, 1966), pp.

232–235. For a general discussion of this triad, see Morton W. Bloomfield, *The Seven Deadly Sins: An Introduction to the History of a Religious Concept* (East Lansing, 1952), pp. 158–201.

69 Geoffroi de Charney, *Le livre de chevalerie*, p. 478. Cf. *Moralium Dogma Philosophorum*, pp. 51, 146.

70 Geoffroi de Charney, *Le livre de chevalerie*, p. 478, 491, 493. See also *Le livre des manières*, lines 409–412.

71 See Keen, *The Laws of War in the Late Middle Ages*, pp. 20, 21. On p. 257, Keen notes that a soldier's punishment for cowardice or treachery was degradation from all honors; he adds that such a man's heirs could not inherit from him any rank not already theirs.

72 Geoffroi de Charney, *Le livre de chevalerie*, p. 490.

73 See Thomas Brinton, Sermon 69, in *Sermons*.

74 John of Hanville, *Architrenius*, ed. Paul Gerhard Schmidt (Munich, 1974), VI, i, p. 214. In book V, Gawain tells the story of Britain from Brutus to the birth of Arthur, digressing, from time to time, to discuss cupidity and knights who are motivated by avarice. Sir Frederic Madden, *Sir Gawayne*, p. xxxvii, also noted Gawain's appearance in the *Architrenius*.

75 See, for example, Howard, *The Three Temptations*, p. 54; Philippe Ariès, *The Hour of Our Death*, trans. H. Weaver (New York, 1981), pp. 130–131.

76 Keen, *The Laws of War in the Late Middle Ages*, p. 20. The *OED* defines "covenant" in both a legal and a figurative way. See also Burrow, *A Reading of Sir Gawain and the Green Knight*, p. 42.

77 Berchorius, *Reductorium Morale*, lib. XIV, p. 567. Cf. Higden, *Polychronicon*, VII, lib. I, pp. 25, 27. The appendix to vol. IV contains a Latin version from MS. Trin. Coll. R. 14.7 fol. 156b to fol. 157b which relates a similar marvel in conjunction with the "oven" of Arthur. Although the descriptions of Higden are not exactly like that of Berchorius, the "democratic" formulas, the descriptions of an open grave, and the references to water connect them.

78 In the play *Everyman*, when it is time for Everyman to die, he speaks of creeping into "this cave" as a metaphor for dying. Burrow, *A Reading of Sir Gawain and the Green Knight*, p. 27, likewise feels that, while the Green Knight may not be Death, the Green Knight has "a peculiar resonance which I cannot explain except by references to the traditional figure of Death in the moral allegories."

79 Donald Howard, "Structure and Symmetry in *Sir Gawain*," *Speculum*, 39 (1964), 425–433.
80 Bede, Homilia III—"De Adventu Domini," *PL* 94, col. 24. See also Berchorius, *Dictionarium Morale*, p. 256; Rabanus Maurus, *Commentaria in Matthaeum*, col. 768; St. Gregory, Homilia XL, in *Homil. in Evang.*, *PL* 76, col. 1305; Bede, *In Marci Evangelium Expositio*, *PL* 92, col. 136, 137.
81 Benson (*Art and Tradition in Sir Gawain and the Green Knight*, p. 241) has also noted that Gawain's two confessions are met with "lufly" laughter.
82 The ending of *Sir Gawain* has been the subject of much critical discussion. In *The Gawain-Poet*, pp. 222–223, A. C. Spearing confronts the issue by noting that there are two ways of interpreting the court's laughter at Gawain. Moorman (*The Pearl-Poet*, p. 110) finds the laughter that of incomprehension, noting that it foreshadows civic failure, an opinion with which I concur. Spearing (*The Gawain-Poet*, p. 223), Benson (*Art and Tradition in Sir Gawain and the Green Knight*, p. 248), Burrow (*A Reading of Sir Gawain and the Green Knight*, p. 159), Howard (*The Three Temptations*, pp. 234–235, 242), and Theodore Silverstein ("Sir Gawain in a Dilemma, or Keeping Faith with Marcus Tullius Cicero," *Modern Philology*, 75 [1977], 1–17) see the laughter as underlining the irony of the poem, as a sign of order restored.
83 In *The Hour of Our Death*, p. 11, Ariès discusses medieval man's fear of dying a lonely and unmarked death. Clearly, the poet juxtaposes Sir Gawain and a real fear, not merely a literary temptation that is easily passed over.
84 For a discussion of the tradition of "fall of Britain" poems, see Hanning, *The Vision of History in Early Britain*, pp. 1–43.
85 For a discussion of Saint John the Baptist's particular appeal to fourteenth-century England, see my article, "St. John the Baptist and Late Fourteenth-Century and Early Fifteenth-Century Ideology," *American Benedictine Review*, 27 (1976), 105–125.

Three: Purity

1 For a sampling of critical discussions of the poet's method of organization and the poem's thematic and imagistic unity, see W. A. Davenport, *The Art of the Gawain-Poet* (New York, 1978), chap. 3; Gardner, *The Complete Works of the Gawain-Poet*, in-

troduction; T. D. Kelly and John T. Irwin, "The Meaning of *Cleanness:* Parable as Effective Sign," *Medieval Studies*, 35 (1973), 232–260; Charles Moorman, *The Pearl-Poet*, Twayne's English Authors Ser., 64 (New York, 1968), chap. 4; Charlotte C. Morse, *The Pattern of Judgment in the "Queste" and "Cleanesse"* (Columbia, 1978), pp. 129–199; Spearing, *The Gawain-Poet*, chap. 2. Throughout, I have used the edition of *Purity* by Robert J. Menner (New Haven, 1920, rpt. 1970); all quotations from the poem will be cited in the text by line number.

2 Both John Gardner and Charlotte Morse (see above) have noticed the pattern of reversion established through the parable of the man in foul clothes.

3 See St. Augustine, Sermo CXII, in *Sermones de Scripturas, PL* 38, col. 646; Bede, *In Lucae Evangelium Expositio, PL* 92, col. 514; St. Gregory, Homilia XXXVI, in *Homiliarum in Evangelia, PL* 76, cols. 1268–1269; *Glossa Ordinaria, PL* 114, cols. 308–309; Haymo, Homilia CXII, *PL* 118, col. 605; Peter Lombard, *Sententiae*, II, xxi, v, p. 406.

4 St. Augustine, Sermo XC, in *Sermones de Scripturas*, cols. 561–562; St. Gregory, Homilia XXXVIII, in *Homil. in Evang.*, col. 1290; Haymo, *Expositio in Apocalypsin B. Joannis, PL* 117, col. 1135; St. Jerome, *Expositio IV Evang. Matthaeus, PL* 30, col. 576; *Commentarius in Evangelium Secundum Matthaeum, PL* 26, col. 167.

5 See St. Augustine, Sermo XC, in *Sermones de Scripturas*, col. 559; St. Gregory, Homilia XXXVIII, in *Homil. in Evang.*, cols. 1282, 1285–1286; Haymo, Homilia CXXV, *PL* 118, cols. 718–721; St. Jerome, *Expositio IV Evang. Matthaeus*, col. 575.

6 For a discussion of the hierarchical nature of the banquet, which has attracted some critical attention, see Menner's n. 114, in his edition of *Purity*. Menner feels that the poet did not intend us to associate this banquet with paradise, but the poet himself makes a number of comparisons between the feast and paradise, clearly drawing upon the common interpretation of the New Testament parable. Cf. the *Pearl*-maiden's description of courtesy; her use of St. Paul's corporal analogy implies a difference of degree among the citizens of heaven.

7 In Homilia XXXVIII, St. Gregory places a similar emphasis upon choice in relation to the banquet described by Matthew.

8 St. Gregory, Homilia XXXVIII, in *Homil. in Evang.*, cols. 1285–1286.

9 Bede, *In II Epistolam S. Petri, PL* 93, col. 79. See also Kelly and Irwin, "The Meaning of *Cleanness:* Parable as Effective Sign," pp. 244–245, n. 14.

10 For discussions of this passage, see Bede, *In Lucae Evangelium Expositio, PL* 92, cols. 546–548; *Glossa Ordinaria, PL* 114, cols. 320–321.

11 Menner (n. 1022–48) discusses the sources for the poet's description of the Dead Sea fruit. For a discussion of Mandeville's *Travels* and this fruit, see C. F. Brown, "Note on the Dependence of *Cleanness* on the "Book of Maundeville,'" *PMLA,* 19 (1904), 149–153. See also Rabanus Maurus, *Commentarium in Librum Sapientiae, PL* 109, col. 717.

12 See Rabanus Maurus, *Comment. in Librum Sapientiae,* col. 716.

13 Thomas Brinton, Sermon 45, in *Sermons,* pp. 202–203. Cf. Sermon 70, p. 323.

14 MS Burney 131, fol. 9, quoted in Robertson, *A Preface to Chaucer,* pp. 383–384. In n. 201, Robertson quotes the English commentary, Oxford, Bodl. MS Auct. F. 3.5, fol. 210; "Other thay are lechoures and thanne thay are understonde be the wodenes of the see or thay are couetoris, that is understandynge be the brennynge fire, or proude, that is understonde be the wastynge levenynge."

15 Spearing has also noted the significance of this remark. See *The Gawain-Poet: A Critical Study,* chap. 2.

16 St. Augustine, *The City of God* (Loeb Library, 1966), XV, xxv, pp. 564–565.

17 For example, see Bede, *Hexaemeron, PL* 91, col. 83; Petrus Berchorius, *Reductorium Morale,* I, v; Peter Comestor, *Historia Scholastica, PL* 198, col. 1081; Hugh of St. Victor (dubious), *Allegoriae in Vetus Testamentem, PL* 175, col. 641.

18 See St. Augustine, *The City of God,* XV, xxv, pp. 564–567; Bede, *Hexaemeron,* cols. 85, 86, 88; *Glossa Ordinaria, PL* 113, cols. 107, 108; Rabanus Maurus, *De Universo, PL* 111, col. 34.

19 For discussions of the crow, see Bede, *Hexaemeron,* col. 101; Berchorius, *Reductorium Morale,* I, vi; Peter Comestor, *Historia Scholastica,* col. 1085; *Glossa Ordinaria,* col. 109; Richard of St. Victor, *Liber Exceptionum,* ed. Jean Chatillon (Paris, 1958), II, I, xvi, p. 231.

20 The dove was frequently seen as a figure for the elect. See Bede, *Hexaemeron,* cols. 101, 102; Berchorius, *Reductorium Morale,* I, vi.

21 See Bede, *Hexaemeron*, col. 169; Rabanus Maurus, *Commentarium in Genesim*, *PL* 107, col. 552; Berchorius, *Reductorium Morale*, I, xiv.

22 See Bede, *Hexaemeron*, col. 165. In col. 167, Bede quotes from St. Augustine's *City of God*, XVI, xxvi, to the same end.

23 See Alanus de Insulis, Sermo IV, *PL* 210, col. 207; Bede, *Hexaemeron*, cols. 168–169; Berchorius, *Reductorium Morale*, I, xiv; Rabanus Maurus, *Comment, in Genesim*, cols. 551–552.

24 For discussions of the prophecy of Isaac's birth, see Bede, *Hexaemeron*, col. 154; St. Gregory, *Moralia*, *PL* 75, col. 918; Rabanus Maurus, *Comment, in Genesim*, col. 552.

25 See *Glossa Ordinaria*, *PL* 113, cols. 131–139; Richard of St. Victor, *Liber Exceptionum*, II, II, vi, p. 237; Hugh of St. Victor, *Alleg. in Vetus Test.*, col. 646; Berchorius, *Reductorium Morale*, I, xiv; Thomas Brinton, Sermon 48, p. 216; Peter Comestor, *Historia Scholastica*, col. 1099. For a cogent discussion of the medieval notion of curiosity, see Zacher, *Curiosity and Pilgrimage*, pp. 4, 19–41.

26 Menner notes (n. 819–828, pp. 95–96) that many of the details the poet supplies about Lot (the incident of Lot's wife's putting salt into the angels' food and the references to Lot's wealth) have their ultimate origins in Hebrew tradition.

27 For a discussion of earthly paradises and their appearance in classical and medieval literature, see A. B. Giamatti, *The Earthly Paradise and the Renaissance Epic* (Princeton, 1969), pp. 11–93.

28 For discussions of Lot's wife, see Rabanus Maurus, *Comment. in Genesim*, col. 558; *De Universo*, col. 56. In his discussion of Psalm 83, St. Augustine discusses Lot's wife as a figure of impenitence, alluding to 2 Peter 2:22.

29 For example, see Peter Comestor, *Historia Scholastica*, col. 1101. There are numerous pairings of the two events, probably because they are frequently linked in the Bible.

30 Friend says: "Another thing: pay attention to the way that Fair Welcoming looks at you. . . . adapt yourself to his manner. . . . Take trouble to follow his lead: if he is happy, put on a happy face; if he is angry, an angry one. If he laughs, you laugh, and weep if he does. . . . Love what he loves, blame what he wants to blame, and give praise to whatever he does" ("The Advice of Friend," in Guillaume de Lorris and Jean de Meun, *The Romance of the Rose*, trans. Charles Dahlberg [Princeton, 1971], part II, lines 7719–7736, p. 145).

31 Traditionally Balthazar was associated wtih satanic pride. See St. Jerome, *Comment. in Daniel, PL* 25, col. 546; Richard of St. Victor, *Liber Exceptionum*, II, VII, xxxix, p. 342. See also Berchorius, *Reductorium Morale*, XXIV, v.

32 Cf. Kelly and Irwin, "The Meaning of *Cleanness:* Parable as Effective Sign," p. 247.

33 See 2 Timothy 2:20. For a discussion of medieval interpretations of this verse, see Robertson, *A Preface to Chaucer*, pp. 326–327.

34 St. Jerome, *Comment. in Daniel*, col. 543. Thomas Brinton also connects Balthazar with heresy (Sermon 23, p. 96).

35 See Alanus de Insulis, *Liber Sententiarum, PL* 210, col. 248; Berchorius, *Reductorium Morale*, XXIV, v; St. Gregory, *Moralia, PL* 75, col. 546.

36 In the *Liber Exceptionum* (II, VIII, i–ii, p. 345), Richard of St. Victor discusses the rebuilding of the Temple in relation to the final sorting out. See also II, VII, xli, p. 343.

37 See Howard, *The Three Temptations*, p. 51, for an account of treatments of the three vices that arranged the sins hierarchically.

38 See St. Gregory, *Moralia*, col. 535; *Homiliarum in Ezechielem, PL* 76, col. 976; Alanus de Insulis, *Sermo IV, PL* 210, col. 209.

Four: Pearl

1 For discussions of *Pearl* as a *consolatio*, see Robert Ackerman, "The *Pearl*-Maiden and the Penny," in *The Middle-English "Pearl": Critical Essays*, ed. John Conley (Notre Dame, 1970), 150–156; Ian Bishop, *"Pearl" in Its Setting: A Critical Study of the Structure and Meaning of the Middle English Poem* (Oxford, 1968), chap. 1; John Conley, *"Pearl* and a Lost Tradition," *Journal of English and Germanic Philology*, 54 (1955), 332–347; P. M. Kean, *"The Pearl": An Interpretation* (London, 1967), chap. 2; Michael H. Means, *The "Consolatio" Genre in Medieval Literature*, University of Florida Humanities Monographs, 36 (Gainesville, 1972), pp. 49–59; James I. Wimsatt, *Allegory and Mirror: Tradition and Structure in Middle English Literature* (New York, 1970), pp. 117–136.

2 For discussions of the traditional elements of dream poetry, see A. C. Spearing, *Medieval Dream-Poetry* (Cambridge, 1976); Angus Fletcher, *Allegory: The Theory of a Symbolic Mode* (Ithaca,

1964), pp. 349, 355; Paul Piehler, *The Visionary Landscape* (Montreal, 1971); Barbara F. Nolan, *The Gothic Visionary Experience* (Princeton, 1977), pp. 156–204.

3 For a discussion of *Pearl* that touches on some of the elements of the love vision, see Marie Padgett Hamilton, "The Meaning of the Middle English *Pearl*," *PMLA*, 70 (1955), 805–824.

4 For balanced discussions of critical commentaries upon *Pearl* within the elegiac tradition, see René Wellek, *The "Pearl": An Interpretation of the Middle English Poem* (Prague, 1933); Laurence Eldredge, "The State of *Pearl* Studies since 1933," *Viator*, 6 (1975), 171–194. For a study of the elegiac tradition, see James H. Hanford, "The Pastoral Elegy and Milton's *Lycidas*," *PMLA*, 25 (1910), 403–447.

5 Ariès, *The Hour of Our Death*, pp. 90, 207.

6 Singleton, *An Essay on the Vita Nuova* (Cambridge, Mass., 1949), p. 114; "*In Exitu Israel de Aegypto*," in *Dante: A Collection of Critical Essays*, ed. John Freccero (Englewood Cliffs, N.J., 1965), pp. 102–121.

7 See Clifford Davidson, "The Digby *Mary Magdalene* and the Magdalene Cult of the Middle Ages," *Annuale Mediaevale* 13, pp. 70–87.

8 Henri Marrou, in Victor Saxer, *Le culte de Marie Madeleine en occident*, 2 vols. (Paris, 1959), p. xi. Saxer's study takes account of previous studies of Mary Magdalene and her cult, especially in France.

9 Saxer, *Le culte de Marie Madeleine*, 1:57.

10 Saxer, *Le cult de Marie Madeleine*, 2:256. The English foundations from 1279–1399 are Berwich, Chester, Pontefract, Sherborne, Deeping, Lokhay, Thetford, Norwich, Beccles, Ely, Evesham, Hereford, Gloucester, Abington, Machelney, Dunster, Dartford, Canterbury, Tunbridge, Chichester, Abbotsbury, Exeter, Tavistock. Under Edward III were founded Tavistock in Devonshire, Berwich in Northumberland, Lokhay in Derbyshire, Thetford in Norfolk (2: 256). The oldest English sanctuary was built in the reign of William the Conqueror, Barnstaple, and was authorized by the Parisian abbey Saint-Martin-des-Champs, of the Cluniac Rule. Mathilda was another royal patron of the saint, establishing a priory in London (1: 121); and Farley was established in 1125 by Humphrey de Bohun. The cult moved north very rapidly according to Saxer (1:121–123). Francis Bond notes that in England, Mary Magdalene was the thirteenth saint in

popularity; of Biblical saints, the eighth. He records 187 church dedications to her and 52 bells. However, he points out that his listings for church dedications continue through the seventeenth century. See Francis Bond, *Dedications and Patron Saints of English Churches* (Oxford, 1914), pp. 17, 29, 218.

11 Saxer, *Le culte de Marie Madeleine*, 1:152–153.

12 L'Abbé L. Bourgain edited this *planctus* in *La chaire française au XIIe Siecle* (Paris, 1879), pp. 373–383. Bourgain states that the homily bears the title "homilia beati Anselmi Cantuariensis"; he further notes that it concludes with the same formula as those of St. Anselm and is generically similar to the *Dialoges Beatae Mariae et Anselmi de Passioni Domini* (*PL* 159, col. 272). See also Anselm, *Opera Omnia*, ed. Francis S. Schmitt (Edinburgh, 1946) III, 64–67. I append Bourgain's edition of the homily or *planctus* to this study (see Appendix) because of its relative inaccessibility and for its peculiar dramatic power. Two recent studies of the homily in relation to Chaucer have contributed to our understanding of medieval texts, their impact, and their dispersal: John McCall, "Chaucer and the Pseudo-Origen *De Maria Magdalena*: A Preliminary Study," *Speculum*, 46 (1971), 491–509; Rosemary Woolf, "English Imitations of the *Homilia Origenis de Maria Magdalena*," in *Chaucer and Middle English Studies in Honour of Rossell Hope Robbins*, ed. Beryl Rowland (Kent State University Press, 1974), 384–391. Saxer too discusses this homily or *planctus* (*Le culte de Marie Madeleine*, 2:346–347).

13 McCall, "Chaucer and the Pseudo-Origen *De Maria Magdalena*," pp. 492–493. On pages 504–509 he appends a list of these. In England, he lists five for Cambridge, eight for the British Museum, one for University College, London, and fourteen for Oxford. McCall discusses the homily in detail.

14 McCall, "Chaucer and the Pseudo-Origen *De Maria Magdalena*," p. 495.

15 Woolf, "English Imitations of the *Homilia*," p. 384. That what is clearly a product of twelfth-century spirituality should enjoy so wide a circulation in the late Middle Ages is not surprising in light of the empathy between the two periods. See Giles Constable, "The Popularity of Twelfth-Century Spiritual Writers in the late Middle Ages," in *Renaissance Studies in Honor of Hans Baron*, ed. A. Maeho and J. A. Tiedeschi (Florence, 1971), p. 5; "Twelfth-Century Spirituality and the Late Middle Ages,"

Mediaeval and Renaissance Studies 5, pp. 27–60. See also Richard McKeon, "Poetry and Philosophy in Poets of the Twelfth Century," *Modern Philology,* 43 (1946), 217–234. See also Helen M. Garth, *Saint Mary Magdalene in Medieval Literature,* The Johns Hopkins University Studies in Historical and Political Science, series 67, no. 3 (Baltimore, 1950).

16 See Woolf, *The English Mystery Plays* p. 28. For two recent studies of fraternal style, see David L. Jeffrey, *The Early English Lyric and Franciscan Spirituality* (Lincoln, Nebraska, 1975); John V. Fleming, *An Introduction to the Franciscan Literature of the Middle Ages* (Chicago, 1977).

17 Saxer, *Le culte de Marie Madeleine,* 2:346–347.

18 For a discussion of these debates, see Hope Traver, *The Four Daughters of God,* Bryn Mawr College Monographs, VI (Bryn Mawr, 1907).

19 Translations of subsequent citations of the *De Maria Magdalena* (see Appendix) are mine.

20 Garth, *Saint Mary Magdalene in Medieval Literature,* p. 68. See also J. E. Cross, "Mary Magdalene in the Old English Martyrology," *Speculum,* 53 (1978), 16–25. Cross transcribes three Latin texts of the "Narrat Josephus" (c. eleventh/twelfth century), all of which emphasize Mary's ardent love of Christ.

21 In reference to Mary Magdalene, both Bruno Astensis (*Commentaria in Joannem, PL* 165, col. 590) and St. Gregory (Homil. XXV, in *XL Homiliarum in Evangelia, PL* 76, cols. 1190–1191) stress the redeeming power of her love.

22 See St. Augustine, *In Iohannis Evangelium,* Corpus Christianorum Series Latina, 36 (Turnholt, 1954), Tract. CXXI, p. 666; Rabanus Maurus, Homilia XII, in *Homiliae in Evangelia et Epistola, PL* 110, col. 162.

23 Bruno Astensis, *Comment. in Joannem,* cols. 593–594. See also Petrus Berchorius, *Super Joannem* in *Opera,* VII, p. 218.

24 See *The Pearl,* ed. Charles Osgood (Boston, 1906); Hamilton, "The Meaning of the Middle English *Pearl.*" For a discussion of the possible dates, see *The Poems of the "Pearl" Manuscript,* ed. Andrew and Waldron, p. 56, n. 39f.

25 See, for example, *Mirk's Festial: A Collection of Homilies,* ed. Theodore H. Erbe, Early English Text Society, 54 (London, 1905), p. 228; St. Anselm, Homilia IX, in *Homiliae et Exhortationes, PL* 158, col. 649.

26 Paul the Deacon notes, "Those who hasten to come to the ease

of contemplation should first discipline themselves in the pursuit of the active life." Quoted in Garth, *Saint Mary Magdalene in Medieval Literature*, p. 87 (*PL* 95, col. 70).

27 St. Anselm, Oratio LXXIV, "Ad Sanctam Mariam Magdalenam," *PL* 158, col. 1012. For a discussion of Saint Anselm and Saint Bernard and their influence on the literature of meditation, see Rosemary Woolf, *English Religious Lyric in the Middle Ages* (Oxford, 1968), pp. 19–66, 120–121.

28 See Karl Young, *The Drama of the Medieval Church*, 2 vols. (Oxford, 1933), 1:683, for a dialogue between Mary Magdalene and Christ built around the metaphor of Christ as a flower. Frequently, Christ was described as the gardener of the human heart, planting the seed of charity; this seed was often linked with the *granam sinapis*, or mustard seed, of Matthew 13:31 and Luke 13:19. Mary's search for Christ in the garden is therefore the result of that seed's germination. See St. Augustine, Sermo CCXLVI, *PL* 33, col. 1154; St. Gregory, Homilia XXI, *PL* 76, col. 1161; Rabanus Maurus, *De Vita B. Maria Magdalena*, *PL* 112, col. 1474. The metaphors of the garden and of the seed and the themes of love, sorrow, and searching also find expression in a hymn to Mary Magdalene, "De Sancta Maria Magdalena," *Analecta Hymnica, Medei Aevi*, vol. III, 69. See also Joseph Szöverffy, "'Peccatrix quondam femina': A Survey of the Mary Magdalene Hymns," *Traditio*, 19 (1963), 79–146.

29 St. Gregory, Homilia XXV, *PL* 76, cols. 1195–1196.

30 See also *Pearl*, ed. E. V. Gordon (Oxford, 1970), introduction, p. xxxi. All quotations from *Pearl* will refer to this edition and are cited by line number in the text.

31 E. Faye Wilson, "Pastoral and Epithalamium in Latin Literature," *Speculum*, 23 (1948), 35–57. Throughout, my discussion of the Biblical epithalamium is indebted to Wilson's study of the genre. For the classic study of the Song of Songs and its influence upon medieval spirituality, see Jean Le Clercq, *The Love of Learning and the Desire for God*, trans. Catharine Misrabi (New York, 1961).

32 On this topic, see particularly, Marc. M. Pelen, "Form and Meaning of the Old French Love Vision: the *Fableau dou Dieu Amors* and Chaucer's *Parliament of Fowls*," *Journal of Medieval and Renaissance Studies*, 9 (1979), 277–305.

33 See St. Gregory, Homilia XXV, *PL* 76, cols. 1195–1196; Alanus de Insulis, *Elucidatio in Cantica Canticorum*, *PL* 210, col. 72.

Interestingly enough, Jean Gerson also links Mary Magdalene with the bride of the Canticle. See "Sympsalma VII," in *Opera Omnia*, ed. Elleis de Pin (Antwerp, 1706), IV, col. 69. Garth notes (p. 85) that Canticle 3:1–4 is still used in the Roman Catholic Church as the lesson for the Mass on July 22, Mary Magdalene's day.

34 *Christ's Burial and Resurrection*, 2 parts, in *The Digby Mysteries*, ed. F. J. Furnivall, Early English Text Society, 70 (London, 1896), pt. II, sc. 3, lines 1442–1447 and 1460–1467. For a study of Mary within the frame of the Digby Mysteries, see Davidson, "The Digby *Mary Magdalene* and the Magdalene Cult of the Middle Ages." The *noli me tangere* play in the *Ludus Coventriae* emphasizes Mary's sorrow and her insistence that, with Christ's death, all joy has left her. The *Cursor Mundi* links Mary's burning love with her successful search.

35 St. Bernard, Sermo XXVIII, in *Sermones in Cantica*, PL 183, cols. 925, 926.

36 As late as the seventeenth century, Thomas Robinson expressed these same concerns in his *Life and Death of Mary Magdalene* (c. 1620), ed. H. O. Sommer, Early English Text Society, E.S 78 (London, 1899), lines 1471–1478, p. 63:

Happy wert thou to touch yᵉ tressells bare
Of thy beloued, heau'nly paramour,
With eye, with hand, with temples, lippe and haire:
Yet thrice more happy, sith thy Sauiour,
With eye, heart, hand of faith thou didst adore:
So doth a loue-sicke soule of best desarte,
Desire to touch her louer in each part,
And closely steale his body, yᵗ hath stole her heart.

37 Charles Moorman, "The Role of the Narrator in *Pearl*," in *The Middle-English "Pearl"*, p. 104.

38 In exegetical literature, the pearl of great price is a symbol for purity, grace, Christ, healing, penance, and Christian doctrine, meanings almost as numerous as those assigned by modern scholars. See St. Augustine, *Quaestionem in Evangelium Secundus Matthaeum*, PL 35, col. 1371; Petrus Berchorius, *Reductorium Morale*, XI, xciii, p. 446; Rabanus Maurus, *De Universo*, PL 111, XIX, viii, col. 472. For a sampling of critical interpretations of the meaning of the pearl, see D. W. Robertson, Jr., "The Pearl as a Symbol," *Modern Language Notes*, 65 (1950), 155–161. For a reading of the pearl as innocence, see J. B. Fletcher,

"The Allegory of the Pearl," *Journal of English and Germanic Philology*, 20 (1921), 1–21; as symbolizing the Eucharist, see R. M. Garret, *"The "Pearl": An Interpretation* (Seattle, 1918); as virginity, see C. A. Luttrell, "The Mediaeval Tradition of the Pearl Virginity," *Medium Ævum*, 31 (1962), 194–200; W. M. Schofield, "The Nature and the Fabric of *The Pearl*," *PMLA*, 19 (1904), 154–215.

39 Charles Williams, "The Recollection of the Way," in *Dante: A Collection of Critical Essays*, ed. John Freccero, p. 176.

40 In *Super Cantica Canticorum*, col. 474, St. Gregory discusses love and imitation in a manner similar to the advice Amant receives in the *Roman de la Rose*, advice that the poet alludes to in *Purity*, lines 1057–1064.

41 See St. Augustine, "In Psalmum XLIV," in *Ennarationes in Psalmos*, Corpus Christianorum Series Latina, vol. 38, pp. 493–495, 508.

42 Geoffrey Chaucer, The Parson's Tale, in *Works*, ed. F. N. Robinson, X (I), p. 259. For a discussion of love and penance, see St. Gregory, *Super Cantica Canticorum*, col. 510. In reference to the Magdalene, see Françoise Bordon, "Le thème de la Madeleine pénitente au XVIIIᵉ siècle en France," *Journal of the Warburg and Courtauld Institute*, 31 (1968), 274–306. Charles Sterling in "A New Picture by Georges de la Tour," *Burlington Review*, 71 (1937), pp. 8–14, discusses *The Repentant Magdalene* as a figure of penance and contemplation.

43 See David Knowles, *The English Mystical Tradition* (London, 1961), pp. 39–47, 105–118, for comments about the perceived dangers of purely affective spirituality.

44 William Durandus (*The Symbolism of Churches and Church Ornaments*, ed. and trans. J. M. Neale and B. Webb [London, 1895], p. 159) considers the threefold instruction inherent in the appointment of the sacrament in a way that illuminates the final lines of *Pearl*: "But it is asked why sacraments are appointed. . . . First, for our humiliation; in order that when man reverently humbleth himself by the command of God unto insensible and inferior things, he may from this obedience become more acceptable unto Him. Secondly, for our instruction; that by that which is seen objectively in a visible form, our mind may be instructed in that invisible virtue, which is to be perceived within. Thirdly, for our exercising: in order that, since man ought not to be idle, there may be set before him a useful and healthy exercise

in the sacraments; so that he may avoid vain and hurtful occupation."

45 Singleton, *An Essay on the Vita Nuova*, p. 114.

46 In "Pastoral and Epithalamium in Latin Literature," Wilson discusses the relationship between love and vision.

47 For a sampling of studies of the expansive nature of *Pearl*'s images, see Louis Blenkner, O.S.B., "The Pattern of Traditional Images in *Pearl*," *Studies in Philology*, 68 (1971), 26–49; Hamilton, "The Meaning of the Middle English *Pearl*"; Constance B. Hieatt, "*Pearl* and the Dream-Vision Tradition," *Studia Neophilologica*, 37 (1965), 139–145; Wendell Stacy Johnson, "The Imagery and Diction of *The Pearl*: Toward an Interpretation," *ELH*, 20 (1953), 161–180.

48 See D. W. Robertson, Jr., "The Doctrine of Charity in Medieval Literary Gardens: A Topical Approach through Symbolism and Allegory," *Speculum*, 26 (1951), 24–49; Giamatti, *The Earthly Paradise and the Renaissance Epic*, pp. 49ff.; E. R. Curtius, *European Literature and the Latin Middle Ages*, trans. W. R. Trask (New York, 1963), pp. 195–202; Rupert, *In Cantica Canticorum*, *PL* 168, col. 903.

49 For a discussion of this incident in the *Roman de la Rose*, see J. V. Fleming, *The Roman de la Rose: a Study in Allegory and Iconography* (Princeton, 1969), pp. 95ff.

50 See, for example, Richard of St. Victor, *Explicatio in Cantica Canticorum*, *PL* 196, col. 487.

51 Alanus de Insulis, *Elucidatio in Cantica Canticorum*, col. 91. See also St. Gregory, *Super Cantica Canticorum*, *PL* 79, cols. 513, 526. For Saint Gregory, the garden is a means of moving from one state to another, thus, the Church.

52 See S. A. Weber, *Theology and Poetry* (Columbus, 1969), p. 23, for a discussion of the pronoun *we* and its associations with the corporal church in medieval lyrics.

53 William of Auvergne, in *De Sacramento Poenitentiae* (*Opera Omnia* [Paris, 1674], c. XVI, p. 492), relates the themes of diligence and spiritual cultivation not only to the Parable of the Vineyard, but also to the garden of the Canticle. For a discussion of the theme of spiritual agriculture in medieval literature, see E. Faye Wilson, "The *Georgica Spiritualia* of John of Garland," *Speculum*, 8 (1933), 358–377.

54 See D. W. Robertson, Jr., "The 'Heresy' of the *Pearl*," in *The Middle-English Pearl*, pp. 291–296; "The Pearl as Symbol."

55 See St. Augustine, Sermo LXXXVII, *PL* 38, col. 531; Bruno Astensis, Hom. XXII, in *Homiliae, PL* 165, col. 771; Bede, *In Matthaeii Evangelium, PL* 92, col. 87; St. Gregory, Hom. XIX, *PL* 76, col. 1154; Rabanus Maurus, *Comment. in Matth., PL* 107, col. 1026. Exegetical discussions of the vineyard are similar to those of gardens.

56 For a discussion of September as the month of vintage in pictorial Labors of the Months, see Emile Mâle, *The Gothic Image*, pp. 73–74. See also Rosemund Tuve, *Seasons and Months: Studies in a Tradition of Middle English Poetry* (Paris, 1933; rpt. Cambridge and Totowa, N.J., 1974), pp. 122–170.

57 See Chauncey Wood, *Chaucer and the Country of the Stars* (Princeton, 1970), pp. 272–297, for a discussion of this reference to Libra.

58 St. Augustine, Sermo LXXXVII, *PL* 38, cols. 538–539.

59 See Berchorius, *Dictionarium Morale*, p. 92, in *Opera; Macrobius' Commentary on "The Dream of Scipio,"* ed. W. H. Stahl (New York, 1952). See also Spearing, *Medieval Dream-Poetry*, pp. 8–11; Fleming, *The Roman de la Rose*, pp. 54–55.

60 See St. Gregory, *Super Cantica Canticorum*, col. 517; St. Bernard, Sermo XXXVIII, in *Sermones de Cantica, PL* 183, cols. 976–977; Richard of St. Victor, *Explicatio in Cantica Canticorum*, col. 501.

61 For a thorough discussion of the ways in which the poem suggests the levels of visionary ecstasy, see Blenkner, "The Pattern of Traditional Images in *Pearl*."

62 See, for example, St. Augustine, *In B. Joannis Apocalyp. in Expositio, PL* 35, col. 2451. Bruno Astensis interprets the river as Christian doctrine (*Expos. in Apocalyp., PL* 165, col. 730); Richard of St. Victor (*In Apocalyp., PL* 196, col. 875) as grace. In each of the four illustrations to *Pearl*, the river has a prominent position.

63 For a discussion of this association and its appearance in late medieval art, see Emile Mâle, *L'art religieux de la fin du moyen age en France* (Paris, 1925), pp. 100–122.

64 Cf. Gordon, ed., *Pearl*, p. 165.

65 See St. Bernard, Sermo XXXIII, in *Sermones de Diversis, PL* 183, cols. 626, 627. Cf. St. Augustine, "Ps. XXIII," in *Enarrationes in Psalmos*, p. 135; Bruno Astensis, "Ps. XXIII," in *Expositio in Psalmos, PL* 164, col. 772.

66 Blenkner ("The Pattern of Traditional Images in *Pearl*") also

stresses the progressive character of the dreamer's experience as it is adumbrated in the poem's images. See also Louis Blenkner, O.S.B., "The Theological Structure of *Pearl*," *Traditio*, 24 (1968), 43–75.

67 Antonio Geraldini of Amelia (1449–1488) published twelve sacred eclogues in Rome in 1485. The eighth, *De Resurrectione Salvatoris*, is a lament by Aeglê (Mary Magdalene) for the death of Acanthus (Christ). This eclogue follows the pattern outlined by the episode in John 20. The lament is a dialogue, first a monologue by Mary, and then a dialogue between Mary Magdalene and the "gardener." Both the series and the particular eclogue are discussed by Leonard Grant in *Neo-Latin Literature and the Pastoral* (Chapel Hill, 1965), pp. 268–269; Grant also notes that the eclogue's pastoral atmosphere is "carefully maintained."

68 *Meditations on the Life of Christ*, trans. Isa Ragusa and Rosalie B. Green (Princeton, 1961), pp. 362–363.

69 St. Anselm refers to this verse in his homily on the Feast of the Assumption (*PL* 158, col. 649).

Conclusion: "He Cryed So Cler"

1 Spearing also uses this phrase in *The Gawain-Poet: A Critical Study*, p. 171.
2 *Pearl*, ed. Gordon, introduction, p. xxxvi.
3 Donald R. Howard, *The Idea of the Canterbury Tales* (Berkeley, 1976), p. 380.

Index

COMPOSED BY GRAPHIC COMPOSITION, INC., ATHENS, GEORGIA
MANUFACTURED BY CUSHING MALLOY, INC., ANN ARBOR, MICHIGAN
TEXT AND DISPLAY LINES ARE SET IN TRUMP MEDIAEVAL

Library of Congress Cataloging in Publication Data
Johnson, Lynn Staley, 1947–
The voice of the Gawain–poet.
Includes bibliographical references and index.
1. Patience (Middle English poem) 2. Gawain and the Green Knight. 3. Purity (Middle English poem) 4. Pearl (Middle English poem) 5. English poetry—Middle English, 1100–1500—History and criticism. I. Title.
PR1972.G353J64 1984   821'.1'09   83-12401
ISBN 0-299-09540-1